Fighting Windmills

Fighting Windmills

Encounters with Don Quixote

MANUEL DURÁN   FAY R. ROGG

Yale University Press   New Haven and London

Published with assistance from the Program for Cultural Cooperation between Spain's Ministry of Culture and United States Universities.

Published with assistance from the foundation established in memory of Philip Hamilton McMillan of the Class of 1894, Yale College.

Chapter opening illustrations are details of figures on the following pages: Introduction, p. 3, Chapter 1, p. 17; Chapter 2, p. 45; Chapter 3, p. 59; Chapter 4, p. 85; Chapter 5, p. 131; Chapter 6, p. 167; Chapter 7, p. 193; Chapter 8, p. 221; Conclusion, p. 251.

Library of Congress Cataloging-in-Publication Data
Durán, Manuel, 1925–
Fighting windmills : encounters with Don Quixote /
Manuel Durán, Fay R. Rogg.
p. cm.
Includes bibliographical references and index.
ISBN-13: 978-0-300-11022-7 (cloth : alk. paper)
ISBN-10: 0-300-11022-7
1. Cervantes Saavedra, Miguel de, 1547–1616. Don Quixote.
I. Rogg, Fay R. II. Title.
PQ6352.D83 2006
863'.3—dc22
2005029715

Printed in the United States of America.

A catalogue record for this book is available from the British Library.

The paper in this book meets the guidelines for permanence and durability of the Committee on Production Guidelines for Book Longevity of the Council on Library Resources.

10 9 8 7 6 5 4 3 2 1

To Gloria, a real-life Dulcinea,
and
to the memory of my mentor and teacher, Américo Castro
— Manuel Durán

To William, Jonathan, and Jeffrey Rogg, my three favorite
Quixotes
— Fay R. Rogg

Contents

Acknowledgments

We wish to thank many people at the Yale University Press. We are especially indebted to Jonathan Brent, the editorial director, whose goodwill and faith in us along the way facilitated the writing of the manuscript. His capable assistant editors, Candice Nowlin and especially Sarah Miller, were exceptional in keeping us on track and informed. Eliza Childs skillfully copy-edited the manuscript. Margaret Otzel expertly guided us through the various stages of production to bound books.

M.D. and F.R.R.

I would like to thank Professors John Hughes, Alicia Colombí Monguió, and Helena Percas de Ponseti, who were helpful before and during the writing of this book. I would also like to thank Reid Cameron, whose gift of a facsimile of the *Don Quixote* first edition proved invaluable.

M.D.

I thank Dr. Antonio Pérez, president of Borough of Manhattan Community College (City University of New York), who granted me a sabbatical to coauthor the book. I wish to express my gratitude to friends and colleagues for their helpful suggestions and efforts: Professor Hilario Barrero, Professor Margaret Carson, Professor Peter Consenstein, Claude DuPont, Professor Charles Faulhaber and his wife Jamy Faulhaber, Professor

Michael Nimetz, Rebecca Rogg, Herbert Samuels, and Professor Carol Wasserman. I want to further thank Professor Emilia Borsi, who spent her vacation editing, rewriting, and proofreading the text. Also, thank you to Shirley Freeman who fine-tuned the manuscript in its last stages.

Finally, this book would not be possible without my kind secretary, Rosemary Zelaya, whose patience, wisdom and hard work on nights and weekends contributed to handing in a readable script and meeting the deadline.

F.R.R.

Fighting Windmills

Introduction

In the second half of the sixteenth century an idea was born
in the mind of a little-known writer from Alcalá de Henares,
east of Madrid. He was of modest means, but well-read and
blessed with an extraordinary imagination. His idea was to pluck
a middle-aged bookworm from his humble, impoverished surroundings and drop him into the world of evildoers and damsels in distress, where he would try to make things right in accordance with the then outdated rules of chivalry, about which
he was very knowledgeable. His name was Don Quixote of La
Mancha. The writer was Miguel de Cervantes Saavedra, whose
beloved knight rode across an unspecified, timeless landscape
and eventually into our hearts and minds. The novel, published
in two parts ten years apart, is today the most widely read literary masterpiece in world literature. Can any of us imagine a
world without *Don Quixote*?

While much has been written about Cervantes and his literary output, *Don Quixote de la Mancha* lends itself to endless
scrutiny because of its many philosophical and psychological aspects, its universal themes, the author's profound knowledge of
human nature, its narrative innovations, and perhaps most significantly, the magnanimous, serene, and forgiving spirit that
comes through in the text of a writer who had known the best
and worst of life experiences. The novel appeals as much to the
contemporary reader as it did to the reader of his day. Although
literary sensibilities have changed, the response to the humanistic values found in Cervantes's work—like love, forgiveness,

kindness, and the pursuit of a more just world—are as valid today as ever. For this reason *Don Quixote* endures. Four hundred years after the publication of the first part of the novel (1605), we find ourselves re-reading the text and asking ourselves, "How did Cervantes write such a rich tale?"

To answer this question, we shall first explore the complex circumstances of the life and times of Cervantes, whose undaunted spirit and will overcame numerous personal and professional obstacles. Then we shall look at how he used the existing narrative styles: the chivalric, pastoral, and picaresque. Today's novels do not fall into such categories. Cervantes took from them themes, ambience, and stock characters and created a new genre with his unique style. We shall also look at how he experimented with technique, language, and character development as he constructed *Don Quixote,* creating a new form of writing, what is now considered the basis of the modern novel. In part 2, we shall call attention to the text itself, detailing the central themes and adventures and discussing the friendship between Don Quixote and his earthy squire Sancho. Finally, we shall embark on a journey across the centuries, looking at how Cervantes's narrative techniques and literary devices were adopted and how the Quixotes of later world-class writers, appearing in different guises, compare with the original Manchegan knight.

When a book is as influential as Cervantes's novel, our first inclination is to analyze the text to find out why it has played such a significant role in Western literature. Immediately problems begin to arise and overwhelm us. Often Cervantes sends contradictory signals. No wonder his critics seldom agree as to the true meaning of the novel. At first it appears to be a book easy to read, easy to understand: as one of its characters tells us, "'it is so clear that there is nothing in it to cause any difficulty: children look at it, youths read it, men understand it, the old celebrate it, and, in short, it is so popular and so widely

Gustave Doré (1832–1883), *Don Quixote Reading*. Engraved by
Heliodore Joseph Pisan. Photo: Snark / Art Resource, NY.

read and so well-known by every kind of person that as soon as
people see a skinny old nag they say: "There goes Rocinante."
... In short, this history is the most enjoyable and least harmful
entertainment ever seen.'"[1]

A "least harmful entertainment" in the author's words, full
of humor and slapstick. Cervantes promoted this aspect of the
novel in the hope that such a description would increase the

number of its readers. But still we find a somber side to the novel, a dark tale hidden between the light-hearted lines; it invites us to take a second look to uncover the underlying themes, purpose, and pulse of the novel, which have consistently placed *Don Quixote* at the top of the list of "the 100 greatest novels of all time." [2] Translated almost immediately after its publication in 1605, it influenced writers from its inception. A case in point is Avellaneda, the first imitator, whom Cervantes reproaches in part 2 of his novel, published in 1615.

What is the secret of the popularity of *Don Quixote*? On one hand, we have the literary critics and philosophers who try to explain the novel's value and Cervantes's appeal. For example, the American critic, author, and teacher Lionel Trilling suggests: "In any genre it may happen that the first great example contains the whole potentiality of the genre. It has been said that all philosophy is a footnote to Plato. It can be said that all prose fiction is a variation on the theme of *Don Quixote*." [3] The Spanish philosopher and critic José Ortega y Gasset agrees. He points out: "There is a need of a book showing in detail that every novel bears *Quixote* within it like an inner filigree, in the same way as every epic poem contains the *Iliad* within it like the fruit its core." [4] The great German writer Thomas Mann reread *Don Quixote* during a voyage by ship that took him to the United States. When he reached the end of the novel, and with it Don Quixote's death, he revealed his deep sentiment: "Pain, love, pity, and boundless reverence filled my heart altogether." [5] Then there are the many writers and artists who were inspired by Cervantes and who created new tales that can be interpreted in the context of his great work. For example, Voltaire's *Candide*, Dickens's *Mr. Pickwick*, and Mark Twain's *The Adventures of Tom Sawyer* and *The Adventures of Huckleberry Finn*, to name just a few. The lengthy list goes on and on as we readily acknowledge that Cervantes's masterpiece is the axis on which the modern novel turns.

It is for these reasons that we decided to investigate this man who can make us laugh and spirit us through so many wondrous adventures. Why do Don Quixote and Sancho captivate us? How does the work penetrate and play on the modern mind? And so, like Don Quixote, we begin our quest. We choose as a point of reference Edith Grossman's translation of *Don Quixote* because the contemporary vocabulary makes for much easier reading. Needless to say, to read the text in Spanish means to enjoy Cervantes's magical use of language. How could we not help pondering once again the powerful, almost incredible transformation that takes place in the first chapter? An obscure, provincial, petty nobleman who has lived an uneventful life in a small village is changed into a valiant knight setting forth to change the world. This incredible metamorphosis has fascinated the world for four hundred years.

In principle we can state that all the great masterpieces of literature can change the way we perceive ourselves and how we see other human beings and the world. This change may be subtle, but it is often cumulative. It remains constant for long periods of time and alters the status quo in a way that is not easily discernable. The works of Homer played a role in the lives of the Greeks, in particular, Alexander the Great, although this influence may be elusive. Dante and Machiavelli also determined the course of Italian history in subtle ways. Many thinkers in Western Europe read Erasmus (1466–1536), the Dutch humanist and scholar, Rabelais (1494–1553), the French satirist and humorist, and Montaigne (1533–1592), the French essayist and moralist. There is no doubt that some readers felt that the works of this first generation of freethinkers during the later Renaissance were disconcerting. Some of their ideas would be reborn during the Enlightenment in the eighteenth century. The Catholic Church placed most of Erasmus' works in its *Index of Forbidden Books*. Montaigne was criticized as having fostered, in subtle ways, relativistic and skeptical trends. Rabelais was an enemy of the Sorbonne theologians and of monks in general (as was Erasmus). The Sorbonne and the ecclesiastic orders of monks and friars were part of the Establishment. By attacking them, Rabelais was undermining one of the pillars of social order. Montaigne criticized fanaticism and colonialism, both very much a part of Western European societies and both taken for granted everywhere. His ideas are quite acceptable to us, but most members of the Establishment in his time loathed them.

When facing a problem the literary historian may choose an oblique approach. The author, the work, the set of ideas that give birth to a masterpiece cannot be confronted directly. We propose to discuss briefly the ideas and lives of a number of authors with a view to obtaining a better insight into our author's work and its consequences. Like Cervantes, these authors had extraordinary experiences that shaped their way of thinking and writing. We shall attempt to see what they have in common with and what separates them from Cervantes.

If we look at different writers in a given historical period as members of an extended family, we soon detect that some authors are perhaps not brothers, yet are similar enough to be called "cousins" because they share certain viewpoints, spiritual values, and concerns. Let us think now of Erasmus, Montaigne, Rabelais, and Cervantes. Although they did not know each other, their thoughts and attitudes unite them. If we were able to gather them at a party, probably they would be drawn to each other. They all shared a critical mind and a deep dissatisfaction with some aspects of their society and the ideological systems that ordered the framework of their surroundings. Each of them had a new way of looking at humankind and its circumstances.

Certainly dissatisfaction about one's personal circumstances, and about the existing society and culture, can be a wellspring of creativity. The critical mind has often spurred writers who question their epoch's intellectual and cultural fabric or makeup. Many of the thinkers in Cervantes's generation were restless and irritated by the constraints imposed on them by tradition and the church. An obvious example is Galileo, who because he challenged long-held beliefs was condemned for heresy by the Inquisition. The sixteenth century is characterized by expressions of disagreement, and even those writers who accepted the ideas and principles prevalent during their lifetimes turn out to be sharply critical. In some cases, at first sight it is hard to find the grounds for their dissatisfaction. A case in point is Michel de Montaigne. What could have been wrong with his life? Born a nobleman, he received a refined education. His tutor taught him Latin before he learned French. He studied philosophy and law, traveled to the court of Francis I, became mayor of Bordeaux, enjoyed later in his life a secluded scholarly existence in a castle tower turned into a huge library, wrote and published brilliant essays. Yet he was critical, although, no doubt, fear restrained his critical attitude.

Could it have been his loveless marriage or cowardice during a plague when he abandoned his mayoral office and fled Bordeaux? Moreover, Montaigne was a secret disbeliever; his philosophy was based on doubt and skepticism, while his position in society and politics called for repeated reaffirmations of the Catholic faith. Even more telling, he was a homosexual, an extremely cautious closet homosexual at a time when gay men were burned at the stake. Could these be the reasons for the hints of rebelliousness, doubt, criticism of his times and of his society, and questions about the official beliefs of his country that we find in his essays?

Rabelais was a dissident, too. He hated monks, although he was one for a while, and he deplored the rigidity of the Sorbonne and its theologians; in a word, he hated the church. He was less politically and socially secure than Montaigne, and therefore he had to find better ways to disguise his skeptical feelings and his thoughts. In his *Gargantua* and *Pantagruel* fables, a word that better suits these texts than the word "novels" because of their moral content, he built a rampart protecting his dissident ideas, a fanciful and grotesque world of giants, strange adventures, and off-color jokes. His truly significant ideas all but disappeared under the weight of the disguising scaffolds.

Erasmus, a Catholic, was very critical of the immorality of the Church of Rome. Some of his detractors thought him a Lutheran. He also shared with Rabelais a hatred of monks in particular and the church in general, and like Rabelais, he felt vulnerable; his defensive action included moving often from place to place and, again, disguising some of his most danger-ous ideas under the double cover of allegory and irony. Despite the fact that Erasmus, Rabelais, and Montaigne are writers and thinkers of the highest order, none achieved the universal fame of Cervantes. Their reputations would have been greater if, like Cervantes, they had opted to create a realistic novel with real characters.

Montaigne, the philosopher, talks mainly about himself and by doing so entertains us and enlightens us as few writers can, but his self-centeredness prevents us from totally bonding with him. Rabelais plays the clown much too much, and we are never sure when we should take him seriously. Erasmus, the reformer, is in turn bold (for instance, when he claims that the warlike and power-greedy Pope Julius II could not enter heaven) and timid, or at least afraid of taking sides. We hear mainly his voice, not the voice of the believable, lovable characters such as those in *Don Quixote*. Cervantes, however, could draw on the humanistic, didactic, humorous, and moralistic views of this trio of "cousins" and still manage to reinterpret, invent, and form his own serene, balanced, realistic picture of society without their bite and vituperative utterances.

Above all, what unites these three writers—Erasmus, Rabelais, and Montaigne—with Cervantes is their irony, an irony that was partially or totally born from the fact that they saw themselves as outsiders. Poverty and fear of persecution in the case of Erasmus and Rabelais, and fear of society's punishment for being a homosexual in the case of Montaigne, made them all look at society with critical eyes. It is possible that Cervantes would have been more outspoken in his criticism if he had been born one generation earlier. He hardly knew this first period of ferment and dissent since he lived, wrote, and published during years when the intellectual climate of Europe, and more specifically Spain, had grown harsher and colder. The great religious wars of the seventeenth century, mainly the Thirty Years' War, were still to take place.

Thus, compared to Erasmus, Rabelais, and Montaigne, Cervantes is much less confrontational in his worldview. He does not write essays against the church or other institutions. He rises above the particular to make a statement about the universality of human experience. While Cervantes appears several times in his novel, he does not comment on his characters' motives or judge them, nor does he reflect on their adventures except in fleeting remarks about their comic value. It has been said that the Devil's cleverest trick is to make us believe that he does not exist. Cervantes hides his opinions to the point of making them almost invisible, but they are there for the discerning reader.

Yet Cervantes is different from his "cousins." He expresses himself in a realistic novel and through complex, true-to-life characters that we can love, admire, criticize, or dislike. The other three writers are writing about themselves and their opinions about society and the world in general. This is easy to see when dealing with Erasmus and Montaigne. In contrast, Rabelais disguises himself as a joker and a teller of tall tales. Probably the reason it is easier to make sense of their writings is that they offer us a single line of thought, one that we can follow from beginning to end regardless of its nature. Therefore, critics have little difficulty interpreting their works.

Cervantes's novel is an extremely complex work, one in which many voices are heard, and we are never sure which one belongs to him. Consequently, critics are often at odds as to its meaning. The author is at times present in the text—we hear his voice as he comments on the action—and at other times he may stand aloof, letting the characters express themselves without interference. Although we suspect that some characters speak on behalf of the author, we can never prove this is so. Moreover, questions may arise regarding the identity of the true author. Is it Cide Hamete Benengeli, a fictitious name Cervantes created and names as the author of a manuscript written in Arabic that he finds by chance as he strolls in a market place? And also, Cervantes tells us that he had the manuscript translated into Castilian, but did the translator change essential words or sentences, perhaps out of ignorance or perhaps deliberately? As we turn the pages of the book we are mesmerized by the precise details and the lively dialogue, but at the same time we are unable to guess in which direction the characters advance or retreat. If Cervantes is playing complex games with his readers, he cannot complain if, in turn, his readers try to interpret the novel subjectively; hence the disagreement among critics and the kaleidoscopic interpretations of *Don Quixote* versus a homogenized, straight-line, explanation or critical rendering of the book.

With Cervantes we are dealing with characters of flesh and

blood, with whom we can identify in part or totally: they engage both our minds and our feelings. We know Don Quixote and Sancho almost as well as we know ourselves. We know how they look, what clothes they wear, how they speak, and how they react to the constantly changing events that spring up during their wanderings. We see them changing slowly or dramatically as events unfold. We see Don Quixote become more and more depressed, visibly aging, overwhelmed by repeated failures and the vision of an enchanted Dulcinea, really an unattractive peasant girl, indelibly engraved in his mind. Our initial merry laughter is replaced by a more profound understanding of the tragedy of human experience, and at the end we feel pity and sympathy for Don Quixote and for Sancho and the sorrow he feels when he realizes his master is dying.

Two outstanding Russian writers offer very different views of the creation of Don Quixote and the author's attitude toward his main character. On the merry, sunny side is Ivan Turgenev, who in his brilliant lecture "Hamlet and Don Quixote" delivered in 1860 comments that *Don Quixote* is "seemingly flooded with southern sunlight" and later recounts that "the spirit of the Southerner is bright, cheerful." To him Don Quixote represents "above all, faith," "dedication to an ideal," which "retains all its untarnished purity."[6] Turgenev's comments show Cervantes's positive attitude about the main character. On the dark side is Vladimir Nabokov, who in his *Lectures on Don Quixote* presents a decidedly despairing view and disapproves of Cervantes's harsh approach to Don Quixote. The atmosphere is somber and the treatment is unkind as he states: "We are going to speak about cruelty. The author seems to plan it thus: Come with me ungentle reader, who enjoys seeing a live dog inflated and kicked around like a soccer football, who likes on a Sunday morning, on his way to or from church, to poke his stick or direct his spittle at a poor rogue in the stocks; come ungentle reader, with me and consider into what ingenious and cruel hands I shall place my ridiculously vulnerable hero. And I hope you will be amused at what I have to offer."[7]

In these same lectures, Nabokov recounts Don Quixote's victories, which are equal in number to his defeats. We would refute his overall somber view. Mindful of the novel's dark moments, we prefer the sunny side. Even Don Quixote does not view the adventures in which he is beaten up as negative but rather as the work of enchanters. For a while—just for a while—he dismisses reality, escaping to knight-errantry and its constant motion, contact, and action with humankind. Life—reality—does not hang heavy over Don Quixote's head, although Sancho is there to remind him and us of their "real" circumstances. Rather, action and passion override the contemplative and the negative. The excitement of the next encounter becomes the focal point. Although his reactions to his adventures are sometimes foolhardy and extreme, they propel him to continue setting free the perceived victims of injustice and physical abuse. At the same time, he draws us to a different realm, into the adventure, thereby freeing us to imagine what he is experiencing. The light that he beams bounces off him to Sancho and begins to emanate, ever so subtly, from Sancho on to the reader. This effect endures.

How can we weigh negativity and doom given such affirmation and conviction of life? Is this why Cervantes's work is so very unlike that of his "cousins"? Could Don Quixote at least in part be a reflection of the author's life? Did Cervantes handle his life experience in a different way than Erasmus, Rabelais, and Montaigne did?

PART I

What a unique monument is this book! . . . How its

creative genius, critical, free, and human,

soars above its age!

THOMAS MANN (1875–1955)

I

Cervantes

A LIFE OF RESTLESSNESS AND COURAGE

Miguel de Cervantes was born in 1547 in the Castilian city of Alcalá de Henares, a city that boasted a relatively new but already famous university founded by Cardinal Cisneros. Alcalá "was the very focus of Renaissance Spain. More than any other place it symbolized the intellectual exuberance and the ideological fervor that characterized that country until it turned in upon itself in the 1560s, after the triumph of orthodoxy and traditionalism at the Council of Trent. In no more appropriate town could Cervantes have been born."[1]

Miguel inherited from his father, an itinerant surgeon always in debt, an incurable restlessness and the inability either to make much money or to hold on to it. He also inherited an inquisitive scientific mind, one that related facts with possible causes and rejected superstition and magic as the ultimate way to explain events in everyday life. From his mother, who struggled stubbornly to keep the numerous members of the financially strapped family together, he fell heir to the ability to survive adversity, a characteristic that would serve him well later in life. From both, probably, he acquired a clear mind and a desire to learn. When Cervantes was born, the University of Alcalá was still a brilliant center of learning, and the city swarmed with boisterous and noisy students. This atmosphere must have stimulated his intellectual curiosity to the point that he managed to acquire enough Latin to read the classics.

We know very little about Cervantes's inner life. He left no personal correspondence, no personal diary, and only a few references to himself in the prologues to his works. We also have a verse letter written while he was in captivity in Algiers, an affidavit dealing with his activities as a prisoner during that difficult time, and a paper trail about his business and legal activities. These are like the pieces of a puzzle, but there are too few of them, especially about his youth and his intellectual formation. We are mostly in the dark about his early life. As Malveena McKendrick states, "a pay slip, a christening certificate, a deed of attorney, a theatrical contract — these are the tiny details on which we often have to build our knowledge of the activities of one of the world's great geniuses. From them, however, a strange story gradually unfolds, a story of courage, mismanagement and poverty, of dramatic episodes in a humdrum, even slightly sordid, existence."[2] Cervantes's options were limited by his family's circumstances to certain professions or activities that would be unrelated to trade, commerce, and banking. Justifiably or not, he may have seen himself as a petty nobleman and trade activities were not appropriate for noblemen. He had to earn a living. He chose the army at first, as a way to escape, to travel, and to see the world, starting with the fabled lands of Italy. Later he tried to build a career in low-level administration, with disastrous results. He even applied for permission to go to the New World, which was denied. Indeed, he had little time to write. The bulk of his works — all his major publications except for his first novel — were concentrated in the last sixteen years of his life, after he quit his government work and made a heroic effort to earn his living with his pen, a challenging profession today and even more so in his era.

Cervantes knew many moments of danger and frustration. His left hand was mutilated as a result of a battle wound. He was a war prisoner, practically a slave, in Algiers. He was jailed in Spain. He was excommunicated for having requisitioned some

Jacob Folkema (1692–1767), *Portrait of Miguel de Cervantes, after William Kent.* Engraving. Bibliothèque Nationale, Paris, France. Photo: Bridgeman-Giraudon / Art Resource, NY.

supplies belonging to the church, although it was required of him in his work. Hardship, frustration, and lack of recognition dogged him throughout his life, yet in spite of all the disappointments, he had a serene outlook toward the end of his life. He was at peace with himself. He lived during one of the most dramatic periods of Spain's history. He had fought against the Turks in the great naval battle of Lepanto. His lifetime spans the years of Spain's greatest influence in Europe and the New World. During part of the reign of Philip II, Portugal and Spain were united. Spanish and Portuguese ships crossed the oceans toward India, China, Japan, and the Spice Islands. These years also witnessed the beginning of a long decline for Spain. This transition from greatness to decadence may be reflected in some of his works. His first novel, a pastoral, shines with the visions of beauty and love inspired by the Platonic Renaissance. The end of *Don Quixote* and some of the *Exemplary Novels* written toward the end of his life, such as "The Deceitful Marriage and Dogs' Colloquy," express a growing disillusion.

Cervantes must have been aware that the world described by the romances of chivalry never existed except in the imagination of writers, and yet he knew there were moments in the past when honor and valor had inspired kings and vassals alike. For instance, in 1536, eleven years before the birth of Cervantes, Emperor Charles V denounced Francis I, king of France, whose behavior he criticized as cowardly, in a speech addressed to the pope, which ended with these words: "Therefore, I promise your Holiness, in the presence of this sacred college and of all these knights here present, if the King of France wishes to meet me in arms, man to man, I promise to meet him armed or unarmed, in my shirt, with sword and dagger, on land or sea, on a bridge or an island, in a closed field, or in front of our armies or wherever and however he may wish and it be fair."[3] Cervantes must have been mindful of the news coming from the New World—

the conquests of Mexico and Peru, the fight for Chile against the Araucanian Indians, and the long search for El Dorado or for the Seven Cities of Cibola—which contained many elements worthy of a romance of chivalry. Life had imitated art for a few moments on a few occasions.

There is more. Young Miguel must have been cognizant of the fact that his family had known better times. His grandfather, Juan de Cervantes, was the son of a prosperous cloth merchant and had graduated in law from the University of Salamanca, then the most prestigious in all of Spain. He had been a magistrate in the university town of Alcalá de Henares and lived a comfortable life, with servants, slaves, and horses. For reasons that remain mysterious, he quarreled with his wife and left Alcalá, abandoning her and taking with him only his youngest son, Andrés. Miguel's father, along with the rest of his family, was left suddenly impoverished and had to make a living as a barber-surgeon, a trade that had none of the prestige of a physician. Young Miguel must have dreamed of restoring the status and the vanished riches of the family.

Intensely curious, bookish, and passionate about learning, he must have been disappointed to learn there was no money for him to enroll at the university. Creditors harassed his father. The family moved frequently and was always in debt. Frustration and shame must have been constant companions to Miguel.

In those early years, his escape to Italy and a stint in the army were a temporary solution, one that would reveal new facets of his personality: his courage in battle and his talent for leadership during five long years as a captive in Algiers, where he was recognized as the boldest and most enterprising of prisoners, organizing several attempts to escape.

Back in Spain, Cervantes had to start his life over again, concentrating his efforts on repaying the debt his family had incurred by ransoming him, and trying to make a living. He was talented, ambitious, and gifted. He attempted to survive by becoming a modest bureaucrat in the great administrative machinery of the Spanish Empire. He gathered supplies for the Invincible Armada being prepared for an invasion of England; however, his lack of foresight as an accountant, combined with bad luck, created almost insoluble problems, landing him in jail for a while. As Salvador de Madariaga puts it, "for the rest of his life he had to live in the presence and company of this contrast: his inner worth, as a soldier and a Spaniard; his utter failure to get recognition for it. He might have incarnated examples of manliness and leadership in slavery; in liberty, he lived a life of helplessness and poverty; a king of infinite space in his Algerian cell, he was on the roads and in the inns and boarding houses of Spain but a scribbler of petitions to the King's ministers and of dedications and laudatory epistles to the King's grandees."[4]

Talent, courage, and bravery in war, but no recognition: this can be a formula for bitterness. And yet nothing in his behavior or in his writings indicates he was discouraged or bitter. On the contrary, we associate Cervantes with a good sense of humor. During his years of hope and disappointment he developed a critical mind and an ironic perspective to make sense of his experience.

A person with a good sense of humor can observe the world around him or her with a certain amount of detachment, yet humor leads to critical analysis and ultimately becomes a tool to better understand both the society we are part of and also a few individuals in this society. Making fun of ourselves is the most difficult, even dangerous, stage of humor. It is possible to find a way to laugh at oneself by projecting a part, and perhaps a very small one into a character we are creating and then making fun of this character. There are subtle ways in which Cervantes may have laughed and criticized himself while creating the main character in his novel.

With humor, it is possible to analyze and criticize without utterly destroying the subject being analyzed. Humor can also be like a drop of oil that makes hard surfaces more manageable. From his lofty viewpoint, the author with a fine-tuned sense of humor sees the characters he is creating evolve in a situation where their weaknesses will be revealed. They will be able to go on acting and feeling since the critical blows that rain on them are not lethal. Ideally, the characters should learn from their mistakes. This seldom occurs, but the possibility of going on with their lives, their hopes, their dreams, is still offered to them. Humor is universal, and at the same time it is conditioned by culture and by history. Humor in Cervantes's time was undoubtedly more rough and cruel toward its victims than it would become in the literature of later centuries.

Cervantes did not have a formal education, but he made up for it with an insatiable appetite for reading and travel. His father had a vast collection of books, which at the time was unusual and much prized. There is no reason to think Cervantes was worse off because he did not attend Salamanca or Alcalá de Henares universities, which were then tradition-bound, old-fashioned, and confining. This was especially true of the University of Salamanca. Reading widely and independently better nurtured his sensitive, imaginative, and creative mind.

His experience more than compensated for his lack of officially accepted knowledge. A writer of fiction needs both imagination and a firsthand acquaintance with different levels of life. Cervantes was blessed with imagination and sensitivity, and his experience encompassed several levels. He traveled abroad and within his own country; he knew poets, writers, intellectuals, aristocrats, and also rogues, thieves, and swindlers; he was a prisoner in Africa for five years and later imprisoned in Spain. He was at odds with the church, even excommunicated for a while. He was entangled in a long struggle with the Spanish Treasury

Department over accounting problems arising from the bankruptcy of a bank where he had kept a sum of money owed to the government. He had a love affair, from which a daughter was born. He married a woman considerably younger than himself. His daughter had love affairs and entanglements that complicated the life of the whole family. In sum, his life was intense, adventurous, and varied. When he started to write his masterpiece, he could draw on the experiences of a rich life, one that had expanded his mind in all directions.

More than any other Spanish writer of his time, Cervantes had come in contact with other cultures and also with many different levels of society. He was ready to create a synthesis, a summing-up where lofty ideals would be put to the test of everyday experiences. The main character in his masterpiece was not modeled on himself, but surely traces of his life experience translate into the personality of Don Quixote. Both Cervantes and Don Quixote seek to escape their humdrum daily life, Cervantes by traveling abroad as a young man, then, later on, by trying to return to Italy. Both Cervantes and Don Quixote are intellectuals and avid readers, and yet each must bend time and again to practical, mundane needs. When Cervantes returned to Spain after years abroad, he had to start from scratch. After Don Quixote's upsetting experiences at the inn, he learned that a traveler, even if he is a knight-errant, should not leave home without some money and clean shirts and underwear. When he fashions his helmet, after ruining in one blow the work of a whole week, our would-be knight is wise enough to accept his work as perfect, or nearly so. Pragmatism and practicality impinge time and time again on the way Don Quixote handles himself, his horse, his weapons, and ultimately his quest. When he gives advice to Sancho, who is about to become governor of his island, he shows how much common sense and practical wisdom he has stored in his memory.

It is obvious that Cervantes's life would be of little interest to us if he had gone on soldiering in Italy or Flanders or had perhaps become a bureaucrat in some obscure city in the vast Spanish Empire. It is also true that in each human life there are decisive moments when a choice must be made: a fork in the road appears, and our character, our background, our hopes and lifelong projects help us decide which road to take. Whether or not we are really free to make this choice is a complex philosophical question. Once the choice is made, our options become more restricted, and at the same time the consequences of our decision determine many aspects of the rest of our life.

A couple of facets reveal an important part of Cervantes's character: his restlessness and his curiosity. More than any Spanish writer of that time, he was a great traveler. As a boy, he was familiar with Madrid, Valladolid, and Córdoba because he followed his father and his family. As a young man, he traveled to Rome and Naples. Later he fought in the naval battle of Lepanto (1571) and subsequently spent five years as a prisoner in Algiers. His love of travel is reflected in his literary output, where the action is placed in Seville, Salamanca, Barcelona, and in other locales.

In the fifteen years that he traveled through towns and villages in Andalusia, he discovered puppet-theater as well as the Spanish version of the Italian *commedia dell'arte* as interpreted by Lope de Rueda. Seville was always important to him, for it was there that he met other writers. Seville was also a boomtown, a haven for the Spanish underworld, which Cervantes got to know intimately during the long months he spent in Seville's jail. In spring 1610, he dreamed once more of leaving Spain for an extended period and traveling to Naples. The count of Lemos, who knew and appreciated Cervantes, had been appointed viceroy of Naples. He wanted to set up a literary court and asked his secretary, Lupercio Leonardo de Argensola, to choose the writers to accompany him to Italy. Cervantes knew Argensola, who had praised *La Galatea*. Nothing came of this project: Argensola chose other writers, whose names have been forgotten, for this literary court, in spite of Cervantes's trip to Barcelona in the hope of obtaining an audience with Lemos to plead his case.

Another important trait, clear and irrefutable, was Cervantes's curiosity. Always an avid reader, he writes of himself, "One day when I was in the Alcaná market in Toledo, a boy came by to sell some notebooks and old papers to a silk merchant; as I am very fond of reading, even torn papers in the streets, I was moved by my natural inclination to pick up one of the volumes the boy was selling" (Gr., 67).

Cervantes knew Latin, Italian, and probably French. His quotations and critical analyses of Spanish poems and prose works showed remarkable knowledge and critical insight. He read and admired Ariosto, Boccaccio, and several other Italian authors. He was well acquainted with Aristotle's *Poetics* and many other classics. Briefly, he was a humanist as well as a writer.

Written and especially printed texts are found throughout Cervantes's novel. "It is not only in the mind of the unhinged hidalgo that the reality of books and the reality of daily experience are hopelessly scrambled. Don Quixote's adventures, of course, begin in a library and frequently circle back to the contents of that library in thought or in speech, and more than once in action; but it is equally remarkable that the world into which he sallies is flooded with manuscripts and printed matter."[5] Cervantes, however, refrained from showing off his knowledge. No displays of erudition are found in his works; on the contrary, he often showed disdain for those who flaunted their readings. Sancho's common sense and quick mind help him solve knotty problems during his stint as governor of Barataria, proving once and for all that a lack of bookish knowledge is not an obstacle to success.

Being curious meant that Cervantes had to delve into the nooks and crannies of the human mind, into human behavior and human motivation. Being restless meant that he would create a main character who is dissatisfied with his mediocre existence and with the society in which he lives. He must change his life by transforming himself into a hero capable of correcting the injustices and cruelty of his society, a hero yearning for beauty and love. He will try to do so through a quest that becomes an inexhaustible journey on the roads of Spain. Cervantes's novel will become a mirror carried along those roads. This mirror will be special: it will reveal the outside everyday world, with its wretched inns, its muleteers, its peasants and shepherds. It will also reveal the inside world of the main characters and, more significantly, the constant interaction between the inner and the outer worlds.

The first part of *Don Quixote* appeared in 1605. Its success was astonishingly quick. Pirated editions appeared in Valencia and elsewhere. Cervantes was hard at work on several projects, including his *Exemplary Novels,* and yet he dreamed of leaving behind his sister, his wife, and his daughter and embarking for Italy, where he was practically unknown. "His age, his infirmities, the sad state in which Magdalena [his sister] found herself, were all serious handicaps for him, it is true. Could he have tolerated a gilded exile? It is hard to imagine this full-fledged sexagenarian suddenly taking leave of his country and his family then laying his projects aside in order to fulfill his obligations as a courtier. All things considered, it was better for him—and for us—that he did not leave for Naples."[6] That he would still seek to set out on new adventures, leaving behind his family and commitments, reveals that throughout his life he remained curious and restless. It also discloses his dissatisfaction with a Spain that had been reluctant to recognize his merit, a Spain where he had been repeatedly jailed in spite of being innocent.

Cervantes lived most of his mature life in penury, always in debt and often hounded by creditors and bureaucrats because he was supposed to repay the Treasury the sum lost through the bankruptcy of the bank. His last few years were made more tolerable thanks to a small pension given to him by a nobleman who admired his work.

There may have been moments of sadness and depression in his mature years, and yet the image that he projected to those around him was one of calm acceptance of his destiny. His prefaces to his two last novels exude confidence and optimism. From this we may conclusively deduce that he had found a way to relate himself, his writings, and his vision of his country, and of his own destiny with an overall positive vision. He judged his society without bitterness, or pity. Faults are there to be seen by all, if the reader takes time to read between the lines. He also tried to leave some space between his own viewpoint and those of his characters. He allowed them to wander, to change their minds, and to grow. Traveling through sun-drenched plains was a way for him to dilute tension and prepare for new initiatives. Movement in space was accorded to his characters and to him as well; perhaps it was a hoped-for answer to his many personal, financial, and family problems. Just moving on might be the solution or at least a provisional respite.

In spite of a number of good biographies of Cervantes, among them, the works of Melveena McKendrick and Jean Canavaggio, the "essential man," the intimate thoughts and feelings of our writer, still eludes us. The fact that his masterpiece has inspired so many different, even contradictory interpretations should alert us to the complexity of the man and his works. As we progress in our analysis of *Don Quixote,* certain clues to the author's personality appear.

A Professional Writer: His First and Last Novel

Cervantes's first novel, *La Galatea* (1585), a pastoral novel full of nostalgia, takes the reader to a never-never land of "beautiful people," of shepherds and shepherdesses who speak in the elaborate, poetic language of courtly love. The subject of a perfect Golden Age that we have lost and might try to recover appears several times in *Don Quixote*. Cervantes knew that the Golden Age, if it ever existed, was lost forever, yet in his writings he tried to go back to it or at least dream about it. He withdrew to the world of literature where he could control his characters and guide their movements in space. There, in the enchanted realm of literature, where the author is fully in charge, we find echoes of a Platonic lost paradise, a place of absolute beauty and happiness. It exists in the mind of Don Quixote every time the knight dreams about Dulcinea, yet the dream is betrayed when he finally sees her in the guise of a coarse peasant girl. Sancho has guided him toward the girl, but when he sees her, Don Quixote gives full expression to his pain in a way that might be an echo of Cervantes's regret and sorrow at finding a Spain that did not coincide with the glorious visions he may have entertained during his long years of captivity.

Why, after writing *Don Quixote,* a novel that is witty, sophisticated, highly original, and groundbreaking, did Cervantes write *Persiles and Sigismunda,* published posthumously in 1617, which is almost totally devoid of the qualities that made his previous novel world famous? This question does not worry the average reader of *Don Quixote* simply because few people who are not professional literary critics ever read the last novel. Yet Cervantes thought this last novel was the best one he had written and boldly stated so in the preface to the second part of *Don Quixote:* "a book that I will complete in four months, *Deo volente,* and it will be either the worst or best ever composed in our language, I mean, of those written for diversion; I must say I regret having said *the worst,* because in the opinion of my friends it is bound to reach the extremes of possible goodness" (Gr., 454).

What are we to think? Was Cervantes an inept critic of his own writings? This is not impossible. Another theory is that he was promoting his last novel: he was preparing the future readers of this novel, whetting their appetite perhaps, and stimulating the future sales of his yet unpublished book. He tells us his last novel is almost finished and will soon appear. This leads us to believe that perhaps he was working simultaneously on the second part of *Don Quixote* and on *Persiles.*

Persiles is a traditional "Byzantine" novel based on a well-known plot: two lovers are separated by numerous happenings and accidents over which they have very little control. Eventually they manage to overcome a cruel destiny and are finally reunited in Rome, destined for happiness and an everlasting life. By reading dozens of Harlequin romances it would not be impossible to find one that closely parallels *Persiles.* The separation of the lovers, however, limits the possibility of dialogue, which was one of the distinctive features of *Don Quixote,* while the seriousness, almost solemnity, of the lovers' travails precludes the presence of wit and humor, two other defining traits of Cervantes's masterpiece. His high hopes for his last novel were not realized. William Entwistle comments: "it is clear that Cervantes's mind was already eager to rival the unapproachable standard of his art as a novelist, though it happens that he succeeded not in the *Persiles* but in the *Quixote* . . . the attempt to gild the lily in his later work proved his undoing. It suffers indeed from what may be called the exemplary fallacy. The portrait of the perfect prince fails to excite admiration because it is monotonous. Persiles and Sigismunda arouse no interest in themselves or in their adventures, and the parade of a rather transparent incognito is merely irritating."[7]

Both Don Quixote and Persiles travel extensively. Alone, Don Quixote leaves his village briefly, and returns to it. The next two major journeys occupy all of the novel. On both, Sancho accompanies Don Quixote. Finally, they return home and Don Quixote dies. Persiles and his beloved Sigismunda also travel throughout the novel, but their journey is not circular: they start at the edge of Europe, in the mists of a northern island, the "Ultima Thule" of legend (Cervantes's geography is as "misty" and vague as the landscapes of this island), and little by little, as if attracted by an irresistible supernatural power, they move toward their target city Rome, "the antechamber of Heaven." Even more than love, it is religious faith that guides them to transcendental and absolute truth. *Persiles* never found a wide audience in Spain or elsewhere. The basic unanswered question is why does Cervantes lose his way after producing a masterpiece?

A tentative answer may well be that Cervantes wanted to appeal to different groups of readers, and he may have thought that the success of the first part of *Don Quixote* was a lucky strike. As insurance against difficult times ahead, he must have started to write *Persiles*.

Another possibility could be that when he wrote *Persiles*, Cervantes had lost touch with his creative genius. But, perhaps better, we can postulate that as an experimental writer, and especially as a professional writer, he was anxious to find a wider public for his works so he decided to try his luck in a different direction, a novel where the sufferings of separated lovers are finally rewarded by bliss, a happy ending in which they reach the center of the civilized Christian world, Rome, and the symbol of their committed love and everlasting happiness. A happy ending is always more acceptable to everyone than the wise yet bittersweet ending of *Don Quixote*.

Fully aware of his accomplishments, Cervantes wisely overlooks his shortcomings. He believes *Persiles* to be his best novel. We know otherwise. We also know that the same ironic and exploring genius that he reveals in *Don Quixote* is found in some of his short stories, also written toward the end of his life. The best short stories in his *Exemplary Novels* are comparable in literary quality to *Don Quixote*.

Any man or woman is defined, at least in part, not only by his or her successes but also by his or her failures. Certainly failures are not lacking in Cervantes's life. Perhaps the defining moment in his constant struggle to survive came when, after being ransomed and freed from his captivity, he found himself back in Spain penniless and without employment; further, he had burdened his relatives with a considerable debt — the ransom money that they had paid. Having tried and failed to find an administrative position in the Spanish possessions in the New Continent, he turned to business, collecting food for the Spanish Armada, and failed, landing in jail while his activity was investigated. In desperation, he turned to literature, becoming what we might call a professional writer. And yet *La Galatea* could not be called a financial success. He had to find other ways of making a living although he never renounced his goal of becoming a successful professional writer, and beyond that goal a loftier one, a trailblazer in the short story and the novel, a writer who would recreate for posterity human lives in all their complexity and richness. His bittersweet experiences and his rollercoaster destiny tossed him up and down during so much of his life. At the same time, these difficult and unpredictable instances gave him penetrating insight into hope, despair, and the will to survive and endure.

We find it hard to understand what it meant to be a professional writer toward the end of the sixteenth century and the beginning of the seventeenth century. It is true, we all know (or have heard) that the life of contemporary writers is often precarious and difficult financially. Yet today's writers enjoy a vast array of possibilities. They receive royalties when their books are published. Some even are granted lavish advances. They can contribute to magazines and newspapers, give lectures, and teach courses on how to write. All these activities and benefits were totally unknown to writers during Renaissance times. There was no way of copyrighting one's work, hence no defense against clandestine editions or sequels written by someone else (and that is precisely what happened to Cervantes and his *Don Quixote*), no royalties, and a small reading public. Books were expensive, which made it much harder to reach a vast audience. All this explains why life was so hard for someone like Cervantes when he decided to make a living writing literary works. The number of professional writers in Spain and elsewhere was minuscule. Very few, like Lope de Vega, would become rich and famous. Lope managed this feat in part due to his wit, his imagination, his poetic and dramatic genius, and above all his incredible fertility. We still do not know how many plays he wrote. Around four hundred have been preserved wholly or in part, but he must have written many more. Even Lope de Vega had to look for a patron, a rich nobleman who would help him financially in case of need.

A professional writer wants above all to be accepted and admired by a large audience. The goal is to sell the maximum number of copies possible. Yet to find an audience is not easy. Sometimes a writer has to probe in many directions and will try to write in more than one literary genre. Such was the case with Cervantes: his first novel reflects the pastoral mode fashionable during the Renaissance, while some of his short stories belong to the picaresque genre, the antithesis of pastoral idealization. If we bear in mind the dilemma of Cervantes as a professional writer in search of a public, we come close to solving a problem that has puzzled many Cervantine specialists.

Bold in Life and Literature

How can we explain these zigzagging trends in Cervantes's literary career? Quite simply that his life had this same pattern: a constant movement and shifting. He exhibited fortitude and drive; he moved on in spite of any obstacle, much like the main character in his masterpiece.

Cervantes was courageous and bold when facing danger. He proved this during his hard years as a captive. He was a survivor. Also, as a man with a curious, independent mind, he was capable of experimenting boldly with new literary trends and devices. Facing poverty, he was compelled to make a living and concluded he was more gifted as a writer than as a petty bureaucrat. As a professional writer his first goal was to find a public. He had to take into account the fashions of his time and the taste of the reading public. This is what drew him to traditional narrative forms: the pastoral, the picaresque, and romances of chivalry. As a bold experimenter, he wished to go beyond these limiting molds; he would use them but ultimately break them. Instead of employing the "tunnel vision" of the picaresque and the romance, he would write a novel that would encompass all sorts of characters, from different social groups, of diverse ages and occupations: a group portrait of Spanish society as seen from a wide area of central-southern Spain, without losing the focus on the main two characters. No romance had been capable of such a feat.

THE EMERGENCE OF A NEW SPIRIT

During his lifetime Cervantes witnessed a deep change of mood in his society. The Spain of his youth, under Emperor Charles V, was a country where new ideas circulated freely. The Renaissance winds were changing medieval ideas into modern ones, creating a feeling of exhilaration and a certain amount of confusion. The Spain of his mature years, under Philip II and later Philip III, was more self-centered, more restrictive in the field of new ideas. Philip II issued a decree in 1559 ordering that no one in his dominions should study abroad, with very limited exceptions. In 1564, another royal decree established that all the edicts of the Council of Trent, which had held its last session that very year, should become laws of the land in Spain. As the critic J. B. Avalle-Arce points out, "Cervantes felt as intellectually alienated in the Spain of the Philips as his hero Don Quijote de la Mancha, and for basically similar reasons: they are both out of step with their historical moment."[8] Don Quixote did not like the Spain around him and wanted to go back to a better, more glorious period, the Middle Ages.

We may venture that if Cervantes had gone beyond an indirect criticism of his society, he could have endangered not only the success of his novel but also its very existence, since a book could not be printed without the approval of the official censor. It was precisely because such a system of censorship and official approval existed that Cervantes managed to strike another blow for independent thinking: he insinuated that the printed word, the world of books, could not be trusted and suggested that people generally had put too much trust in books as such. When Don Quixote has to defend the romances of chivalry against their detractors, he claims there has to be truth in these romances; otherwise the censors could not have accepted them for publication. By truth he meant, of course, that the novel as a genre had to have some verisimilitude; it had to resemble the physical and spiritual reality of everyday life. We realize that Cervantes was conscious of the increasingly rigid and authoritarian intellectual climate in his country, and we may surmise that he was also aware that this rigidity applied to other countries as well. Throughout the second half of the sixteenth century and most, if not all, the seventeenth century, Western Europe was dominated by two sets of rules and rigid principles, both based on the written and printed words. Catholic countries were under the thrall of the articles approved by the Council of Trent as further defined and extended by papal bulls. Protestant countries were equally dependent on texts, in this instance the Bible in its different versions, whether Luther's famous translation into German or the different translations in England that culminated in the King James Version. The same phenomenon took place in Holland, Sweden, and other Protestant countries.

The seventeenth century proved to be one of the most authoritarian periods in the history of Western Europe, and since the two sets of guiding texts were at odds in some respects, the Thirty Years' War resulted, which was at bottom a religious conflict. Its aftermath entailed a slow recovery toward less repressive principles, with a renewal of hostilities in France with the revocation of the Edict of Nantes by Louis XIV and a renewed persecution of Jansenists and Protestants. We should not forget that the persecution of so-called witches was practiced on both sides of the religious divide, with spectacular numbers of victims, especially in German countries. The great strides of the early Renaissance were slowed down, and some of the Renaissance ideals went underground, reappearing in new forms during the Enlightenment. It was precisely then, throughout the eighteenth century, that the ideas and literary techniques of Cervantes's masterpiece took root and inspired the first wave of modern novels.

If we assume that the Renaissance was a period in which secular, individual values coexisted with orthodox religious values, and moreover that in Northern Europe there were new, independent interpretations of religious values that would be opposed and resisted by Southern Europe, we could conclude that *Don Quixote* is a novel expressing Renaissance values, whereas *Persiles* was centered around Counter-Reformation values. If we know that Cervantes was writing both novels at the same time, what are we to think? Two hypotheses may appear: his personality was so complex and his view of the world so subject to change that he was able to hold two conflicting views of literary creation at the same time. The other more plausible interpretation, as mentioned above, is simply that he was looking for a new audience. He knew that the intellectual climate of his country had been changing for a long time. Spain had become the cradle of the Counter-Reformation; both the Council of Trent and the Jesuit order were mainly inspired by Spain. At least in Spain, in Cervantes's mind, the reading public was ready for a novel inspired by the Counter-Reformation.

In contrast, perhaps the rest of Europe was not, which may explain the international success of *Don Quixote* and the failure of *Persiles*. The seventeenth century witnessed the ascent of Holland as an influential power. It also experienced the long and indecisive Thirty Years' War and the increasing importance of scientific and mathematical discoveries by Galileo, amongst others, and Newton. Trade, especially sea trade, was displaced from the Mediterranean to the Atlantic. Rome could be seen as the center of the Western world only by giving priority to traditional religious and cultural values.

This priority was being contested by important discoveries in two fields, astronomy and geography. Copernicus had upset the geocentric view of space relations that had prevailed since the Greco-Roman culture. Galileo not only reinforced Copernicus's heliocentric map of the skies, he discovered spots in the surface of the Sun. This destroyed an ancient belief that postulated imperfection in the Earth and perfection in all the other parts of the sky. Ancient geography could not keep up with the new discoveries. Aristotle had no description to match what the sailors were bringing back from the New World and beyond. In a subtle way, every new discovery of land, animals, and plants devalued ancient wisdom. Answers had to be found elsewhere, not in ancient texts. The human body was being described in detail. Slowly, advances in medicine replaced the old theories of Hippocrates and Galen. The number of books written in Latin and published in Renaissance times, considerable in scientific fields, diminished steadily until, by the beginning of the nineteenth century, it became almost insignificant.

Even the old Greek belief about the perfection of certain geometric figures, such as the sphere and the cube, was disproved when Kepler tried to establish the orbits of the planets. He started by trying to make them conform to circles inside squares but had to concede that they were elliptical. At first, these discoveries were limited in their scope because they did not reach beyond a very small number of scientists; nevertheless, their shocking influence could be detected by increasing numbers of elite groups. As for geography, the ancient and medieval descriptions of the earth, its fauna and flora, had to be constantly revised in view of the new findings that came back from the explorers in the New World and elsewhere. Traditional teaching in universities was losing ground, opening new spaces for thinkers and scientists determined to find startling new solutions to old problems.

Self-Conscious Literature, Self-Conscious Art

In his acclaimed *Les mots et les choses* (*The Order of Things*), Michel Foucault expounds a complex theory dealing with changes in the Western world consciousness during the seventeenth century, separating it culturally from the previous centuries. Even if we do not embrace completely Foucault's ideas, it seems clear that the Copernican revolution that changed our view of the cosmos during this century must have had parallels in the world of art and literature. Things are susceptible to different ways of being organized in our minds. The century that followed witnessed heroic efforts to organize the world of plants and animals by Linneus, Buffon, and other great naturalists. At least in part, the seventeenth century turns inwards. Both thinkers and artists (including writers) are beginning to reflect on the impact of their inner world on their interpretation of the outside world of things, of plants, animals, people, and landscapes.

Thus, we may define the seventeenth century as an era of continual surprises, of contradictions between received knowledge and knowledge empirically produced by science, observation, and exploration. *Don Quixote* is a novel full of surprises. It is surprising to witness a deep change of personality such as the one taking place in the first chapters of the novel. Moreover, we find our hero surprised by the turn of events in almost every chapter. Things are not what they appear to be. This is one of the basic lessons of the novel, and it is in tune with the cultural, social, and political developments of its time and anticipates the centuries that follow.

Something also changed in the minds of creative artists and writers in the seventeenth century. Painters began to paint works in which they included their own image. The most obvious experiment in the interaction between an artist and his masterpiece is found in Velázquez's huge canvas *The Ladies in Waiting* and Vermeer's *Allegory of Fame*. In both instances, the artists paint themselves as part of the canvas, and their presence is crucial to the composition in terms of theme and perspective.

We know that canvasses are flat. Yet the correct use of perspective, shading, and chiaroscuro (contrasting light and dark areas) gives us depth, or three-dimensional perspective. This is especially true during the Baroque era as soon as Caravaggio develops his dramatic chiaroscuro technique, which becomes popular all over Western Europe, including in the works of Rembrandt. Yet when the artist inserts himself in the canvas in the act of painting, we ask whether he has introduced a fourth dimension, Time perhaps? After all, it takes time to paint a picture. Is the artist uniting past (the action as it was developing) and present (the finished product)? Where is the artist—inside his work, painting it? Or perhaps outside, looking in? Where are we? All these questions may be asked if we examine Velázquez's *The Ladies in Waiting* (in Spanish, *Las Meninas*) or Vermeer's *Allegory of Fame*.

Velázquez's canvas is so complex that the viewer is perplexed until he or she begins to decipher it. It may be useful to underline now that this complexity and beauty can be compared to the complexity and beauty of Cervantes's novel. We will understand *Don Quixote* better if we try to see a few links between the canvas and the novel.

Velázquez, Rembrandt, Bernini, and Vermeer belong to a period when artists are conscious of the great achievements of the Renaissance and try to go beyond them and create new challenges. Bernini's sculptures are perhaps more refined and expressive than Michaelangelo's. Rembrandt is as expressive and dramatic as any artist had been. In *The Night Watch* we have the feeling that an inner tension is about to explode and project parts of the painting out of the canvas toward the viewer.

Velázquez's canvas is especially interesting for us because the artist probably had read Cervantes's novel. *The Ladies in Waiting* has all the immediacy and spontaneity of a modern snapshot. Nobody is posing: neither the young princess nor the lady in waiting, the young dwarf nor the dog. Velázquez behind his huge easel is serenely examining everything before resuming his work. Yet he seems to be looking toward us, the public, and his gaze projects out of the painting. In the background the king and his young queen are reflected, blurred, in a mirror. Perhaps the king and his wife were standing there where we are standing now, outside the canvas. A servant in the background, framed by an open door, is either entering the room or leaving. Velázquez seems to be saying, "I am practically a member of the royal family, I live among them, painting is a noble occupation, a great artist is to be compared to the highest nobleman." This exalted position was reinforced by the inclusion of the artist himself inside the work he was painting, surrounded by members of the royal family. While there were complaints that the canvas was at bottom a self-portrait, not a portrait of the young princess and the court ladies around her, Velazquez was responding to a trend initiated by Cervantes, whose desire was to become indissolubly fused with his characters: "For me alone was Don Quixote born, and I for him; he knew how to act, and I to write; the two of us alone are one" (Gr., 939).

If *Don Quixote* is a self-aware novel, a novel in whose text we find traces of the author, of the creative process, of parts of the novel itself, then we should call the two masterpieces by Velázquez and Vermeer "self-aware art." Vermeer's self-portrait, *Allegory of Fame*, has been given other titles, such as *The Painter in His Studio*. More modest than Velázquez, he does not show his face, only his back. His presence is still significant and attests to the fact that he is the one who conceived and organized every square inch of the canvas.

Medieval sculptors and even cathedral builders were so modest that their names often have not come down to us or their work was a collaborative division of labor produced in workshops. By Renaissance times most artists were signing their works. In the seventeenth century both writers and artists are striving for recognition and independence. Lope de Vega and Cervantes are waging war on two fronts: as professional writers they must endeavor to make money from their writings. At the same time they appeal to distinguished noblemen who are interested in literature for patronage, preferably in the form of a pension.

A possible explanation of the plight of writers and painters is the collapse of the medieval social and economic structure. The rise of a new urban and monetary system left them struggling to find a place in society that would give them greater visibility and dignity. Both writers and artists needed powerful patrons in order to survive. They were aware of their talent, indeed their genius, yet recognition was granted grudgingly if at all. Some artists, such as Titian, Rubens, and Bernini, were courted by kings, while others, equally worthy, led a precarious existence. Among the second group we find Cervantes. Consciously or not, he had to state and restate his presence inside his novel, reminding us who was writing it and who was in control. Was this a way of advertising? If a novelist could write himself into a novel, why should the artist not paint himself in a painting?

2

Experimenting with
Existing Narrative Tools

Throughout his literary career, Cervantes delighted in experimenting with different narrative models popular in the sixteenth century, at times improving them, parodying them, imitating them, and reinventing them. There were three main types of novels whose style and themes Cervantes could tap into: the romances of chivalry and the pastoral and picaresque novels. Each of these genres had been solidly established by the time he started to write his masterpiece and each of them is linked to him in some way. The many works published at the time have been defined by these predictable literary conventions because readers wanted and expected them and would have been disappointed by their absence. Today we would consider them contrived.

The romances of chivalry combined the refined ideas about courtly love promoted by Eleanor of Aquitaine, who married first the French king Louis VII and later the English king Henry II, and by Chrétien de Troyes, who fathered the "roman courtois," or courtly novel, in the twelfth century, with the heroic spirit of the old epic poems. The institution of chivalry had become more and more codified by traditions and conventions inspired often by the church in an attempt to rein in and soften the endemic violence of early medieval life. To this foundation were added descriptions of exotic lands and lofty castles, long genealogies of knights and princesses, and many supernatural elements—such as wizards, witches, flying horses, and magic arches—under which only true lovers could cross. This combination of courtly love, battle scenes, and the supernatural was a formula that could please different groups of readers, but the end result was totally divorced from the realities of everyday life. In these novels, Cervantes found a perfect subject for parody.

Whereas the romances of chivalry are a projection of medieval attitudes into Renaissance times, the pastoral novel is much closer to Renaissance tastes and sensibilities. Pastoral novels tend to be static with little action, since what matters most is the description of inner feelings, such as love, jealousy, longing, nostalgia, and sadness, in a landscape always verdant and pleasant, in which nature becomes an enclosed garden. Once again the conventions of the era interfere with originality. Cervantes knew this genre well, and *La Galatea* exhibits the limitations and restrictions characteristic of it.

The picaresque, created in Spain by such distinguished novels as *Lazarillo de Tormes* (1554) and *Guzmán de Alfarache* (1599), had become very popular there. The world of the picaresque novel is diametrically opposed to that of the pastoral. There can be no doubt that in a spectrum of literary values the picaresque would be placed at one end, let us say the ultraviolet, and the pastoral would be at the other end, as infrared. There is a marked contrast between the bitter, degrading visions of the underworld described by the authors of the picaresque and the idealized, Platonic visions of the pastoral. Cervantes was so familiar with both genres and so adept at using them that he was able to combine both visions in the several picaresque sketches that later appeared as part of his *Exemplary Novels* even while he was writing his masterpiece.

In *Don Quixote*, the picaresque dimension appears sporadically in Palomeque's inn and when the knight meets the galley

Gustave Doré (1832–1883), *Don Quixote on Horseback*. Engraved by
Heliodore Joseph Pisan. Photo: Snark / Art Resource, NY.

slaves including Ginés de Pasamonte, who is their most typical representative. Given the popularity and success of Cervantes's masterpiece, it is legitimate to ask whether it is through this book that the picaresque mode exerts influence in the European literature of the following generations. This genre continued to be popular in Spain. Francisco de Quevedo published *El Buscón* (*The Rogue*) in 1626, ten years after Cervantes's death.

The seventeenth and eighteenth centuries give us the German, French, and English picaresque with Christoffel von Grimmelshausen's *Simplicissimus*, Alain René Lesage's *Gil Blas de Santillane*, and Daniel Defoe's *Moll Flanders*, respectively. In this epoch, the picaresque appears as a "novel of education" or *Bildungsroman* (less somber than the Spanish models), in which a naïve young man learns slowly and painfully about the world through trial and error. Young Candide, whom we discuss at length in a later chapter, and Tom Jones are also good examples of this type. This mode goes into hibernation in the first half of the nineteenth century during the Romantic era but appears again in the second half of the century as realism and naturalism coincide. Loneliness and distrust prevail as the picaroon is overwhelmed by his or her circumstance, struggling to survive, but generally the atmosphere has improved in comparison with earlier Spanish picaroon fate. The basic rules remain the same: a picaresque novel is a confession in which the main character tells all about his "successes and misfortunes," to quote Lazarillo, the original rogue. It offers us a glimpse into extreme existential situations, where human beings face daily the threat of death by starvation and the dishonor of being arrested, jailed, and branded as criminals. Their heroes, or rather antiheroes, are afflicted with tunnel vision. They see a world where survival is perhaps possible but always precarious. Luck is not enough. The rogue must constantly be alert and astute, ready to escape or to attack. The relatively affluent readers of these novels could only imagine the pressures exerted on the wretched characters by abject poverty, vice, and life in slums or jails, yet they must have felt a mixture of curiosity and fear while reading about the strenuous efforts to survive in the life of the picaresque heroes and heroines. It was an unsettled world, one where sudden changes could overwhelm instantly the life of an individual or a family. As the British historian J. H. Plumb describes it:

> In the twentieth century, moments of luck in life, sudden reverses of fortune, are rarely explored by novelist or poet. This reflects a great change in the structure of European societies, and indicates the gradual growth of economic and social stability in individual lives. We are all much more settled and secure than our ancestors. In Cervantes's day, bankruptcy was commonplace, sudden promotion could be overturned by sudden dismissal, affluence followed by destitution. . . . It was a world, too, in which power was easily abused, far more easily abused than we can often grasp. And it was a world in which crime and violence, great and petty, flourished to a horrifying degree and, more often than not, without any redress. Such conditions created not only fear and anxiety but also a yearning for the good and the noble, a longing for the just to triumph, for relief from the horrors and terrors of the world of experience.[1]

Cervantes intuited that a limited picaresque mode offered no hope to the reader who identified with the novel's hero, and he also probably guessed something even more important: the future of Western culture would be one in which many competing voices would be heard. This was especially true in the area of religious and philosophical thought. The Reformation introduced a new set of theological attitudes and values in defiance of the established ones, and within Protestant countries new voices would be heard that departed from one central set of values. Europe became theologically divided. Humpty-Dumpty could not be put together again. The seventeenth century witnessed the brutal clash of differing ideologies in an inconclusive war that devastated many countries and retained the record for ferocity until the great wars of the twentieth century. An uneasy truce after the war could not disguise the tensions and hatreds that flared up time and time again. Catholics were marginalized in England and Holland. Protestants were persecuted in France toward the end of the reign of Louis XIV and the Spanish Inquisition did not disappear until the end of the eighteenth century. In the field of purely intellectual ideas, Europe would remain divided for some time between Copernicans and anti-Copernicans, between Skeptics and Cartesians on one hand and neo-Scholastics on the other. The eighteenth century would witness the increasing power of lay, scientific ideas, while in the area of religion the increasing power of Russia would underline the presence of Orthodox Christianity. In Europe during these centuries many voices were present, often talking past each other, often creating confusion and misunderstandings.

Novels written during the same period as *Don Quixote* suffer from a uniformity of perspective, a lack of variety in viewpoint and ideology. This is especially true of the picaresque novels. Written in the first person, as confidence or confession, they enjoy all the advantages of the first-person viewpoint — immediacy, pathos, heightened emotional atmosphere — but also all the disadvantages and limitations of this first-person view. Anguish, emotional claustrophobia, a feeling of powerlessness, loneliness — these are the reader's reactions when reading most picaresque novels. This is in marked contrast to Cervantes's novel where the narrative technique is at the service of the large idea representing a variety of viewpoints. The main character in the picaresque is a sad and lone wanderer, "a true exile who never achieves authentic dialogue with other men because most of them distrust him and he distrusts them all, once he has acquired a little experience."[2]

Let us consider, for example, *Lazarillo de Tormes,* a charming and ultimately sad narrative in the first-person singular, supposedly autobiographical. It is a confession made by a rogue to an unnamed figure of authority who remains silent all during the narrative much like a modern psychoanalyst might. It is still not clear who the author was, but we must assume he had a certain level of education since he quotes Cicero. The book has been often attributed to Diego Hurtado de Mendoza, a courtier in the court of Charles V, ambassador to Venice and to the Council of Trent. If *Lazarillo de Tormes* is the first realistic novel of modern times, as many critics claim, then why is it almost unknown outside the Hispanic world? This question still puzzles many Spanish scholars since the picaresque tradition penetrated many other cultures after *Lazarillo*'s inception in 1554.

The novel's dominant theme is hunger. The story begins when the young Lázaro is only eight years old and very innocent. He loses his father, who was a thief and swindler. His mother can no longer support him, and so she hands him over to a blind beggar, who mistreats him and starves him. From him, Lázaro learns to survive by stealing and lying, but after a number of cruel, brutal jokes played on him by the beggar, the boy retaliates in kind, therein the irony of the pupil who teaches the teacher. Lázaro does not have a better time with his subsequent masters except for the impoverished *hidalgo,* a low-ranking nobleman with an exaggerated sense of honor, who stands in front of his unfurnished house with a sheathed sword, picking his teeth with a toothpick as though he has eaten when, in fact, he has not. Now the tables are turned and the boy looks after his master, who lectures him on the topic of honor and the virtue of having clean hands when eating, neither of which means anything to Lazarillo whose concern is to find the next meal. No doubt Cervantes was familiar with this work, in particular with the character of the *hidalgo* and the irony of the story. The relationship between Lazarillo and the *hidalgo* brings to mind the camaraderie between Don Quixote and Sancho in a very abbreviated way, especially in the unrealistic attitude of the *hidalgo,* his exaggerated sense of honor, and the importance of appearances vis-à-vis the real world. This is in contrast with the boy's down-to-earth concern that makes his master's speech regarding honor and cleanliness ludicrous. Loneliness, degradation, and dishonor are also themes in the novel. When his life seems to stabilize, it is because he consents to be the cuckolded husband of a woman who is the mistress of an important ecclesiastic.

In some ways we should not consider Lázaro's life a total failure: he is now well established, he has a permanent job, a wife, a house, and a steady income. He is a cuckold, and other people know this, yet he is still alive and up to a point prosperous. What he does not acknowledge, and the author clearly points out, is that he has fallen morally, the ultimate irony. He must be lonely because he is reluctant to talk about his life to other people. Who are his friends? To whom can he tell the truth about his life? He tells a person of a higher class because he uses "Vuestra Merced" (your honor), the polite, grammatical, formal form of addressing a person. Perhaps he has chosen a man, an important courtier, to tell his story to because he realizes this man has few contacts among Lazarillo's neighbors and will keep the confession to himself. Loneliness is the key to the end of the novel.

Indeed, when we examine the picaresque and its origins in Spain, it is impossible to separate the evolution of the novel as a genre from the main changes in society: ideology, politics, and the economy. Specifically, between the date of *Lazarillo* and the date of *Guzmán de Alfarache* many changes took place in Spain and also in most Western European countries: the Protestant Reformation and the Catholic Counter-Reformation made it difficult, if not impossible, for a writer in a Catholic country to attack the Catholic Church, either directly or indirectly. In *Lazarillo* we find a frank, precise, powerful criticism of certain practices associated with the church: the sellers of indulgences are shown to be avaricious and deceptive; poor Lázaro is taken for a fool because his wife is having an affair with a church dignitary. Nothing similar will be found in *Guzmán*. In many ways, the picaresque novel is becoming the mouthpiece of the Counter-Reformation. The Council of Trent had underlined all the differences between Catholic and Protestant theologies and in the process had also upheld traditional values that harkened back to the medieval period, such as a totally negative view of life in this world, in this "valley of tears." One of the many unanswered questions in Spanish literary history is why is there the long hiatus between the first picaresque novel, *Lazarillo,* and the second, *Guzmán de Alfarache*? No other novel of this type appears in between, in spite of the fact that the first one had been very successful. Any presumptive author of a picaresque novel had to think hard about repackaging this subgenre to make it acceptable to the new trends generated by the Counter-Reformation. It is not surprising that this enterprise found no takers for a long time: it was risky, dangerous, and difficult to adapt a genre that had started as critical of both society and the church. It required utmost caution and an elaborate system of inner criticism, which is what we find in *Guzmán*. The final result is much more somber and despairing than what we find in the first novel—and yet, we should not forget, the second novel was a "bestseller" without rival. It followed the pattern of the first novel, with the first-person narrative, the lonely boy wandering from one master to the next, always hungry and insecure, but it got rid of criticism of the church and emphasized the repentance of the hero through endless moralizing that makes the novel in its original text almost impossible to read today.

The "hero" of the second picaresque novel, *Guzmán*, sees only a limited part of the world, and what he finds is corruption, treachery, disillusion, and sinfulness. His rejection of what he sees is unequivocal. What is left is purely didactic. Since this world is totally evil, the only hope is another world, and by implication there is no salvation outside the Catholic Church. Every instant of the picaroon's life after repentance should be guided by the precepts of the church. This message also appears in art and architecture. From the Spiritual Exercises of the Jesuits to Calderón's *Autos Sacramentales*, Bernini's statues, and Baroque churches in Bavaria, Spain, and the New World, the message is the same: only strict adherence to the principles of the church will bring respite from the anguish of loneliness, futility, sin, and ultimate annihilation. The picaresque novel becomes a cog in a gigantic intellectual and theological machine. The Protestant world has its own version of the same intricate theological and ethical system, whether in the sermons of Jonathan Edwards or the pages of *Pilgrim's Progress*.

Cervantes rejects this narrow, claustrophobic view of the world without becoming a heretic or an unbeliever. His emphasis on dialogue in his novels, and the fact that he often blurs the answers by pitting one opinion against another without offering a clear conclusion, mean that his attitude is not basically in tune with the theological mode that has become all-important in political, ecclesiastical, and even philosophical circles in the second half of the sixteenth century. The situation tends to get worse during the first half of the seventeenth century. On the one hand, great advances are made in science and philosophy by Galileo, Kepler, Leibnitz, Descartes, Pascal, and, toward the end of the century, Newton. On the other hand, dialogue between the southern and the northern parts of Europe is interrupted by the bitter, protracted Thirty Years' War and also by the hunt for witches that develops in Germany and elsewhere.

In general, during the sixteenth century the negative attitude about novels is constant, from both church and state. Churchmen criticize novels as a waste of time and as perverters of youth, and sending novels to the New World is prohibited. Nothing should distract the inhabitants of the Spanish dominions from hard work, discipline, and remittances to the crown and the mother country. In the rest of Europe, the sixteenth and seventeenth centuries are not wholly favorable to the new genre.

How and why the picaresque literary fashion was born is a subject that has been only partially explored. Although many of the novels in this genre seem to be autobiographical, it is probable that we are facing a literary device, not a real situation. We know enough about the lives of the most distinguished writers of picaresque novels to realize none of them would qualify as picaroons. Diego Hurtado de Mendoza, the presumed author of *Lazarillo,* was a nobleman with a distinguished pedigree and a career as a courtier and a delegate to the Council of Trent. Mateo Alemán, the author of *Guzmán de Alfarache,* perhaps the quintessential picaresque novel, never lacked for good food and shelter, and although as a converted Jew his psychological existence may have been at times precarious, his physical needs were always met up to a level that we could call, in modern terms, middle class or upper middle class. Francisco de Quevedo, who wrote *El Buscón,* another famous picaresque novel still widely read today, was a nobleman, a knight of the Order of Santiago. Often he was seen at the royal court, and his portrait was painted by Velázquez. What impelled these writers, so far above the average Spaniard of their time, to write about a wretched underclass? What made so many readers interested in what these writers had to say? Finally, how did this type of realism with all its imperfections and limitations become so entrenched in Western letters and ultimately in the consciousness of Western minds?

Cervantes had read *Lazarillo* as well as other picaresque novels, for example, *Guzmán de Alfarache,* the success of which he may have envied. He was no doubt aware that his generation offered him a pattern, a model, leading to one specific type of literary realism: the picaresque mode. He experimented with it time and time again, always dissatisfied with the original formula, always tinkering with it, trying to find other messages behind and beneath the official pattern. He finally devised his own formula for realism in the novel and the short story, one that incorporated a few elements of the picaresque yet gave them new meaning and enlarged their original message. The result was so original and so creative that it made it almost imperative to forget the picaresque as a path to first-rate literature.

Cervantes includes in his novels numerous sketches of characters and situations that are either picaresque or close to it; nevertheless, we never feel overwhelmed or oppressed by them. They become elements in a much vaster canvas; they are "decompressed" by the presence of other characters, and the poisoned atmosphere so typical of picaresque novels is dissipated by Cervantes. Take, for example, one of his *Exemplary Novels,* "Rinconete and Cortadillo." It is the tale of two lads who escape their families and try to find a new life in the big city, in this case Seville, then the most populous city in Spain. He describes in detail the underworld with its thieves, pimps, and beggars, all tightly organized in a Spanish Mafia. Its powerful godfather, with a wooden leg, Monipodio, respects the individual reactions of the lads. One of them decides to go back home since he does not like life in the underworld, while the other lad decides to stay. In a word, Cervantes believes that experience molds our personalities and makes us capable of making decisions that reflect our inner freedom. This is a new concept, one that is missing in the traditional picaresque novels, the pastoral romances, or the romances of chivalry. It is precisely this inner freedom that makes Cervantes's characters authentic and so true to life.

3

Constructing *Don Quixote*

Because there were few ancient Greek and Roman models to imitate in the field of fiction, Renaissance writers were forced to be original. In his effort to conceive the modern novel, Cervantes showed ambition, imagination, and tenacity. His novel is one of the longest produced in his generation, and it is the most audacious in terms of its structure and its characters, which seem so spontaneous that we do not think of them as an author's creation as the novel unfolds before us. No wonder, then, that *Don Quixote* has influenced profoundly so many other works in the following centuries.

WHO IS THE AUTHOR?

In the preface of *Don Quixote*, Cervantes beckons us to enter the enchanted world of his novel. There in the novel we find him, the author, with a "friend," or rather an acquaintance, or perhaps a stranger: Cide Hamete Benengeli, a mysterious Moorish historian. Hamete has written the "true" history of Don Quixote and Sancho, and Cervantes has helped by finding his manuscript, which becomes the story that is told to us. Thus, from the beginning, we receive mixed signals and contradictory instructions. "Some assembly required" could be the slogan for the novel. Cervantes appears again later in his novel. By writing himself into the story, he has created the first "self-aware" novel, with important consequences for novels that followed, as the critic Robert Alter has observed. Cervantes breaks new ground when his novel calls attention to itself, that is, becomes a self-referential work of art. Who wrote it? Who translated it? Where and how was the text we are reading really written? Certainly Cervantes is jesting and toying with his reader, but we are given to understand that the text was written in Arabic by Cide Hamete, and we are told that Moorish historians lie or at least exaggerate most of the time. What about the person who translated Hamete's work? Did he really know Arabic? Did anyone look over his translation? And where is the rest of the text of the novel? Abruptly, in the middle of an adventure, in part 1, chapter 9, we have to pause, the action is frozen and the two rivals of that adventure are paralyzed, their swords still in the air, because we have run out of text.

This device, of pausing the narrative while searching for the lost manuscript, is an example of how Cervantes distances himself in order to provide perspective to full advantage and with dramatic impact. The technique of opening up the scope of the novel may remind us of the reason why medieval cathedrals—as opposed to the Romanesque cathedrals—have high vaults. The windows are now two stories high so that more light comes through. Similarly, Cervantes, by creating a second author opens up the novel to a larger perspective and also to some confusion. Further, in doing so, he creates suspense. In other words, the technique has two aims: perspective and dramatic effect. We are familiar with it in many examples offered by popular literature, even in such early Hollywood movies as *The Perils of Pauline*. Perhaps a character whom we have come to like or admire finds himself or herself in a dangerous predicament. Suddenly the movie reel ends with Pauline tied to the railroad tracks; the train is about to arrive at great speed, and she is in mortal danger. We are left in suspense and will have to wait a while, perchance a whole week, until a young savior arrives and frees Pauline in the nick of time. This is what happens in chapters 8 and 9 of part 1, where Don Quixote and a Basque opponent are about to

Francisco de Goya y Lucientes (1746–1828), *Don Quixote*. British
Museum, London, Great Britain. Photo: Alinari / Art Resource, NY.

do battle. Swords are unsheathed and raised, blows are about to fall. But . . . the manuscript that tells our story ends here, and we will have to wait until Cervantes, by chance, finds the rest of it, in the shop of a Toledo merchant who is using it as wrapping paper.

Why should we believe an Arab historian when he casts doubt about a chapter of the novel? To complicate things further, where did Cide Hamete Benengeli obtain the information included in that chapter? Is the whole chapter a lie? Is the initial statement a lie? Who can tell us where to find the truth? Cide Hamete is troubling because he introduces a germ of doubt in the process of creating the novel: "he is both the untruthful author from whom Cervantes distances himself in order to judge the work that he himself is in the process of writing, and at the same time the scrupulous historian who reveals to the reader his effort to capture his hero in all their fullness, thus making the reader enter into the very act of literary creation."[1]

We see the superimposed and almost invisible threads by which Cervantes moves his characters—and when we begin to suspect that the threads lead to Cervantes, we find the author has momentarily eluded us and we are facing the Arab historian, Hamete Benengeli, who is, as an Arab historian, totally unreliable. At moments like these we realize Cervantes's novel has become self-conscious and includes in many mysterious ways powerful allusions to itself, to its author, and to the art of writing novels, including criticism of literature in general.

We search in vain for anything as complex in the other novels of that time. We must wait until much later to find anything resembling Cervantes's games, for his labyrinth of mirrors is almost impossible to duplicate. At the beginning of the second part of the novel, Don Quixote learns about a just-published book describing his recent adventures. He worries: how accurate is this book? Is he being portrayed in a false or indecent light?

Don Quixote is about to become a reader of the first part of *Don Quixote*. The self-referential novel is a conspicuous topic of contemporary literature. Cervantes pioneered it three centuries earlier.

Historical versus Poetic "Truth"

One of the goals pursued by Cervantes in his novel is to separate, in the mind of his readers, history from poetry (including in this category the romances of chivalry, legends, and popular versions of the past). History is an honest and objective account of the past. Poetry, interpreted as encompassing not only poems but also fiction that mixes romance, legends, and supernatural, fantastic, irrational beings and situations, may be extremely popular but is essentially a beautiful lie and in most cases, a serious distortion of reality, an adulteration or negation of everyday experience. Common sense, plain, careful observation, and in a few cases the controlled observation and analysis of the beginnings of modern science refute the distortions and fantastic depictions of both legends and romances of chivalry. A knight who has been cut in two by the mighty sword of his adversary cannot be put back together by such a magic concoction as the Balm of Fierabras. A man is not made of cardboard; it is impossible to glue together his broken halves.

Enchanters, wizards, even one of the greatest of all wizards, Merlin, appear in the pages of the novel. They are there to explain, from Don Quixote's viewpoint, why his adventures do not turn into victories the way they should. Merlin is, surely, a ruse to entrap Don Quixote into new, frantic efforts to disenchant Dulcinea; as a deus ex machina Merlin is not totally convincing, yet Don Quixote seems to take to heart the wizard's instructions. The very absence of magic as such, magic as accepted by the author and the characters in a novel full of adventures, indicates a new turn of mind, favorable to science and common sense, unfavorable to magic and superstition.

Thus Cervantes bewilders us. He tells us that history is an effort to find out the truth. On one hand, fiction has its own rules. This praise of history, this avowed superiority of history over fiction, is given to us in a work of fiction—which, on the other hand, claims to be the narrative of true historical facts. Before we decide what is the precise message Cervantes wants to convey, we should perhaps assume Cervantes is toying with his readers and disregard his convoluted message altogether. We bear in mind that Cervantes was acquainted, directly or indirectly, with Plato's ideas about poetry (that is, in this context, fiction, novels) and scientific and philosophical truth. In *The Republic* Plato proposes to exile the poets because they embellish reality to the point of lying and thus cannot be accepted as intellectual leaders of the community. Much has been written about Aristotle's influence on Cervantes's ideas about literature, yet Plato may have had the last word: the search for truth is to be preferred to a poetic embellishment of human lives and human experience. "'History is like a sacred thing; it must be truthful'" (Gr., 479).

After such enthusiastic praise of history and historians, we come suddenly to a contradictory and defiant remark. History is our guide to truth and historians are truth's faithful servants, but the author of the present historical narrative may be less than perfect; even more, he may be seriously at fault; he may have left out some of the most glorious deeds of the tale's hero: "In this account I know there will be found everything that could be rightly desired in the most pleasant history, and if something of value is missing from it, in my opinion the fault lies with the dog who was its author rather than with any defect in its subject" (Gr., 68–69). Almost at the same time, Cervantes praises history and historians but makes us suspicious of the historian whose work we are now reading, and there is no doubt that, having spent five sad years as a slave in Muslim Algiers, he is fully aware that the word "dog" applied to our Arab historian is one of the worst insults available in the Muslim culture.

We are beginning to suspect Cervantes is giving his readers contradictory and ambiguous messages. Distrusting text written by a historian could ultimately result in casting doubt upon the historian's sources, viewpoints, and techniques in establishing the truth. If historical truth cannot be firmly established, what are the consequences?

LANGUAGE AND ITS IMPLICATIONS

According to Michel Foucault, Cervantes should be recognized as opening new vistas and creating a new way of looking at the world that teaches us to look into the meaning of words as they relate to things. As Carroll B. Johnson notes, Foucault, in *The Order of Things,* reminds us that modern linguistic science has shown conclusively that "there is no inherent, organic similarity between the word and whatever it stands for . . . but in Cervantes's time the arbitrary nature of the linguistic sign had not been discovered. In fact, the professional linguists of the sixteenth century assumed an organic relation. Michel Foucault considers that Cervantes had in effect discovered the arbitrary relation of word to thing, that language is related not so much to things as to mental processes, and by so doing ushered in the modern age."[2] If we assume, as many scholars did in medieval and Renaissance times, that a word designating a thing was a spiritual emanation or projection of that thing, words could become so closely intertwined with the object they designated that no personal interpretation would be possible.

Don Quixote and Sancho disagree almost all the time about the world around them because each one of them interprets what he sees according to a code. This code is based on the individual, his culture, his experience, a worldview that can be very special, and many other factors: thus the multiplicity of viewpoints and interpretations.

Don Quixote has internalized all the messages of the romances of chivalry; he sees the whole world through them. He is bound to disagree with Sancho, who sees things through a different lens, using a different code. Linguistic relativism, as discussed by Leo Spitzer, is related to a deeper phenomenon: people react to language according to cultural patterns that have been etched in their minds and are still being etched and developed during their life experiences. A sound reading of Cervantes's novel will validate the interpretation of everyday life by the characters in the novel, who in turn represent all of us, in our interpretation of the words, signs, and symbols around them. No longer will language be anchored in a solid, unbreakable relation with "things," with the world outside us. Privileged by this newfound freedom, we can defend individual interpretations and freedoms, and instead of a rigid definition of our duties and our place in the world, a new space is created where dialogue will replace the dictatorial powers of the past.

Human beings are not passive vessels waiting to be filled with words that link them to things. They are active decoders of language, signs, and symbols. Emotions may compel one person to interpret a word or a sign in a subjective way. Words like "freedom," "happiness," "privacy," and "honor" have different meanings in different cultures. Languages are not the only example of codes or signifying systems. Sancho and Don Quixote both speak Spanish, but often they use words in a different way. Don Quixote's vocabulary is much larger than Sancho's, and it also contains many words that were old-fashioned and hard for the average Spaniard of that time to understand. Moreover, Don Quixote often reacts to stimuli in a peculiar way because he associates what he sees or hears with events he has read about in his beloved romances of chivalry. Today we continue to use natural languages to communicate with each other, but we have added other systems of signs and symbols. As Carroll B. Johnson observes, "we use artificial languages such as Morse code, musical notation, shorthand, and BASIC. We are surrounded by myriad visual signs whose meaning is established by reference to agreed-upon codes. The red light means 'stop,' the green means 'go.' But at sea the same red and green lights mean 'left' and 'right,' respectively. Back in port, the red light means something else. . . . The entire world presents itself as a giant text to be read, by Don Quixote and by all the rest of us."[3]

Who Is Don Quixote?

"I know who I am," Don Quixote states early in the novel. Here he manages to define himself, his mind, his quest, his ambitions, and his love; he will be faithful to himself until the end. We seem to hear an echo of Polonius's famous advice, "This above all: To thine own self be true." The readers also get to know Don Quixote and Sancho as one would know old friends from high school. Cervantes does not make any of his main or secondary characters betray themselves. We know what to expect, and this is why we can notice important changes in the psychology of both Sancho and Don Quixote toward the end of the novel. Their adventures and misadventures mature them. They slowly evolve, visibly aging, and Sancho becomes surer of himself. All the while we witness the crisscrossing of viewpoints and opinions, a constant readjusting of perspectives with each character striving to have his view prevail yet at the same time being subtly influenced by the attitudes of other characters. No man is an island in Cervantes's novel; each character changes slowly and is enriched by the presence and influence of other characters. In other words, he creates characters who strive to seek freedom and a better knowledge of themselves, not—as in many medieval works to illustrate certain moral norms. Cervantes's novel can be placed historically between two great waves of didactic-moralizing literature, the first in medieval times anchored in Christian morality and the second during the Counter-Reformation as a reaction against Renaissance uncertainty or skepticism. Briefly, a didactic work presents a problematic situation that will be solved by one or more characters in a right or wrong way, and the result will be underlined in an explicit statement of the moral of the story (as in many fables) or else will be implicit because it is crystal clear. Literature is thus placed at the service of a given ideology. The closest we come to didacticism in *Don Quixote* is the tale of "The Man Who Was Recklessly Curious," but the atmosphere of this tale is very different from the rest of the novel. Anselmo, driven by an unhealthy curiosity, with no goals or clear purpose, totally differs from Don Quixote and his quest. In a heroic and sustained effort, our knight wants to prove that human life can be as beautiful and fulfilling as a literary work or, to be precise, as beautiful and fulfilling as a romance of chivalry. Every one of his thoughts and actions brings him closer to his ideal: to live like a new hero of a literary work and to resemble, for instance, Amadís of Gaul, the greatest hero of chivalry romances.

Foucault caught a glimpse of that important aspect of our knight's personality, although the identification with the romances of chivalry does not take into account the times when Don Quixote acts like everybody else. His folly is intermittent and flares up only at certain moments, while the impressions of the external world can be equated, by an effort of the will, with the characters, situations, and objects found in the romances of chivalry. Don Quixote's adventures are the highlights of the novel, but if we count the intervals between one adventure and those that follow, we come to realize that many hours pass during which Don Quixote's mind approaches normalcy. Still, we must agree with Foucault: "His adventures will be a deciphering of the world: a diligent search over the entire surface of the earth for the forms that will prove that what the books say is true. Each exploit must be a proof: it consists, not in a real triumph—which is why history is not really important—but in an attempt to transform reality into a sign. Don Quixote reads the world in order to prove his books."[4]

The books in Don Quixote's library are mainly about heroes whom he wishes to emulate. He finds, however, that he stumbles, and his imperfect acts point to a flawed hero. A flawed hero is easier to approach, easier to understand, and above all easier to identify with. Perhaps more important, a flawed hero is believable, as we are all aware that flawless heroes are either nonexistent or very rare. Even such traditional epic heroes as Achilles were provided by their creators with at least one weak spot: for Achilles it was his heel, and also, psychologically, his hubris. The Teutonic hero Sigfried had a vulnerable spot in his back where a leaf prevented the dragon's blood from bathing his skin with its protective magic powers.

Our knight embodies many traits characteristic of famous heroes. He is above all brave; he defies giants or what he thinks are giants, whether windmills or wine skins; he does not hesitate to enter the lions' cage; he does battle with the Knight of the Mirrors and wins, and with the Knight of the White Moon and is defeated. He is also praiseworthy for his efforts to fight for justice. What we like most about him is his effort to reach out to others, establishing links of solidarity with other people, whether they are weak ones he wants to protect or the one and only perfect, exquisite beauty, paradigm of grace, harmony, and intelligence, Dulcinea, the idealized, sublime woman who continues in his mind the illustrious family of idealized women like

Dante's Beatrice and Petrarch's Laura. Don Quixote believes in pure, essential, Platonic, Romantic (*avant la lettre*) love, and this belief lifts him far above all other characters in the novel. It is so deep and sustaining that he accepts death when he cannot proclaim it, having lost his final battle. His world is not only a world of love and beauty, it is also a perfectible world, since the courage of knights errant can win all the battles against injustice and ugly aggression from giants and monsters.

It is true that our admiration for him is tempered by our laughter at his ridiculous efforts, which end always or almost always in defeat, his lack of acceptance of his limited strength, and his constant mistakes and misunderstandings. Any reader who has enjoyed the films of Stan Laurel and Oliver Hardy recognizes in Cervantes's novel many of the essential characteristics of basic slapstick. Pride, they say, comes before a fall; we can surmise that frustration follows, which is what happens to Don Quixote and Sancho throughout the novel. Whether it is a helmet, or windmills, or wine skins, Don Quixote's efforts are frustrated. His will and his imagination are powerless against the resistance of real life represented by the objects, and the knight is ignominiously defeated by things, or rather by his miscalculation about things, their real being, their resistance and stubborn opposition to his will. Living beings are also stubborn. Sheep and pigs frustrate him, refuse to behave like enemy armies, confound and humiliate him by simply being flocks of sheep and herds of pigs. How can we respect and admire a hero when we laugh at his mistakes, his clumsy powerlessness when facing familiar objects and situations?

The heroic and flawed heroic characteristics of Don Quixote make for the paradox that may explain why the readers' opinions about our knight have varied so much from one century to another, and from one critical school to the next. Janus-like, he offers admirable traits followed immediately by serious errors of judgment. His resolve and his courage are undeniable. If we want to understand the scope of his efforts, we should not forget that he has lived for years, in his imagination, in the enchanted realm of the romances of chivalry, books where men and women are endowed with nobility, valor, grace, elegance, devotion, and heroism.

Like a butterfly from a chrysalis, Don Quixote emerges from his mediocre past with bright colors and a strange costume, ready to leave his friends and neighbors behind, ready to fly away. One day he looks around in his own backyard in his village and finds nothing that can compare with his readings. Surely the real world has sunk very low; certainly something must be done to lift it to a higher level. Don Quixote mounts his horse and goes forth. We know, as his readers, that he will fail time and again in his quest for justice. But should he not have tried? Should no one have tried to bring a little justice, a little beauty, a little love to a sad world? If we want to understand him, let us imagine spending several days or weeks in a great museum in Athens or Cairo soaking up the majesty of Greek statues, the elegance of Egyptian reliefs, and then going out to look at the people walking in the streets of Athens or Cairo. A strange feeling of melancholy or depression may torment us. We would like the passers-by to be perfect, as elegant as their idealization inside the museum. If we could do something to change reality, that would be our quest.

Because we admire his courage and his good will but laugh at his repeated failures and his lack of contact with the real world, he is for us a flawed hero and as such creates mixed and ambiguous feelings. Instead of placing his main character on a pedestal, as the writers of chivalry romances did, Cervantes paints a Don Quixote with obvious weaknesses, yet at the same time endowed with courage, high ideals, a vast knowledge in many fields of learning, and unrivalled eloquence. It is up to the reader to decide which side of the knight to emphasize in his or her mind.

A Psychological Approach

Cervantes's characters unfold and develop through both action and thought. We can almost guess what they are thinking. They react incessantly either to what they see and hear or to their inner thoughts, intent upon reaching goals that act like a beacon or perhaps like a red cape, exciting the wild bull inside each one of us. Even their long dialogues, their ceaseless conversations, are full of excitement and help us understand their inner thoughts, their dreams, and their secrets. We are constantly in and out of the characters' minds. It can be said that Cervantes is the true creator of the psychological novel, in spite of the fact that superficially what we read resembles a novel of action, an endless adventure unfolding through travels in space, that is, a "western-and-travelogue" novel. The most intriguing hints learned from this novel are that the most fulfilling adventures take place in the human heart, imagination, and consciousness. In the second part of the novel when Cervantes allows us to take a look at Don Quixote's dream world and uncovers the knight's subconscious, thus anticipating Freud by several centuries, we feel that a new layer of knowledge, and of doubts, has been added to the previous ones, making his world and ours more dramatic and more problematic.

This significant and highly original aspect of Cervantes's novel further defines and explains the personality of the main characters, in this instance that of Don Quixote as revealed in his dream during his descent to the Cave of Montesinos. Dreams have fascinated people for centuries and are present in some of the world's oldest texts, for example, the pharaoh's dream interpreted by Joseph in the Old Testament. Latin literature has contributed Scipio's dream, complete with a trip to the moon and a vision of the future of the Roman Empire. Yet the difference between these dreams and Don Quixote's dream is essential. Most dreams coming to us from ancient times are either revelations about the future or premonitions of future disasters or coming successes. Not so with Don Quixote's dream; in it our hero is deeply troubled by his role in life and in history and especially worried about Dulcinea, who asks him for money, offering as security her undershirt. We inhabit for a few hours an underworld where the characters are distortions of their previous heroic selves. This degraded vision shows us how the subconscious mind of Don Quixote is much less sure of his role in the world and of the moral qualities of the woman he loves. Nothing similar can be found in Renaissance literature. Many years will pass before literature and, let us add, psychology will be able to exploit dreams as one of the most important tools for revealing humankind's deep secrets. The great Spanish nineteenth-century novelist Benito Pérez Galdós, who admired Cervantes, was one of the first to make extensive use of dreams in his novels, not as portents of future events but as windows into the deep areas of his characters. In contemporary letters we find dreamlike short stories by Jorge Luis Borges and Julio Cortázar in the Hispanic world, as well as similar texts in the many literatures inspired by surrealism.

We find especially remarkable the chapters where a character shifts his viewpoint and proceeds to interpret the outside world in an unexpected way. We find an important example of such changes in part 1, chapter 35, the wineskins fiasco, and in the chapters about the Cave of Montesinos, part 2, chapters 22–23. Sancho and other secondary characters are specifically affected by the happenings in these scenes, while the visions of Don Quixote during his descent into the Cave of Montesinos reveal significant changes in the subconscious mind of our hero. It is not in vain that most modern critics find part 2 more intense and more pathetic than part 1. Cervantes is slowly leading us to the climax of his novel in the last chapters of part 2. Jean Cassou, Leo Spitzer, and Jose Ortega y Gasset underline the importance of perspectivism in Cervantes's novels as a whole and relate it to the ambiguity and proliferation of viewpoints during Renaissance times. In drawing and painting, the laws of perspective, ignored during classical and medieval times, gained a firm foothold in Italian and Flemish art in the early Renaissance and spread to other European countries. These laws clearly underline that the vision of a landscape or a palace interior will change if the artist or the spectator is displaced right or left, up or down. Much depends on the point of view of whoever is describing a place or an event. Knowledge increases, almost exponentially, and at the same time certitude seems to elude even the most competent observers. Rigid medieval principles are vanishing, "but reason is specific, and experience limited. By a curious *boomerang* trick, reality becomes less certain the better it is known. Man has discovered Nature, but he is also discovering his own mental powers. And God, who used to establish a fixed bond between the two, has retired from the scene."[5] Reality changes according to the viewpoint of each spectator. Must we believe Don Quixote or Sancho? Must we believe the duke and the duchess or Sansón Carrasco? Thus the problem of appearance versus reality is placed at the core of everyday life.

Cervantes's Vibrant Dialogue

We are soon aware that the conversations between Don Quixote and Sancho constitute the almost impossible contact and mutual influence of two different kinds of culture. Sancho cannot read. His culture is totally oral; it has come to him by oral transmission from older generations. Sancho and Don Quixote frequently disagree, and their disagreement is often funny since it reveals a weakness on either side, most often on Sancho's, because he is revealed as an ignoramus. Yet, as Harry Levin points out, "Now, on the comic stage, Sancho would have the final word. In the pictorial vision of Daumier, the pair coexist within the same frame of reference as the bourgeoisie and the caricatured intellectuals. Yet in a book, where words are the only medium, Don Quixote enjoys a decided advantage; the very weakness of his position in life lends strength, as it were, to his position in literature; in the field of action he may encounter discomfiture, but in the verbal sphere he soon resumes his imaginary career."[6]

Sancho is cunning, and moreover he is backed by common sense and an oral tradition that is centuries old. His point of view is restated many times, yet Don Quixote ignores it or argues successfully against it. He is aware that Sancho is an uneducated peasant and has had no contact with the beautiful texts of epic poems and chivalry romances.

It is hard to find reliable statistics about literacy in Spain during the sixteenth and seventeenth centuries. Probably in some parts of rural Spain the percentage of illiterate adults could have been as high as 80 percent. "Nevertheless, at times it begins to look as though all mankind were composed of two overlapping classes: readers and writers. It seems as if from behind every roadside bush and every wooded hill another author is waiting to spring out, clutching a sheaf of verses; even a dangerous convict is busy planning the second part of his autobiography as he marches off to the galleys; and the unlooked-for pleasures a traveler may find in the attic of his inn are as likely to be a trunk full of books as the embraces of a hospitable serving girl."[7]

It would not be difficult to describe many pages of Cervantes's novel as a duel between two types of culture, the learned culture of books versus the traditional oral culture. Sancho misunderstands many statements made by his master because he does not understand key words, a result of his restricted vocabulary. Don Quixote usually has the last word, but the reader often has the impression that oral, traditional culture is closer to common sense and worthy of respect.

Cervantes knew that ordinary life is complex and subject to change from one second to the next; it is made up of intricate exchanges and highly complex relationships. It involves the subjective judgment of people who face each other, who interact with each other, and the outcome of such face-to-face relationships is always in doubt. Other writers before him may have intuited this basic psychological truth, but only Cervantes gave it full play in his novel. We all need codes for deciphering the world. Don Quixote stubbornly rejects any code except the one he has found in the romances of chivalry. Thus result the misunderstandings that will make him clash with other characters in the novel. Each character has to interpret the outside world through a vast series of filters and connections that refer back to personal previous experiences, memories, and cultural data.

The importance of dialogue in Cervantes must be underlined because it is at the core of the novel, and also because dialogue in itself assumes the need to communicate with our fellow humans and the possibility that this need will bring harmony to our relationships. In essence, dialogue is the antithesis of authoritarian control, of tyranny, in which the orders flow from above to those below, who must listen and obey and above all must not speak back or object. Throughout the novel Sancho objects to most of his master's renderings of facts and actions that follow such interpretations. What makes this dialogue possible is that although Don Quixote possesses a great deal of authority—he is the master, the senior figure, the wealthy one, and a man endowed with a vast culture in comparison to the very poor, almost destitute Sancho—the facts and common sense are usually on Sancho's side. Therefore, the contenders are, in a way, well matched, and the dialogue is not stifled by having one of the parties silence and crush the other party. On the contrary, the match can last a long time and yield moments of lucid merriment. Gerald Brenan comments that Cervantes "is a master — and what a great one! — of the art of dialogue. It was only to be expected that he should have done this well, because one of the particular pleasures to be derived from his book comes from the continual victories we witness of words over facts."[8] As the narrative unfolds, some new situation arises that we know or guess Don Quixote will manage to interpret in accordance with his peculiar fantasy and his general view of the world, "and we wait to see how he will do it. Then, no sooner has his interpretation been given than the inevitable insurmountable objection is made by Sancho or some other person, and at once the question is how he will get round it. That he always does so, and far better than one could have hoped, and in quite unsuspected ways, is due not only to his ingenuity in argument, supported by the wide range of his mind and reading, but to his remarkable rhetorical powers. The knight, who loses every time he takes to the sword, wins a battle whenever he opens his mouth."[9]

A dialogue always assumes a certain degree of equality between the speakers. The opposite of a dialogue is the sermon, the harangue, the official speech. We should not forget that Plato, presumably inspired by Socrates, in Athens invented dialogue as a literary genre during a period when democracy flourished and diverse opinions were being discussed in public. A parliamentary democracy is based on dialogue. Cervantes's Spain was strictly divided into classes, and this sociological rigidity made dialogue across class lines extremely difficult. Cervantes created a situation in his novel that required a constant crossing of class lines in the continuing dialogue between Don Quixote and Sancho. It would be hard or perhaps impossible to find a similar situation in prose writings, in Spain or elsewhere, during most of the seventeenth century. It is true that the Spanish plays of that period made a place for dialogues in which a servant, usually a "funny man," the *gracioso,* would criticize the behavior of the young nobles or members of the middle class. This group of plays, under the umbrella name of "comedia," was a genre favored by Lope de Vega and other playwrights of that time. The *gracioso*'s criticism was on the whole disregarded by the play's main characters; he could not possibly understand the motivations and values of the members of the upper classes, and therefore what the Spanish plays offered was a "dialogue of the deaf" since real contact between social classes was deemed impossible by both playwrights and the public at large.

A Philosophical Approach

There is still another way in which Cervantes's novel has made inroads in literature. The main characters, and also the secondary ones, are often transfixed by a sense of wonder. What do they see? Is it real or a fiction of their imagination? How can they agree about what is real and what is not? How can they tell the difference between what seems to be real and what is totally, positively real? For Don Quixote it is exasperating that strange transformations change dramatically what he sees, or thinks he sees, into something totally different. Who is masking reality? How can we reach to the bottom of what exists? These are questions that have fascinated philosophers and thinkers of all ages. The birth of modern science and modern philosophy has made them more urgent. Both Descartes and Kant respond to similar questions. Descartes thinks that even if an "evil geni" like the ones Don Quixote feels are tormenting him could change what we see through our senses, there is a God who guarantees the reality of the world in which we live. For Kant the situation has become more precarious; we are no longer sure to penetrate deeply into things, into the "real reality" of things.

Both Cervantes and Descartes take part in a new approach to our interpretation of the world that we see. In both cases we discern a presence, often ambiguous, of two opposed attitudes: the supernatural versus the common-sense approach. Common sense is the common denominator of Sancho Panza, as well as the curate, the barber, and all the characters that represent the average inhabitant of Spain during the development of the novel. Descartes praises common sense—although he doubts it is as common as its name implies. The supernatural, in the shape of evil enchanters and perverse magicians, plays a prominent role in Don Quixote's mind. These evil enchanters seem to find great pleasure in confusing everything so as to rob Don Quixote of his victories. The reader wonders how it is possible for him to go on after so many disappointments.

Descartes's hero—that is to say, Descartes himself—fights a great battle, which we might call "the Battle of Systematic Doubt," in which an evil enchanter or geni, *un malin génie* in French, plays an important role. Descartes doubts everything that he has learned or thinks he knows, including all of the ideas that have come to his mind. He even suspects that an evil enchanter has changed the world around him in such a way that it is impossible to find any truth. After such an acceptance of uncertainty and doubt, we wonder how Descartes comes out of the deep pit he has dug for himself. His immediate solution is to withdraw into himself. He has been thinking. He thinks. Thinking belongs to a being who thinks. He thinks, therefore he is; he exists. This immediate emergency solution is followed by a long-range one; he thinks about a perfect Being, God, who being perfect must exist and moreover does not lie. God is therefore the guarantor of the real existence of the world, and the evil geni is thus cast into the shadows where he belongs.

Let us remember that in his struggle against the irrational, Don Quixote preceded Descartes. How does our knight cope with the evil presence of enchanters, hovering all the time over his journey, robbing him of the glory that his quest and adventures should have given him?

Our memory plays a crucial role. In his Meditation III, René Descartes deals with the problem of interpretation of sensory perceptions: How do we recognize what we see? Can we be sure of our interpretations? "I remember that, when looking from a window and saying I see men who pass in the street, I really do not see them, but infer that what I see is men. . . . And yet what do I see from the window but hats and coats which may cover automatic machines? Yet I judge these to be men. And similarly solely by the faculty of judgment which rests in my mind, I comprehend that which I believed I saw with my eyes."[10]

Descartes was incorporating the old problem of appearance versus reality into the philosophical world, giving to it a new rigorous strength. Cervantes had already dealt with this problem in his novel. Descartes's philosophical writings are musings of a single man, a long soliloquy begun in a small cabin surrounded by winter snow during a war in Germany while the French troops were hibernating; yet they are so influential that many textbooks trace the beginning of modern philosophy to them. Although emblematic of the clarity and rigor of modern science, they represent one single thought, a unique viewpoint. What Cervantes offered was a multiplicity of viewpoints, often in conflict with each other. For instance, we may believe instinctively that Don Quixote is wrong in his interpretations of the everyday world that surrounds him, but we should not overlook the fact that many other characters in the novel deceive, lie, or are deceived and lied to. It is out of this complex point-counterpoint of voices and opinions in conflict that the novel is born, not only Cervantes's but also most of the novels that will follow.

Our wits are constantly put to the test by encounters with men or women whose view of the world differs from ours, and they are also challenged by the material world, the world of objects that resist us. Don Quixote experiments with the hardness or softness of material objects as he makes a valiant effort to equip himself with the armor and weapons a knight-errant needs. His helmet is a main source of trouble. "The Ingenious *Hidalgo,* when necessary, can be chary of anything that threatens to interfere with his fantasies. Because he wanted to test the sturdiness of the helmet that he had made from pasteboard, he destroyed a week's work with one swipe of his sword. The lesson is sufficient: he repairs the damage, and he also refrains from any new trials, in order not to spoil 'a helmet of the most perfect construction.'"[11]

Indeed, interpreting what our senses communicate to us is what keeps us busy all day long. We have to judge the moods of people talking to us, especially if we expect them to grant us a favor, and we also have to estimate the hardness or softness of a material object that we plan to use.

Both Don Quixote and Sancho embark on their travels, or should we say, their quest, following two lines of reasoning, two sources of knowledge and guidance: their memory and their senses. Their senses give them information that we may suspect to be the same. But how can this be true since their experiences and lives have been worlds apart, molding two different personalities? Our interpretation of the world and our immediate surroundings may vary from that of our friends and neighbors, perhaps even more from what a stranger might see and understand. This is made explicit during Cervantes's novel every time Don Quixote's interpretation clashes with what Sancho sees.

Cervantes knows that the senses give us raw material that develops differently in each individual. Is there some basic knowledge hardwired in our brain that induces us to interpret what we see and hear in a certain way? The idea of this fundamental knowledge goes back to Greek philosophy, to the "innate ideas" of classical tradition; moreover, modern science has validated this concept when analyzing the behavior of insects and birds. Humans were supposed to be guided by innate ideas combined with knowledge supplied by trial and error and by the thousand experiences of everyday life. By choosing two characters who are at opposite poles, a valiant knight who is above all an idealist and is guided by "innate ideas," in his case the ideas of chivalry romances that have been internalized and become wired to his brain, and a matter-of-fact, cowardly rustic, guided by common sense and traditional values and folk wisdom contained in proverbs and folk sayings, Cervantes creates a study in contrast. Yet, if we let this impression guide us, we may misread the novel or at least we may miss a substantial part of its meaning.

A Simple Not So Simple Read

It is possible to read Cervantes's novel as a straightforward narrative. These are the adventures and misadventures of Don Quixote and his squire, Sancho Panza. Why complicate them? They are enjoyable in and by themselves. And yet if the majority of readers follow this path, and there is little doubt that they do, there is much that they will miss. The very structure of the novel is highly complex and teems with hidden messages. As Jean Canavaggio puts it, "The more the reader familiarizes himself with this multiple universe, the more he discovers overlapping planes, stories within stories, mirrors that reflect each other to infinity. . . . The Chinese-box effect is also a result of the skill with which the novelist hides behind the pseudo-narrators to whom he lends his voice and delegates his powers."[12] Who is speaking? Can we trust the speaker? At a certain moment Cide Hamete Benengeli, the Arab historian, casts doubt about the authenticity and veracity of a chapter he is about to write. How are we to interpret such a statement? It may remind us of an old conundrum that has come to us from ancient Greece: "All the people from Crete are liars, without exception: they lie all the time. I can assure you this is true, for I am a Cretan."

Words, language, and identity baffle us. How can we absorb the vast possibilities that Cervantes presents on so many levels? Certainly we are caught off guard as the barrage of adventures, encounters, speeches, and general display of humanity bombards us. Are we reading the truth about these fictional characters? Further, Cervantes forces us to explore the inner mind and hearts of these individuals and finally foists upon us the question of what is real and what is not real. Just a simple read? Not quite.

It is now opportune to come to a preliminary conclusion: Cervantes's novel offers many new approaches to the art of storytelling and the craft of narrative prose. It is outstanding today and was probably more so when it appeared because it is so original in so many ways. Its originality was confounding and misunderstood. We are still unraveling its many messages. The next generation's interpretations may supersede our own.

4

A Look into Cervantes's Masterpiece

The celebrated first chapter of *Don Quixote* invites the reader to enter the life of a humble country gentleman, describes his possessions, his rural routine, but more important, his obsession with books of chivalry. Further, we are told that he has a young niece, a housekeeper, a horse, a greyhound and that he is a friend of the village priest and barber, both versed in books of chivalry. The gentleman, obsessed with reading books on knight-errantry, decides to become a knight and improvises the making of a suit of armor. He renames his horse and chooses a peasant girl who happens to live nearby as his ladylove. He will pay homage to her with his feats of bravery in righting the wrongs of the world, thereby gaining fame and glory.

All is well and good at this point, and we, his readers, feel secure in the story line. Cervantes takes great care to describe Don Quixote's background. He is writing a novel, not a play; therefore, the visual aspect, that is, the immediate fact in a play has been replaced by minute descriptions of the environment of the hero. We know how he looks with his long, lean body and elongated face, which recalls the style of El Greco's portraits. We further know that he has been selling his land to buy books. Books were more expensive at that time than they are now. We see hundreds and hundreds of books. We are told what he eats, what clothes he wears, and what books he reads. We are about to witness a remarkable event—the birth of Don Quixote, the new name that he gives himself, and his mission to go forth and change the world and to build a society that is more just, nobler, kinder, and more full of love.

Now, let us backtrack a bit and start over. "Somewhere in La Mancha, in a place whose name I do not care to remember . . ." Where exactly are we? "Some claim that his family name was Quixada, or Quexada, for there is a certain amount of disagreement among the authors who write of this matter, although reliable conjecture seems to indicate that his name was Quexana. But this does not matter very much to our story; in its telling there is absolutely no deviation from the truth" (Gr., 19–20).

What is the main character's name? Who is the author or authors? What is the author's credibility given the vague references to location and questions about the name of the main character and his origin? So we begin the adventures of Don Quixote with important information withheld. Presented to us as a "true story" and as a small part of the vast canvas of history, we know that "historians must and ought to be exact, truthful and absolutely free of passions, for neither interest, fear, rancor, nor affection should make them deviate from the path of the truth, whose mother is history, the rival of time, repository of great deeds, witness to the past, example and adviser to the present, and forewarning to the future" (Gr., 68). And yet this true tale told by a Muslim historian is full of imprecision.

Instead of a precise, clear, and true name we have been offered several names, which makes us unsure about the name of our hero, who later on will acquire two new names, the Knight of the Sorrowful Countenance and the Knight of the Lions. We are also offered several names for Sancho's wife and for another secondary character, the Countess Trifaldi. The critic Leo Spitzer states, "I see this as a deliberate refusal on the part of the author to make a final choice of one name . . . in other words, a desire to show the different aspects under which the character in question may appear to others."[1]

Honoré Daumier (1808–1879), *Don Quixote on Horseback*. Neue
Pinakothek, Munich, Germany. Photo: Bridgeman-Giraudon /
Art Resource, NY.

Moreover, Cervantes defies the basic principles of chivalry romances from the beginning. In contrast with the exotic, beautiful landscapes of the romances, he offers us the parched, un interesting plains of La Mancha and central Spain. Instead of a brilliant description of palaces and castles, the dull details of a poor *hidalgo*'s everyday life; instead of a glorious aristocratic genealogy, Cervantes offers us nothing, or next to nothing— Don Quixote's relatives are not mentioned by name. He is born in the mind of a middle-aged *hidalgo*, like Pallas Athena out of Zeus' head, the only difference being that he has to scramble to find an appropriate armor, whereas Athena was fully armed at birth. Once more the myth, the heroic myth, clashes with the tedious needs of a prosaic present. The ancient family weapons are rusty; the helmet is defective.

We are present as Don Quixote is creating himself. He is following through on his obsession. It is as though we have special access to his home where we are watching him design his knightly attire as well as his life's trajectory, that is, reinventing himself or perhaps out of restlessness heeding a desire to endure and become part of a book. Robert Alter comments: "In the first part of the novel, he prepares for every action with an acute consciousness of the sage who is to write the history of his exploits, for it is only through the writing down that he can become as real as Amadís, Don Belianis, Felixmarte, and all the rest."[2]

Add to this the transformations of the "skinny nag" now named Rocinante (*rocín* = nag and *ante* = before) with its double meaning, the peasant girl Aldonza Lorenzo into the fair damsel, Dulcinea del Toboso (*dulce* = sweet), and our poor *hidalgo* to the newly minted, or not so newly minted knight-errant, Don Quixote de la Mancha. Remember that Cervantes's humor, his sharp wit, and his mighty pen spare nothing and no one.

The chapter is filled with nuances and historical and literary allusions. At the same time, it easily conveys a straight story line of the beginning of the knight-errant and his quest. Without apparent effort, the author incorporates all of the above. How to read the chapter or, for that matter, the book largely depends on what the reader brings to the reading table. No book before had attempted such a wide reach or to appeal to so large an audience. In these early pages, Cervantes is setting the scene for the development of the novel.

Life as Literature or Literature as Life?

The story continues in chapter 2 as Don Quixote, worried because he has not yet been dubbed a knight, starts out by allowing Rocinante to take him wherever the nag chooses in search of adventure. When he meets up with two prostitutes whom he views as "fair damsels and gracious ladies" entering an inn cum "castle," he addresses them with the incomprehensible rhetoric of romance novels. He accepts the hospitality of the innkeeper who perceives the bizarre manner and appearance of Don Quixote and plays along with the charade. Because his helmet is stuck on his head, the knight has to sleep and eat and drink with it on. The innkeeper designs a reed for the knight to drink more easily.

But let us recall how Cervantes wreaks even more literary havoc on his readers by creating a main character who in turn creates himself. Is the main character put inside the story inside the book? Is the reader paying attention to the straight-line story and the invention of the main character? Can the reader see the boomerang effect: literature-penetrating life and life-penetrating literature? Suddenly, Alonzo Quijano is moving out of himself and into "character" as the knight, Don Quixote, hero of a tale of chivalry.

The interaction and interpenetration of literature and life is therefore one of the main subjects of Cervantes's novel. Precisely because Don Quixote sees everyday life through a literary prism, and one made of novels where fantasy and irrational events rule, he must misinterpret everything he sees; he lives his new life as a chapter of a book, a novel of chivalry where he is the hero. "He is himself like a sign, a long, thin graphism, a letter that has just escaped from the pages of a book. His whole being is nothing but language, text, printed pages, and stories that have already been written down. He is made up of interwoven words; he is writing itself, wandering through the world among the resemblances of things. Yet not entirely so: for in his reality as an impoverished *hidalgo* he can become a knight only by listening from afar to the age-old epic that gives its form to Law. The book is not so much his existence as his duty. He is constantly obliged to consult it in order to know what to do or say, and what signs he should give himself and others in order to show that he really is of the same nature as the text from which he springs."[3]

Thus we come to understand from these first chapters of the novel that the knight has internalized the contents of many novels of chivalry to the point of identifying his own existence, and his own projects, with a book that is the condensation and quintessence of many other books, the archetype of all chivalry romances, *Amadís of Gaul.* The hero, Amadís, is unsurpassed by any other knight. His lady, Oriana, is a mirror image on the feminine side, perfect in beauty and warm love. Enemies and obstacles are everywhere, yet they can and will be vanquished and surpassed. A mysterious, magic arch forbids the entrance to a mysterious, magic building leading to an uncharted island. Only the bravest and fairest can come under this arch, and the main requisite is true love. With it, everything is possible; without it, disaster is imminent. Luckily, the two lovers pass the test and head to the uncharted island called Terra Firma. It would not be difficult to transpose them into eighteenth-century costumes in a canvas by Watteau, *Embarking to Cythères,* elegant couples in slender boats heading to an island, a magical yet real island, where love is the goal and the lovers will know eternal bliss.

Imitation of this ideal knight and his ideal life of heroic adventures and tender love is basic to Don Quixote and permeates the entire novel. In short, Don Quixote is a man who becomes a book. He lives his life as an imitation of Amadís. Every move he makes must be a mirror image of his hero's adventures. As Harry Levin points out, "imitation is the test that Cervantes proposes, knowing full well that when nature imitates art, art reveals its innate artificiality."[4] Don Quixote has read all the books, at least insofar as books of chivalry romance are concerned, and he intends to live his life according to their precepts. It is not only Amadís who guides his footsteps, he aspires to become a living equivalent of Amadís as depicted in the novel with that title; he wants to become not only the living standard-bearer of the Amadís novel, he wishes to become the embodiment of the whole shelf of Amadís novels. This penetration of literature into the life of our hero compels the reader to go back and forth from everyday life as seen by other characters to the literary interpretation given to events by Don Quixote. As in all other parodies, it helps to put our hero's adventures side by side with the heroic adventures of a romance like *Amadís of Gaul*.

CONTRAST AND SYMMETRY

Few novels are as full of visual suggestions as this one. Cervantes describes his hero, his horse, and his armor. Later we see Sancho, short and stocky, depicted as the antithesis of the long and lank Don Quixote. Also, Sancho's sturdy donkey is a study in contrast with the emaciated Rocinante. As the book develops into almost a travel chronicle, we see the outside and the inside of an inn; we see windmills, endless plains, and twisting roads. These images, so abundant and detailed, have made Cervantes's novel a treasure trove for illustrators, the best-known and perhaps the best being the nineteenth-century French artist Gustave Doré. Under the influence of these images it would not be too hard to simplify the events and the message: Don Quixote is an idealist, a courageous knight, at least in his own view; Sancho, on the other hand, is coarse, often cowardly, practical, and pragmatic.

Thus simplified, the novel unfolds as a travelogue full of humorous incidents in which Don Quixote and Sancho are basically predictable. This does not make them less funny; it increases our hilarity when we realize how well we can foresee their behavior. We can almost conclude that everything that happens in the novel is related to the contrast between the knight and his squire.

The trouble with this simplistic interpretation is that it seems to paralyze both main characters and therefore cannot account for their interaction and their development. It would be more accurate to add to the two main characters another pair of "characters," that are invisible and abstract. The first new character would be called Interaction; the second would be Time.

Interaction is the result of the constant shared experiences: Don Quixote and Sancho are seen together in almost all the chapters of the novel. If we reread the book, we will miss Sancho in the first chapters and will wonder why it took so long for Cervantes to introduce him as an essential element in his novel. Without Sancho as a foil, we would not have the dialogues between knight and squire, which are at the very heart of the novel, as they allow both characters to define them and influence each other.

Both characters change during the course of the novel, yet they change in different ways. Don Quixote's changes are more spectacular. He "creates" himself in the first chapters; he has moments of depression during the first part, severe bouts of melancholy and depression during the second part; and finally he reverts to his early self, Alonso Quijano, at the end of the second part. Sancho's evolution is subtler; at the very beginning of the novel he is introduced as "a good man—if that title can be given to someone who is poor—but without much in the way of brains" (Gr., 55).

Think for a minute as our poor, old threadbare *hidalgo* knocks on the door of his neighbor, a simple farmer, and promises him the world: adventures, the possibility of being a governor of an island, and riches. Sancho leaves his wife, his children, his rural life as his fantasies come into play. Certainly this happens to explorers and adventurers as they dream of places far beyond their reach and of fame and fortune at the end of their travels.

Sancho's first words to Don Quixote are: "'Señor Knight Errant, be sure not to forget what your grace promised me about the ínsula [island]; I'll know how to govern it no matter how big it is'" (Gr., 56). This leads Don Quixote to promise even more grandiose things.

Sancho is easily seduced by Don Quixote's promises, improbable and exaggerated as they are: "'it well might be that before six days have passed I shall win a kingdom that has others allied to it, and that would be perfect for my crowning you king of one of them. And do not think this is any great thing; for events and eventualities befall knights in ways never seen or imagined, and I might well be able to give you even more than I have promised'" (Gr., 57). Sancho, however, has a sense of proportion and concludes right away that he just cannot imagine his wife as a queen: "'in my opinion, even if God rained kingdoms down on earth, none of them would sit well on the head of Mari Gutiérrez. You should know, sir, that she isn't worth two *maravedís* as a queen; she'd do better as a countess, and even then she'd need God's help'" (Gr., 57). There is a contrast between Don Quixote's expansive imagination and Sancho's common sense. Interaction helps us to define and understand both characters. At the same time we understand the charismatic power of Don Quixote, ever eloquent and opening great vistas to his squire's mind, and the cautious reaction of Sancho, who is unable yet to accept the highest honors offered him and his family.

What is most significant is that Don Quixote and Sancho never talk past each other. They listen carefully and adjust their answers accordingly. After Don Quixote realizes that Sancho has some difficulty imagining himself as king and his wife as queen, he paints a more modest picture of the future awaiting Sancho and his family: "'Leave it to God, Sancho,'" said Don Quixote, "'and He will give what suits her best; but do not lower your desire so much that you will be content with anything less than the title of captain general.'" Sancho then concludes the dialogue in a mood of happy, polite acceptance. Let us imagine also his blind faith, his warm, giving soul as he adoringly answers his master who suggests that he should not settle for a meager title. "'I won't, Señor,' Sancho replied, 'especially when I have a master as distinguished as your grace, who will know how to give me everything that's right for me and that I can handle'" (Gr., 57). Interaction here, as often in the novel, is based on a series of agreements, partial disagreements, contradictions, and occasional reproaches, often followed by an acceptance that the future might bring good tidings to both the master and the squire.

His common sense guides him, a quality that serves him well in his travels with his master. But he also brings innocence, naiveté, trust, shrewdness, simplemindedness, and most important, a warm generous heart. From this rich mixture, for the most part, he manages to cull the right attitude at the right moment. This is especially true later on in the book as he travels, converses with his master, and meets all sorts of people. With Sancho's presence as the point of departure, a friendship, unparalleled in literature, begins. His unconditional love lasts throughout the novel and beyond.

Through Time, Sancho evolves given his exposure to a multitude of adventures and meeting people from all echelons of society, and his digesting of Don Quixote's encyclopedic erudition while casting a skeptical eye at the magnitude of his master's wild imagination. Compare the peasant-cum-squire-to-be of part 1 "without much in the way of brains" with the chapters in part 2 where Sancho, now a governor of his Barataria Island, acts as a judge in several difficult cases of civil and criminal law and gives proof of wisdom and enlightened common sense. We must conclude that Sancho has developed his inner resources and become an enlightened legislator because Cervantes respects his characters, does not use them for didactic means, and allows them to develop through experience and the passing of Time. In the case of Sancho, the constant challenges of Don Quixote's ideas, conversation, cultural references, plus the effect of traveling further nurture Sancho's wisdom. He probably never left his village before meeting Don Quixote. Now, through Don Quixote's descriptions, he travels the enchanted world of literature and legends. As for his master, he seems to be more cautious in part 2. There are important moments of introspection and doubt, especially when he is left alone during Sancho's stint as governor of Barataria; he is visibly upset and depressed by seeing Dulcinea enchanted, and he is less active and less enterprising during the final chapters of the novel. Sancho understands how depressed Don Quixote has become and proposes a new life as shepherds as a way to free Don Quixote from a negative attitude that ultimately will determine his death.

Although we may project Sancho on a lower plane than Don Quixote, Sancho is a flawed character, a flawed hero, but yet a hero. With his mixture of common sense, cunning, and ambition, his limited mental resources lead him to mistakes in the interpretation of Don Quixote's lofty vocabulary. He occasionally lies to his master, as when he claims to have visited Dulcinea and produces an improvised and rather coarse portrait of the lady. But Sancho turns out to have much greater inner resources than we had assumed when finally, in part 2, he reaches his goal and becomes governor of Barataria and for a few chapters is the center of the book's action, the peasant-turned-wise-man-and-philosopher. At the end of part 2, in the final chapters of the book, his love for his master redeems him from all the mistakes and deceptions in his past. We are also placed in an ambivalent and ambiguous relationship with Sancho; we admire his common sense and his wisdom when put to the test as a governor but dislike his stubbornness and ignorance. In any case, if we think of him as a hero, as the most "modern" of the book's characters, pointing to a future for bourgeoisie and democracy, we may also have misgivings about him and therefore we must admit he is a flawed hero.

With the elements of Time and Interaction, and endless conversations between the two main characters, a sensitive reader may come to an unexpected conclusion, one that has been overlooked by critics of the novel: both knight and squire are having a good time, an extended vacation, and both are much happier than ever before, having broken all the rules of a monotonous existence.

They meet everyone on their own terms. Don Quixote can find peace of mind in his love for Dulcinea and in his ardor for travel, moving on, discovering and fighting for others. He has designed the parameters: to follow where Rocinante leads him and to obey the code of chivalry. He is unselfish and wants to help in any way that a knight-errant deems worthy. He passes this aura on to his faithful companion who perhaps sees the world slightly differently but shares a love of adventure, freedom, and faith in mankind.

They are masters of their own lives, omnipotent when it comes to deciding where to go, what to do, and how to defy enemies. Both are united by the hope of victory, success, and glory. Don Quixote dreams about honor, fame, and unending love. Sancho, more practical, wants power and riches. Their dreams are connected: Sancho can hope to reach his goals only if Don Quixote is successful in his quest. Therefore, Sancho is as disappointed as his master when promising adventures turn into disaster. We should note that Don Quixote is not perfect and has human frailties; for example, at times, he can be very angry with Sancho.

Two Women, Two Realities

Dulcinea of Toboso and Teresa Panza, the women in the lives of Don Quixote and Sancho Panza, respectively, play key roles in the novel, pointing up real and imagined reality, a central theme of the novel. The infinite, mesmerizing conversations and winning camaraderie of the knight and his squire delight us, but it is the presence of the women they adore and respect that paints the wildly conceived and fanciful versus the actual and earthy, echoing their male counterparts. First, Dulcinea, the knight's imaginary ladylove, the light of his life, and figment of his mind, perhaps inspired by Aldonza Lorenzo, the neighboring farm girl, and second, Teresa, the happy, loving, supportive wife of Sancho. Dulcinea's role is especially vital because in her creation Cervantes manages to encompass many themes: the comic, the tragic, the concrete, the elusive, the poetic, and the prosaic.

For the greater part of the book we live in Don Quixote's fantasy of the beauteous, perfect Dulcinea. Everything he does, he does for her, and everyone he meets must acknowledge her perfection. This constitutes the code of a knight-errant, but her part is extremely complex and more often than not full of factual inconsistencies and contradictions. Who is she—Aldonza

Lorenzo or the imagined Dulcinea? We learn about Dulcinea through Don Quixote's reminiscences and discourses with Sancho. "'I depict her in my imagination as I wish her to be, in beauty and in distinction'" (Gr., 201). He repeats this idea to the duke in part 2 in a slightly different manner, "'God knows if Dulcinea exists in the world or not, or if she is imaginary or not imaginary'" (Gr., 672). Reality blurs and merges with fantasy; we are left at the mercy of Don Quixote's whim. At the same time, he gives us some facts: Dulcinea does not know how to read and write, their love has been platonic, and in twelve years he has seen her not more than four times. Her father is Lorenzo Corchuelo and her mother Aldonza Nogales, and he knows that she is not highbred but he can overlook this because she is virtuous. He also argues that it is of little importance whether she is of flesh and blood because poets dedicate verses to women who exist in name only. But later in the tale, he denies that he has ever seen Dulcinea and states that he is in love with her image and with her beauty. What are we to believe?

Next, there is the Sancho factor where the complexities of the relationship of the knight, squire, and the real or imagined Dulcinea are revealed. Dulcinea becomes at once a problem to Sancho, a challenge that he is able to meet only through deceptive practices, by lying and by presenting his master with imposters. A case in point is the episode at Sierra Morena, where Don Quixote and Sancho have taken refuge after another failed adventure. Here we note the contrast between the knight's vulnerability and the squire's cunning, as Don Quixote proclaims that he wishes to do penance in the Sierra Morena for his beloved as did other famous knights, for example, Ariosto's Orlando in the poem titled *Orlando Furioso* (Mad Orlando). The knight, then, orders Sancho to carry a love letter to Dulcinea, which he is obliged to memorize in the event that he loses it. From this request a new complicated set of problems arises regarding writing the letter, which is eventually written and which Sancho accidentally forgets to take with him. The language of the letter is too difficult for him to reconstruct. And where is El Toboso? Accountability is a huge problem. But Sancho lies his way through the episode. "'She didn't read the letter,' said Sancho, 'because she said she didn't know how to read or write; instead she tore it into little pieces, saying that she didn't want to give it to anybody else to read because she didn't want people in the village knowing her secrets'" (Gr., 260). His master's relentless number of questions and idealized reinterpretation of the nonexistent visit put Sancho to the test. Again the counterpoint between the two provides humor and pathos as Sancho tells of a peasant girl with "'a mannish kind of odor'" who "'was sweaty and sort of sour,'" which Don Quixote translates to "'the fragrance of the rose among thorns, that lily of the field'" (Gr., 259). When his master questions him about the customary token gift, usually a jewel, that a beloved bestows upon a squire for the delivery of a love letter, Sancho settles this misconception quickly saying that in this case it was merely a piece of bread and cheese. The knight notices the rapidity of Sancho's visit but accounts for it easily explaining that a friendly sorcerer whisked Sancho there and back. Nothing is resolved at this point as Don Quixote continues to believe, and Sancho is overjoyed that his master explains the situation in terms of a "'wise necromancer who watches over my affairs'" (Gr., 260).

When Sancho sallies forth with his master for a second time and the knight expresses his desire to go to El Toboso to be blessed by Dulcinea, the squire's quandary becomes more pressing. Don Quixote naturally assumes Sancho's familiarity with the destination as well as his acquaintance with Dulcinea given Sancho's conversation with him after his retreat to the Sierra Morena and the supposed delivery of the love letter. Sancho, however, denies that he knows her and understands that he is in trouble. He suggests that Don Quixote wait in the nearby woods, and in broad daylight they will enter and find Dulcinea's abode. With sadness, Don Quixote acquiesces. Sancho is troubled by his master's grief and by the fact that his lie has placed him in a situation for which he sees no solution. The confounded squire is playing for time to think. Sancho sits down and has a conversation with himself: "'Do you know where her house is Sancho?' 'My master says it has to be royal palaces or noble castles.' 'Have you, by any chance, seen her?' 'I've never seen her, and neither has my master'" (Gr., 515). The soliloquy is humorous and at the same time we are anxious to discover how Sancho will find his way out of this predicament. He tries to reason with himself and mentions that "'everything has a remedy except death.'" He comes up with the enchanters' motive, as is the style of his master, and he is greatly pleased with his ingenuity in this matter. He spots three peasant girls on their donkeys and beckons his master. It is one of Sancho's key moments when he points to the trio, and Don Quixote remarks that he sees only three peasant girls on three donkeys. But Sancho straightens him out: "'Is it possible that three snow white palfreys, or whatever they are called, look like donkeys to your Grace? God help us, may this beard of mine be plucked out if that's true!'" (Gr., 517). He plays out the scene indicating that one of the village girls is Dulcinea and has his master kneel in front of her. Poor Don Quixote thinks that he has cataracts in his eyes and that everything he sees is ugly. When Sancho resorts to the enchanters and their wickedness as an explanation in this instance, Don Quixote accepts Sancho's explanation. Erich Auerbach points out the role reversal: "Now it is the other way round. Sancho improvises a scene after the fashion of the romances of chivalry, while Don Quijote's ability to transform events to harmonize with his illusion breaks down before the crude vulgarity of the sight of the peasant women."[5]

Let us recall that Dulcinea is Don Quixote's creation, part of his vision, but when Sancho finally convinces him that Dulcinea has been enchanted, Don Quixote loses control of his creation. Sancho now has the upper hand although he will come to regret his deception because deep down he loves his master and does not want to see him sad. But for now Sancho is happy in his success. His master accepts that Dulcinea is enchanted. Sancho could have confessed his deception but he never does.

As they continue encountering more adventures, Don Quixote's devotion to Dulcinea remains strong. Before he descends into the Cave of Montesinos, he prays to God for success and also calls on Dulcinea to protect him. Indeed, the descent into the cave with its beautiful meadows, palaces, and enchanted, legendary characters from the books of chivalry is the ultimate experience of Don Quixote before he begins the eventual ascent into reality. The concept of a descent into a cave that serves to reveal truths brings to mind similar experiences found in other books, in particular, the extravagant world of Lewis Carroll's *Alice in Wonderland*. Don Quixote learns that for five hundred years Merlin, the enchanter, has held hostage a number of characters from the chivalric novels. Montesinos, for whom the cave is named, welcomes Don Quixote and guides his guest through the sumptuous surroundings much like Virgil guided Dante through the rings of Hell and Purgatory. When Montesinos mentions the famous Dulcinea and compares her with another beauty, Don Quixote rises to his beloved's defense.

Don Quixote reports to Sancho all the marvels that Montesinos showed him in the depths of the cave. The squire is surprised to hear that his master saw the "'three peasant girls who were leaping and jumping in those pleasant fields like nanny goats, and as soon as I saw them I recognized one of them as the peerless Dulcinea of Toboso, and the other two as those same peasant girls who came with her, the ones we spoke to as we were leaving Toboso'" (Gr., 611). Don Quixote tells Sancho that Montesinos had informed him that they were probably high-born women who were enchanted. When the knight relates that he saw the same three women who Sancho had presented to him on the donkeys and that one of them asked for six reales for Dulcinea, but he only had four, which he gave to her, the squire is astounded. Further, "'And after taking the four *reales*, instead of curtsying she gave a leap and jumped two *varas* [almost six feet] into the air.'" Sancho cannot bear what his master is saying: "'Holy God!' shouted Sancho. 'Is it possible that there are in the world enchanters and enchantments so strong that they have turned my master's good sense into foolishness and madness? Oh, Señor, Señor, for God's sake think about what you are doing, and take back your honor, and don't believe this nonsense that has reduced and lessened your good sense!'" (Gr., 613–14). His master is devastated with this vision of an impoverished Dulcinea begging, and now it is Sancho who is talking about enchantment, not Don Quixote.

At the palace of the duke and duchess, the experience of a plain, coarse, peasant girl stays in his mind as he expresses his despair of Dulcinea's enchantment to the duke: "'your highness must know that not long ago, when I was going to kiss her hands and receive her blessing, approval, and permission for this third sally, I found a person, different from the one I was seeking: I found her enchanted, transformed from a princess into a peasant, from beautiful to ugly, from an angel into a devil, from fragrant into foul-smelling, from well-spoken into a rustic, from severe into skittish, from light into darkness, and finally, from Dulcinea of Toboso into a lowborn farm girl from Sayago'" (Gr., 671).

The duke and duchess have read the first part of the novel. The humor of the earlier episodes, the poignancy of the time that Sancho fools his master into believing that Dulcinea is enchanted, and the flight of fancy of the Cave of Montesinos have been replaced by a more sober overtone as the knight answers the many questions put to him by the duke and duchess regarding Dulcinea.

Another dark moment appears in chapter 64, part 2, when Don Quixote, finally defeated by Sansón Carrasco disguised as the Knight of the White Moon, decides to commit suicide by asking Sansón to kill him: "Don Quixote, battered and stunned, not raising his visor, and as if speaking from the tomb, said in a weak and feeble voice: 'Dulcinea of Toboso is the most beautiful woman in the world, and I am the most unfortunate knight on earth, and it is not right that my weakness should give the lie to this truth. Wield your lance, knight and take my life, for you have already taken my honor'" (Gr., 887). Sansón Carrasco's purpose is to have Don Quixote retire from his knight-errantry and return to his village. But Don Quixote's defeat is not the end of his dream of Dulcinea's disenchantment. During his journey home, he sings a love song to his beloved and he still orders Sancho to receive the 3,300 lashes that will disenchant Dulcinea. Don Quixote has hope but when Sancho cries out, Don Quixote steps forward and in a moment of lucid reality he orders Sancho to stop beating himself and to think of his wife. His master is left with reality. We can see progressively in the above instances how each time Don Quixote reaches out to find his Dulcinea, the real world interferes with his imaginary world. Dulcinea mirrors Don Quixote's image, and it is through her that Cervantes brings to light other facets of Don Quixote's and Sancho's friendship.

Next let us consider Sancho's wife, first referred to as Juana Gutiérrez, who like her husband represents rural shrewdness and common sense. Unlike Dulcinea, she is three-dimensional, alive, and vibrant. As noted earlier in this chapter, Sancho refused to accept a position as king, telling his master that his wife would not be able to handle too high a status in society. Also, it would not be a wise position for their daughter who was of marriageable age.

At the inception of his first journey with Don Quixote, Sancho convinced his wife that this venture held the possibility of untold gains for him. Although she has limited intelligence, her finely tuned intuition and solid values outshine any deficiency. Her happiness resides in her caring for and looking out for the good of the family. But she is not immune to receiving gifts and fully enjoys the little money and small trinkets that Sancho brings home from his first sally with Don Quixote.

When Don Quixote sets out with Sancho for the second time, the squire demands a salary at the urging of his wife, who is here called Teresa or Juana Panza (but also known as Mari Gutié-rrez).[6] His master quickly dismisses this demand and gives him a "take it or leave it" ultimatum, which Sancho readily accepts, promptly and joyfully leaving with his master.

Later in the book, the correspondence between Teresa and Sancho, the newly appointed governor, reveals their mutual concerns. Sancho details all of the points that touch Teresa: "I'm sending you a green hunting tunic that my lady the duchess gave me; make it into a skirt and bodice for our daughter.... The gray [Sancho's donkey] is fine and sends you his best.... [Y]ou'll be rich and have good luck" (Gr., 698–99). With these assurances, Sancho feels that his wife will be happy with his new position, but he does show his letter to the duchess who tells him he is mistaken to imply that he received the governorship in return for giving himself 3,300 lashes to disenchant Dulcinea; the duke did not originally appoint him governor with this stipulation. Also she expresses dismay at his greediness. Sancho, in his usual good spirit and willingness to oblige, offers to rip up the letter, but the duchess says that she wants to discuss it with the duke. Then she sends a page to Sancho's village to take his letter to his wife along with a string of coral beads from the duchess. The page says one letter comes from "'Señor Don Sancho Panza, governor of the ínsula of Barataria'" (Gr., 784) and another from the duchess who even more so exaggerates her courtesy by asking Teresa to send her two dozen acorns, informing her of the excellent marriage that she plans to arrange for Sanchica. Teresa is enchanted with the humility of the duchess and orders Sanchica to take good care of the page. Meanwhile Teresa is flaunting her riches and the letters in the village, which leaves Sansón Carrasco and the priest incredulous. When they speak with the page they understand the irony of the situation, but facts are facts and Sancho is governor and the letters and gift are real. When they offer to respond to Sancho and the duchess, Teresa instead hires an altar boy who can write rather than having other folk meddle in her affairs. Her common sense tells her not to trust them. Teresa is ever present in Sancho's mind. He writes to Don Quixote that if she sends correspondence, could he kindly pay for it.

The content of the two letters Teresa sends, one to the duchess and the other to her husband, merit attention. Her goodness and candidness are unmistakable. In her letter to the duchess, she describes her joy and happiness and shamelessly admits that all in the village think little of her husband's ability, but his governorship is proof of his astuteness. She wishes to come to court in a carriage and asks that her husband send her money. Even more ebullient is her letter to her husband in which she recounts her ecstasy: "I practically went crazy with happiness. . . . [W]ho could ever imagine that a goatherd would become a governor of ínsulas? And you know, dear husband, my mother used to say you had to live a lot to see a lot: I say this because I plan to see more if I live more, because I don't plan to stop until I see you as a landlord or a tax collector, for those are trades, after all, in which you always have and handle money, though the devil carries off anyone who misuses them" (Gr., 802-3). She sprinkles in gossip of the village and news of the crops and relates that Sanchica is saving for her dowry. Teresa again expresses her desire to visit the court and her great love for her husband, that she wishes him a longer life because life on earth for her would be unbearable without him.

Her banter, vitality, optimism, country wisdom, and jocular presence reinforce our perspective of Sancho. She reasons, plots, and revels in his fantasy because she believes in him and strives for a better life for the family. As such she is very much Sancho's match, of flesh and blood.

ENCHANTERS, WIZARDS, AND MAGIC

There is a built-in insecurity in Don Quixote's world. After all, it is a magic world, at least for our knight, one in which the hero has no allies and his enemies watch his progress from all sides. Don Quixote soldiers on while spied upon by strange, dark, malignant beings intent on checking his progress, evildoers who pillage his library, turn giants into windmills or wine bags, and finally deliver a mortal blow when they turn the exquisitely beautiful Dulcinea into a coarse peasant girl. Thinking back on his own experiences, Cervantes may have thought that one of the most glorious moments in his life, the Christian victory over the Turks in the naval battle of Lepanto, may have been dimmed and tarnished by an evil enchanter—as the Turks regrouped all too soon, rebuilt their navy, and renewed their piratical attacks. The vessel carrying him back to Spain was captured by Muslim ships and he had to endure long years of servitude in Algiers. It is also possible to imagine the melancholy musings of Philip II, whose vast fleet, the Invincible Armada, was carried to almost total destruction by the evil winds and huge waves of a storm that forced the Spanish vessels to flee toward the north and pushed them to Scotland and a long, disastrous return through Scottish waters and around the western coast of England. Could malignant enchanters inspire the evil forces opposed to the Spanish enterprise?

Similarly, failure is often encountered by Don Quixote, who sees victory snatched away just when he is about to savor it, and whose interpretation of the facts and people around him is often changed abruptly by a quick reversal of the situation. It would be impossible for our knight to survive adversity if not for the fact that he blames evil enchanters for his misadventures.

Enchanters and magic play an essential role in the mind of Don Quixote, as they do in most romances of chivalry. Suspension of disbelief was common among the readers of such novels, made easier by the fact that the very fabric of society and culture at that time was permeated by irrational thoughts connected with superstition and magic. This aspect of the novel has had less influence on the literature that followed Cervantes because on the whole, the novel as a genre develops toward realism, and although it would not be hard to find the presence of magic and supernatural elements in nineteenth-century literature, and even in our own time, the sources for such elements can be found elsewhere: let us remember, for instance, that Romantic writers were fond of medieval legends where magic often played a main role.

Nevertheless, magic is so pervasive in Don Quixote's mind that it is impossible to describe his thoughts and his actions without it; it is essential to his view of the world from the very beginning of the novel. In chapter 1 of part 1, just as the novel begins, we read: "His fantasy filled with everything he had read in his books, enchantments as well as combats, battles, challenges, wounds, courtings, loves, torments, and other impossible foolishness, and he became so convinced in his imagination of the truth of all the countless grandiloquent and false inventions he read that for him no history in the world was truer" (Gr., 21).

Before Don Quixote sallies forth for the second time, he finds with dismay that his whole library—books, room, and all—has disappeared and concludes that the evil enchanter Frestón is to blame. The bewildering incidents at Juan Palomeque's inn, such as when a melee erupts as he intercepts Maritornes's visit to the muleteer, when Sancho is tossed in a blanket and Don Quixote is unable to come to his rescue, or when the giants turn out to be wineskins, convince our knight that everything that happens there is the work of enchanters. Between his two stays at the inn, Don Quixote assumes that an enchanter, this time a friendly one, has whisked Sancho from Sierra Morena to El Toboso and back with supernatural speed in part 1, chapter 31. At the beginning of part 2, when he becomes aware that their adventures have been published in a book, Sancho wonders how their historian could report what they said and did in solitude. Don Quixote is quick to reply, in part 2, chapter 2, that their historian is a magician of the kind that has complete and thorough knowledge of all events and can read men's inner thoughts. And obviously, Dulcinea's enchantment and Merlin's instructions are a pivotal section in the second part of the novel.

We accept instinctively magic as part of Don Quixote's mind since it plays an important role in the romances of chivalry, but Sancho's attitude is more ambivalent and often more critical and negative. His frame of reference differs from Don Quixote's. Still, magic is part of Sancho's superstitious cultural background, and occasionally he will refer to enchantment as a way to explain an event that is not explainable otherwise. In part 1, chapter 35, when his master in a daze, half asleep, has slashed about his room with his sword and has cut up several wineskins full of red wine, Sancho announces to the innkeeper and the other guests that a battle has taken place between his master and a giant; he has seen the giant's severed head: "'Don't stand and listen, go in and stop the fight or help my master, though that won't be necessary because, no doubt about it, the giant must be dead by now and giving an accounting to God of his sinful life; I saw his blood running along the floor, and his head cut off and fallen to one side, a head the size of a big wineskin'" (Gr., 306). All rush to the knight's room; the giant's head is not to be found. Sancho comments: "'Now I know that everything in this house is enchantment; the last time I stood on the very spot where I'm standing now, I was punched and beaten and I never knew who was doing it, and I never could see anybody, and now the head is nowhere to be found, though I saw it cut off with my very own eyes, and the blood ran out of the body like water from a fountain'" (Gr., 306–7). The innkeeper rebukes him, "'Don't you see, you thief, that the blood and the fountain are only these slashed wineskins and the red wine flooding this room?'" (Gr., 307). Richard L. Predmore comments, "For the first time, Sancho needs enchantment to defend his illusions."[7]

The most devastating example of the evil work of enchanters comes with Don Quixote's perception of the enchanted Dulcinea. Beauty and love have guided him as much as the love of justice and glory through his many adventures and calamities. Beauty is now tarnished, although love, a tortured love, will endure.

Don Quixote complains bitterly: "'Sancho, what do you think of how the enchanters despise me? Look at the extent of their malice and ill will, for they have chosen to deprive me of the happiness I might have had at seeing my lady in her rightful person. In truth, I was born to be a model of misfortune, the target and mark for the arrows of affliction. And you must also know, Sancho, that it was not enough for these traitors to have changed and transformed my Dulcinea, but they had to transform and change her into a figure as low-born and ugly as that peasant'" (Gr., 519–20). His sense of smell reinforces the sad, depressing vision of his transformed lady: the enchanters had to "'take away something that so rightfully belongs to noble ladies, which is a sweet smell, since they are always surrounded by perfumes and flowers. For I shall tell you, Sancho, that when I came to help Dulcinea onto her palfrey, as you call it, though it looked like a donkey to me, I smelled an odor of raw garlic that almost made me faint and poisoned my soul'" (Gr., 520). From this moment on, until the end of the novel, the reader may observe an increasing sadness, even a depression in Don Quixote. From the beginning to almost the end, his mentality is locked into the magic of the enchanters until he can delude himself no more and succumbs to reality.

VISION, VIEWPOINT, INTERPRETATION

Whereas some adventures are attributed to the machinations of wizards and enchanters, others are explained through the shifting viewpoints of the main characters. Chapter 35, part 1, the wineskins chapter to which we have just referred, serves as a good example of changing perspectives. Here, Sancho changes his viewpoint so that it approaches Don Quixote's interpretation of everyday life. He becomes a "believer" and accepts the "fact" that his master is battling giants.

The chapter begins in the virtual area of a literary tale: the curate has been reading aloud to a select audience. We are at the inn where so many adventures have already turned sour for our knight. Suddenly Sancho rushes in, out of breath: "Only a little more of the novel remained to be read when a distraught Sancho Panza rushed out of the garret where Don Quixote slept, shouting: 'Come, Señores, come quickly and help my master, who's involved in the fiercest, most awful battle my eyes have ever seen! By God, what a thrust he gave to the giant, the enemy of the Señora Princess Micomicona, when he cut his head right off, just like a turnip!'" (Gr., 305).

Don Quixote had been dreaming about giants. Awake, he realizes that strange, dark, mysterious shapes surround him (in reality, the wineskins the innkeeper kept stored in the garret). He springs into action and attacks the "giants" with his sword. Sancho sees his master, sword in hand, surrounded by strange dark shapes from which flow a reddish liquid and interprets the scene in a flash, from a quixotic and heroic viewpoint. Don Quixote is addressing one of the "giants": "'Hold, thief, scoundrel, coward! I have you now, and your scimitar will be of little use to you!'" (Gr., 305). As the knight slashes at the walls with his sword, Sancho insists to the others that he saw a giant with "'a head the size of a big wineskin'" (Gr., 306).

Why does Sancho mention wineskins? Could it be that subconsciously he is beginning to doubt his own statement about giants? Moreover, how is it possible for Sancho, always levelheaded and practical, to think there are now giants in the inn? We must remember Sancho has been happily imagining himself as governor of an island, or a province, or perhaps a small kingdom. But this happy ending is possible only if Don Quixote has not been lying or fantasizing. Sancho's rosy future is linked now to Don Quixote's inner world. There can be no governorship for him if Don Quixote does not first win a battle against some powerful enemies or perhaps some wicked giants. The Sancho who sees giants at the inn is not the thinking Sancho, but instead, the optimistic dreamer Sancho who fantasizes about a better future for himself and for his whole family. Cervantes infers here that our interpretation of the outside world is guided not only by our senses and our reason, but also by our hopes and desires. For a few seconds Sancho has become Don Quixote. The last words coming from Sancho determine a strong reaction from the innkeeper, who until this moment had whimsically defended the existence of knights errant but is now interpreting what he has heard through a series of interconnected clues. He knows enough about Don Quixote from an earlier visit when the knight left the inn without paying his bill, and he also knows that the room where Don Quixote slept is full of wineskins: "'Strike me dead,' said the innkeeper, 'if Don Quixote, or Don Devil, hasn't slashed one of the skins of red wine hanging at the head of his bed; the spilled wine must be what this good man thinks is blood'" (Gr., 306). Meanwhile Sancho is looking everywhere for the giant's head, and when he does not find it, he complains that everything in the inn is enchanted; the last time he was there he was punched and beaten and never knew who was doing it, and now the head was nowhere to be found, "'though I saw it cut off with my very own eyes, and the blood ran out of the body like water from a fountain'" (Gr., 307). Sancho resorts to the same defense Don Quixote uses every time an adventure turns to defeat: enchanters have intervened and turned the tables against him. In the meantime he is still looking for the giant's head: "'All I know . . . is that if I don't find that head, my luck will turn and my countship will dissolve away like salt in water'" (Gr., 307). The psychology lesson is clear: our yearnings and passions make us interpret what we see or receive through our senses in strange, nonrational ways. "Sancho awake was worse that his master asleep: such was the faith he had in the promises his master had made to him" (Gr., 307).

Most noteworthy in this chapter are the sudden changes of opinion by Sancho and by the innkeeper, contrasting with the relative lack of change on the part of the priest and the barber, on one side, and of Don Quixote, on the other side. It is as if Cervantes wanted to submit a group of characters to a controlled pressure, in this case the pressure of the presence of giants in Don Quixote's system of values, creating in him the need to fight them, and then observe the reaction of each individual. We could compare the events in this chapter with a laboratory experiment with guinea pigs where the priest and the barber, more stable than the others, would be control animals and would not be inoculated with the germs being studied. The description of these events in the text of our novel is not made in an external, objective, and cold way; on the contrary, it introduces us to the changing emotions of Sancho and the innkeeper. A category or label such as the supposed "quixotization" of Sancho cannot fully describe a situation this complex. Sancho comes closer to his master's viewpoint not by merely imitating him, but rather from the core of his own personality, his hopes and his ambition; he makes use of three different resources—the creative invention of concrete details, the recourse to possible enchanters, and his faith in his master's judgment—in order to reach his goal, his ambitious future status as governor of an island.

Another example of a changing point of vision, viewpoint, and interpretation occurs in part 1, chapter 21 as Don Quixote and Sancho are ambling along in a light rain. Don Quixote catches sight of a man riding toward them wearing on his head something that glitters like gold. Our two main characters have radically different opinions of what the object is. Don Quixote remarks, "Unless I am mistaken, coming toward us is a man who wears on his head the helmet of Mambrino [an enchanted helmet made of gold having magic powers, part of the Italian epic tradition]. . . . Tell me, do you not see that knight coming toward us, mounted on a dappled gray and wearing on his head a helmet of gold?" Sancho's description is much more restrained: "'What I see and can make out . . . is just a man riding a donkey that's gray like mine, and wearing something shiny on his head'" (Gr., 153). The shiny object is ambiguous because the itinerant barber wandering toward them is wearing a brass basin as a hat to protect himself from the rain, thus making possible Don Quixote's interpretation. Each persists in his interpretation. For Sancho, it is clear that the man riding a donkey is not a knight and the shiny object is only a barber's basin. But Sancho witnesses the encounter.

Don Quixote charges the barber who gets off his donkey, throws down his basin, and runs away. What are they going to do with the spoils of the battle? According to the code of chivalry, Don Quixote is entitled to take possession of the helmet. Sancho covets the donkey, judging it better than his own donkey. But the code of chivalry does not allow it. Could he at least keep the donkey's saddle and trappings he asks, obviously in much better condition than the ones his donkey is wearing? Suddenly Sancho is pushed by greed to come closer to his master's interpretation, for if there is no gold helmet and no knight, then there has been no knightly encounter. The code of chivalry does not apply, and what Sancho proposes is simply stealing. In spite of himself, Sancho is brought to his master's reading of the object—although he cannot totally agree when Don Quixote asks him to admire the "helmet" and is bound to remark that it is a helmet that looks very much like a barber's basin. The bottom line is that Don Quixote keeps the "helmet" and Sancho appropriates the packsaddle and harness.

In part 1, chapter 25 (Gr., 195), the disagreement about the "helmet" flares up again. Sancho is afraid others will not see the shiny object as a basin and fears he runs the risk of having people think he is out of his mind. Don Quixote counters: "'you have the dimmest wits that any squire in the world has or ever had. Is it possible that in all the time you have traveled with me you have not yet noticed that all things having to do with knights errant appear to be chimerical, foolish, senseless, and turned inside out? And not because they really are, but because hordes of enchanters always walk among us and alter and change every thing and turn things into whatever they please, according to whether they wish to favor us or destroy us; and so, what seems to you a barber's basin seems to me the helmet of Mambrino, and will seem another thing to someone else'" (Gr., 195).

Finally, in part 1, chapter 45, a crowd has gathered at Palomeque's inn. Don Quixote and Sancho are there, and the barber arrives unexpectedly and claims as his the objects Don Quixote and Sancho had taken. Everyone wants to state his opinion as to the objects in question. Sancho had declared, at the very end of part 1, chapter 44, that the object has been very useful in the battle when his master freed the chained galley slaves, "'if it wasn't for this basihelm, things wouldn't have gone too well for him because there was a lot of stone-throwing in that fight'" (Gr., 390). "Basihelm," a composite of "basin" and "helm," is a word invented by Sancho that allows him to agree (partially) with his master and at the same time not to lose touch with his own sense of reality. Don Quixote seems to betray Sancho: he insists that the "helmet" is a true helmet but allows that the saddle looks like a packsaddle to him. Finally, Don Fernando and the others present at the inn decide to play a joke on the barber and proclaim that the "helmet" is a real helmet. The poor barber is overwhelmed. Each character acts subjectively, deciding for himself the meaning of words. They do so according to their own interest, according to their own whim, or are carried away by the opinion of the crowd. This meeting at the inn is a microcosm of a society where people have different interests, claim different meanings for common words, and pursue different goals. Their actions are often in conflict, and tension increases as a result. Frequently laughter is the only way to defuse tension, and we can find winners and losers as a result of social interaction.

Thus the Mambrino helmet episode blows up into a three act play in which there is action, reaction, compromise, and epilogue; action and stubbornness on the part of Don Quixote, diverse reactions of the people in the inn to suit their whims, and Sancho's compromise of the "basihelm." Laughter and tears are the bonus. Again, vision, viewpoint, and interpretation emanate from this adventure.

Cervantes Inside His Novel

We touched on the enigma of locating the author in chapter 3, "Constructing *Don Quixote*." If we investigate the text, we find concrete examples of the hide-and-seek game that the author plays along with the further turmoil created by the words he puts into the mouth of the main character about the author's true identity.

We mentioned earlier the scene in chapter 8, part 1, where Don Quixote prepares to do battle with a Basque. Both characters had unsheathed their swords, they faced each other, and we expected a bloody fight to take place—but the action froze at that very moment since the "first author" of the novel, that is, the Arab historian Cide Hamete Benengeli, left the battle pending, apologizing because he found nothing else written about the feats of Don Quixote other than what he had already narrated. At the beginning of chapter 9, the suspense continues: "we left the brave Basque and the famous Don Quixote with their swords raised and unsheathed, about to deliver two downstrokes so furious that if they had entirely hit the mark, the combatants would have been cut and split in half from top to bottom and opened like pomegranates; and at that extremely uncertain point, the delectable history stopped and was interrupted, without the author giving us any information as to where the missing parts could be found" (Gr., 65).

It is at this moment that the "second author," Cervantes, appears. He is sad and irritated since he had grown fond of the tale and its hero and wants to know more about Don Quixote's adventures. By chance, while strolling in Toledo's market he finds a boy who is trying to sell to a silk merchant some old papers written in Arabic—probably the papers would be then used as wrapping paper as was customary. Cervantes proceeds to explain that he suspects they might contain something of interest, buys them, and has them translated. The translator laughs as he starts reading the papers: "As I have said, . . . 'This Dulcinea of Toboso, referred to so often in this history, they say had the best hand for salting pork of any woman in all of La Mancha'" (Gr., 67).

The reader is now facing several viewpoints, hence several layers of meaning. The Arab historian intrudes mainly by his absence since it leaves the narrative interrupted at a crucial moment. Then he reappears as his name is found on the first page of the batch of papers. Cervantes, who seems to be a concerned reader, anxious to find out how the narrative unfolds, takes an active part in the search for new manuscripts. The translator makes it then possible to go on with the tale even if we do not know how good a translator he is. Finally, the anonymous author of the note about Dulcinea injects a down-to-earth tone that contrasts and contradicts the exalted, spiritual, and exquisite image of the lady in Don Quixote's mind. The result is a discontinuity in the narrative, and a veil of doubt is superimposed about what we have read and are about to read. Cervantes appears, facilitates the continuation of the story, and comments about the possible defects attributable to its Arab author: "and if something of value is missing from it, in my opinion the fault lies with the dog who was its author rather than with any defect in its subject" (Gr., 69). Right away the action resumes. The name of Cervantes will appear again later, in chapter 40, part 1, when an escaped captive describes the desperate life of Christian slaves in Algiers under the tyrannical Azán Agá, king of Algiers: "Each day he hanged someone, impaled someone, cut off someone's ears. . . . The only one who held his own with him was a Spanish soldier named something de Saavedra [an allusion to Cervantes himself, for his complete surname was Cervantes Saavedra], who did things that will be remembered by those people for many years . . . ; if I had the time, I would tell you something of what that soldier did, which would entertain and amaze you much more than this recounting of my history" (Gr., 344). This brief appearance by the author reminds us of the cameo appearances, in modern times, of the famous movie director Alfred Hitchcock, who can be seen for a few fleeting moments in some of his most celebrated films.

How much more Cervantes confuses us when he has Don Quixote opine on the author and be the judge of the very story. Here Cervantes can be sarcastic and self-deprecating: "'Now I say,' said Don Quixote, 'that the author of my history was no wise man but an ignorant gossip-monger who, without rhyme or reason, began to write, not caring how it turned out, just like Orbaneja, the painter of Úbeda, who, when asked what he was painting, replied: "Whatever comes out." Perhaps he painted a rooster in such a fashion and so unrealistically that he had to write beside it, in capital letters: "This is a rooster." And that must be how my history is: a commentary will be necessary in order to understand it'" (Gr., 478).

The hero himself criticizes the very novel in which he is a hero as well as the author of the novel. At least in one respect Don Quixote's comment is right: the novel has given birth to not one, but many efforts to explain its meaning. So, Cervantes goes forth where no author has gone before. We feel his presence throughout the book, and in part 2 Don Quixote feels the presence of part 1, already published. He worries that the author has injected some licentiousness into his relationship with Dulcinea, and expresses his desire to read the first part of the novel, in other words, *to read about himself.*

Early in the book, Cervantes points up moral weakness in Spanish society when Don Quixote encounters a poor shepherd, Andrés, tied to a tree, flogged by an avaricious and cruel master simply because the young lad expects to be paid a salary. The master-cum-peasant expresses his side of the story, relating that he bought three pairs of shoes for the shepherd and paid Andrés's medical bills. Still, a sheep is missing from the flock each day. Don Quixote is blind to any explanation other than his vision that one human being is abusing another in front of his eyes. Now in full command as a knight-errant, he cannot fathom the punishment, and Cervantes pits the knight's world, code, and rules against reality.

Cervantes presents a moral dilemma. We do not know why a sheep is missing each day. Is it thievery or carelessness on the part of Andrés? Is someone else stealing sheep? Is the peasant justified in not paying the boy his salary for seven months? The reader stands by knowing full well that the punishment meted out after Don Quixote's intervention will be a good deal harsher. This is confirmed later in the novel when Andrés wants to flee at the sight of Don Quixote, because of the unfortunate aftermath of the knight's good intentions.

First, Cervantes is making a point in his vagueness, pitting our reality against the knight-errant's view. Second, we must remember that when he was a tax collector, he was jailed for having helped poor people who did not pay all they owed in taxes. This episode resonates with Cervantes's life experience.

Perhaps the sharpest criticism Cervantes's novel offers about Spanish society and institutions can be found in chapter 22, part 1, where Don Quixote confronts the chain gang of galley slaves, prisoners who are serving their sentences by rowing in the king's galleys. One of the prisoners, pointing to a comrade who is so downcast and melancholy that he is unable to speak, says, "'This man, Señor, is being taken away for being a canary, I mean a musician and singer.'" Don Quixote does not understand. "'But I have heard it said,' said Don Quixote, 'that troubles take wing for the man who can sing.'" One of the guards clears this point: "'Señor, among these *non sancta* people, singing when you're in difficulty means confessing under torture. They tortured this sinner and he confessed his crime, which was rustling, or stealing livestock, and because he confessed he was sentenced to six years in the galleys, plus two hundred lashes, which he already bears on his back; he's always very downhearted and sad because the rest of the thieves . . . abuse and humiliate and insult him, and think very little of him, because he confessed and didn't have the courage to say his nos. Because they say *no* has even fewer letters than *yes,* and a criminal is very lucky when his life or death depends on his own words and not on those of witnesses, or on evidence, and in my opinion, they're not too far off the mark'" (Gr., 165). This unhappy prisoner had been compelled to confess under torture. Was he guilty or not? We are not sure. We realize the cruelty of a system that relied on torture to extract confessions. Penalties were also cruel and excessive: two hundred lashes could kill a man, and being a galley slave meant hard work under the lash of the galley master while being chained to the rowing bench; if the vessel sank the galley slaves were doomed.

The other prisoners' tales are equally stark and sad. One of them has been condemned for being a go-between: "'But I never thought I was doing wrong: my entire intention was for everybody to be happy and to live in peace and harmony, without discord or distress; but this virtuous desire did not prevent me from being sent to a place from which I do not expect to return'" (Gr., 167). Cervantes was critical of the system of justice because he had personally experienced its errors and slow pace, having been jailed in spite of being innocent and having been hounded by bureaucrats almost all his adult life. Don Quixote concludes: "'it might be that the lack of courage this one showed under torture, that one's need of money, another's lack of favor, and finally, the twisted judgment of the judge, have been the reason for your ruination, and for not having justice on your side'" (Gr., 169). The vow he took as a knight in the order of chivalry compels him to favor "those in need and those oppressed by the powerful"; therefore he frightens away the guards and frees the prisoners. The adventure does not have a happy ending since he then orders them to set out for the city of El Toboso to appear before the lady Dulcinea del Toboso and give her all the details of their liberation. The ex-prisoners refuse because they can think only about hiding from the police, and they throw stones at the knight and his squire.

This incident exposes an important contradiction in Spanish society of that time. Don Quixote's instinct tells him that justice is often unjust, that the punishment often does not fit the crime, and finally that freedom is a basic need that should be respected. But again there is a moral discrepancy: Don Quixote is no doubt releasing men who acted against the law. Cervantes uses humor and irony in language as the galley slaves recount their felonies. All of this confounds the reader. There is such ambiguity that we cannot be certain if the severity of the sentencing was fair, but at the same time, is Don Quixote correct in freeing them then and there after hearing the quick and facile explanations of the galley slaves?

Each character or group of characters interprets the situation in a specific way, a way that conflicts with the other interpretations. The guards are sure the galley slaves are guilty and should be punished. The galley slaves claim they are innocent and that justice has not been done. Don Quixote seems to agree with this viewpoint, but after freeing the prisoners he demands they visit Dulcinea, which immediately turns them against him. Above all, Sancho is appalled by the situation and afraid the Santa Hermandad (Holy Brotherhood, that is, the rural police) will find them and they will all go to jail. It is the interplay of different, even opposed viewpoints that creates the dramatic situation, and the word "misunderstanding" is the only common denominator to all the viewpoints presented. Don Quixote appears to be a flawed hero. His decision to free the prisoners is perhaps too hasty since he is not aware of all the details related to their trials, and in any case, the demand that they pay homage to Dulcinea is totally unreasonable given the circumstances of the moment. Cervantes presents a partially positive portrait of our hero: courage when facing the guards, eloquence in his words about justice and freedom, yet undue haste and unreasonableness in his request. The average reader may find this episode amusing and one more proof of Don Quixote's folly, but there is no doubt about the defiant message it sends us.

When Cervantes criticizes Philip II and Philip III, in chapters 16–18 of part 2, he does so in such a subtle way that many—indeed, perhaps all—of his readers at that time did not understand the hidden meanings in the novel's pages. An instance of this occurs when Don Quixote is elated after his victory over the Knight of the Mirrors and goes forth along the road where he meets "a prudent knight of La Mancha," the Knight of the Green Coat. It soon becomes obvious that these two gentlemen have little in common. The Knight of the Green Coat seems at first to be a reasonable, prudent, well-organized man, fully in control of his estate, well dressed, and prosperous. Sancho is impressed. But little by little we see another side; the newcomer is boastful, vain, improperly dressed as a dandy while traveling a rough road. His life is uneventful and dull. He represents "the average Spaniard" of the time. He is not even courageous. When a cart carrying a lion appears and Don Quixote, anxious to defy the king of beasts, commands the man in charge of the lion to open the cage and let him in, the Knight of the Green Coat runs away as fast as he can. Don Quixote will not stay long in the house of his new acquaintance, the Knight of the Green Coat. He suspects a spirit of pettiness and lack of imagination that is the opposite of the life he wants to live. The confrontation with the lion underscores the spiritual distance between Don Quixote and the Knight of the Green Coat, who flees on his mare while the lion refuses to come out of his cage and turns his hindquarters on Don Quixote. Like the Knight of the Green Coat, the lion is disgraced for refusing to fight. In fact, there are two lions caged in the cart. They belong to the Spanish king, whose flags fly on the cart. Two lions appear in the coat of arms of Spain.

As Helena Percas de Ponseti points out, "the lion is symbolic of regal dignity and victory. A lion victorious represents the 'exaltation of virility'; a lion tamed betrays the indignity of castration. In this context, the knight's challenge to the lethargic male lion, who refuses to come out of his cage, is a challenge to the slumbering spirit of Spain. . . . The disgraced opponent [of Don Quixote] is the king himself—the official mirror of Christian Spain—nominally identified with the king of beasts, the 'generous lion,' a euphemism for an indifferent king, who 'more courteous than arrogant,' two more euphemisms for apathetic and cowardly, pays little heed to Don Quixote. . . . The lion (the king), who shows 'restraint,' or indifference, before Don Quixote, does not fall into the category of the vigilant monarch mindful of his duties; he lacks 'supreme consciousness' for he stretches and yawns. He falls instead into the category of 'sick king' afflicted by 'sterility of spirit . . . a state he projects onto the environment around him and from which Don Quijote (Cervantes) fails to shake him with his challenge.'"[8] Cervantes could not forget, nor forgive, the indifference of Philip II when he attempted to get recognition for his services. Moreover, as a war hero he must have felt contempt for Philip II, the "Prudent King," who differed from his father the Emperor Charles V in that he never went to battle and much preferred the sound of the scribbling pens of his bureaucrats to the thunder of guns on the battlefield.

Once more, Cervantes shows the moral weakness present in society in part 2, but this time in the aristocracy, in the palace of the duke and duchess. Only Cervantes can shed an analytical and critical light on the people who lived around him and the way they dealt with each other. He is fully aware of the way that Spaniards who think they have "pure Old Christian blood" feel fully empowered to rule the country and lead it into the future, and also he is the only Golden Age writer who understands the decay of the feudal system in Spain, rotting from within while preventing any other system of values from taking over. This is made clear when we read an episode in part 2, chapter 48. A mother comes to see Don Quixote by night, seeking his help. Her daughter has been seduced and abandoned by one of the duke's vassals, the son of a farmer. The duke is aware of the facts, yet he has not forced the young man to marry the girl. The seducer's father is rich; he has often lent money to the duke and guaranteed his debts. The duke should protect and rule his vassals. The social order has been subverted. A commoner is prevailing over an aristocrat. Don Quixote makes a brave attempt to restore genuine feudal order by forcing the duke to assume responsibility and provide justice within his domains. He throws down his glove in the middle of the duke's manor's hall. The duke picks up the gauntlet, yet he manages to defy Don Quixote's challenge, protecting the wealthy farmer and ultimately creating a new opportunity to make fun of Don Quixote. The official system of justice administered by a feudal lord in his domain does not work. As Carroll Johnson states, "feudalism no longer exists except in a perverted form, and the structures of Spanish society ensured that a more modern socio-economic order would not come along to replace it."[9]

The duke and duchess's vacuous, shallow existence, along with their cruel antics toward the main characters, typifies Cervantes's view of upper-class life. They have read *Don Quixote* part 1 and perceive him as a madman and Sancho as a coward. Their malicious jokes go to the very heart of the beliefs and desires of the knight and his squire, respectively: they mock knight-errantry with all its fuss, pomp, and circumstance, including the ritual of washing Don Quixote's beard; introduce the nasty punishment of disenchanting Dulcinea by making Sancho inflict on himself 3,300 lashes; and finally give him the governorship of an island (village), putting him through all sorts of trials and tribulations.

No more charitable is the wealthy Don Antonio Moreno who extends his hospitality to Don Quixote and Sancho in Barcelona. He too has read part 1 of the book and has knowledge of Don Quixote's reputation. He puts a sign on Don Quixote's back with large printed letters—"This is Don Quixote" (Gr., 867)—and parades him through the streets as people comment and pass judgment on the knight's actions. Then the wealthy couple arranges a ball at which Don Quixote is made to dance every dance until he drops from exhaustion in the middle of the floor.

There is a marked difference in self-consciousness between the first chapters and the later parts of the book. It increases in the second part, as Harry Levin comments: "During the decade that had passed between the publication of the two parts, Cervantes's figures had stamped themselves as types upon the popular consciousness. In contrast then to Part One, where the Don meets with misunderstandings on all sides, most of his interlocutors in Part Two are prepared to play his game. In fact, they go so far out of their way to cater to his madness with practical jokes that—and the invidious comparison is repeatedly drawn—they seem madder than he."[10] Our main characters rise above the hollowness and malevolence of the upper class, and Cervantes points up the dignity and moral fiber of Don Quixote and Sancho and the unkindness and abuse of the highborn and the wealthy.

This critical approach to Spanish society is both subtle and multifaceted. Sancho, a peasant, proves to be a worthy companion, even a friend, to Don Quixote, thus transcending class barriers. Sancho also demonstrates he can be a good governor, a good legislator, and a good judge. If we compare his success as governor of Barataria to the failure of the only aristocrats portrayed in the novel, the duke and duchess, to engage in anything that is not superficial and frivolous, we see a contrast that is disturbing and may lead us to the conclusion that Spanish society has given too much wealth and power to individuals who are unworthy.

"I Know Who I Am"

Don Quixote says "I know who I am" to his neighbor Pedro Alonso, who finds the "knight" beaten up and reciting ballads from pastoral novels and referring to books of chivalry. The peasant, baffled by these words uttered with such conviction, manages to escort Don Quixote back to his village. But those five words will carry Don Quixote and Sancho through the novel. He has faith in who he is and what he sets out to do. He never falters from believing in himself and his quest. This certainty is unwavering until nearly the end of the novel when he reverts back to reality as Señor Quijano.

Don Quixote, just as Descartes after him, takes refuge in his own existential self. He affirms his being, his willpower: "'I know who I am, . . . and I know I can be not only those I have mentioned [Valdovinos, Abindarráez, that is, two heroic characters in Spanish ballads and novels] but the Twelve Peers of France as well [knights chosen by the king of France because they were all equally heroic], and even all the nine paragons of Fame, for my deeds will surpass all those they performed, together or singly'" (Gr., 43). His confidence in himself, his hope for future glory, and his total devotion to his lady are what give him the strength to pick himself up and go on with his quest. Compared to Don Quixote's heroic efforts, centered on his valor and his love, Descartes looks pale, sheltered by a God that will protect him from evil enchanters and will not hide or alter the truth. Being alone in such an unending struggle does take a toll. By the end of part 2 of the novel, with Dulcinea enchanted supposedly by an evil magician but in reality because of Sancho's malicious intervention, Don Quixote becomes more and more disheartened. His previously comic persona is acquiring darker, even tragic aspects. This makes him much more interesting than Descartes as a hero of the unending struggle to pit human existence against all the confusing circumstances that surround each one of us in our daily life.

PART II

En el siglo XVII fue saludado con una carcajada,

en el XVIII con una sonrisa y en el XIX con una

lágrima. Escapándose siempre su profunda

comprensión.

(In the seventeenth century [*Don Quixote*] was

greeted with an outburst of laughter, in the

eighteenth, with a smile, and in the nineteenth, with

a tear, always eluding its profound meaning.)

LUIS ASTRANA MARÍN (1889–1959)

5

Cervantine Sallies
into Eighteenth-Century France
and England

By the eighteenth century much had changed in Western Europe's literary scene. The novel was becoming more fashionable, although critics were still hesitant to treat it with respect because of Aristotle's influence. But his dominance as the supreme organizer of Western thought was beginning to wane. English literature had flourished with Shakespeare, Milton, and John Donne. The plays of Corneille, Molière, and Racine dominated the French stage. In Spain, the glorious literary period known as the Golden Age endured until Calderón's death in 1681.

Cervantes's novel continued to gain fame with readers throughout the seventeenth and eighteenth centuries. New editions and important translations had appeared immediately after the publication of part 1. In May 1607, the Brussels bookseller Roger Velpius (authorized by Robles, who first published the novel in Spain) published a new edition, which served as the basis for the English version by Thomas Shelton. Shelton claimed to have finished his translation in forty days, an assertion that sounds exaggerated or impossible. The English translation did not appear for several more years. In 1608, Juan de la Cuesta published in Madrid a third edition of the novel. That same year Nicolas Baudoin published in Paris a translation of the interpolated story "The Man Who Was Recklessly Curious." The following year an anthology of fragments of *Don Quixote* appeared in a translation by the French writer Jean Richer. Cervantes's reputation was spreading across Europe. A second edition of his novel appeared in Brussels in 1611. In 1612, at last, Shelton published *The Delightful Historie of the Most Ingenious Knight Don Quixote de la Mancha,* which became a bestseller. During the following years, John Fletcher collaborated with Shakespeare on a play, unfortunately lost, inspired by Cardenio's madness based on an episode in *Don Quixote.* In part 1, chapters 28–29, Cardenio, a suitor to beautiful Luscinda, goes mad when she marries a rival, Don Fernando. A complete French translation of *Don Quixote* by César Oudin, one that required four years' work, appeared in 1615.

The eighteenth century is characterized by an increasingly critical stance with regard to traditionally held political and religious beliefs, which were parodied, in favor of a more rational approach. A certain amount of skepticism entered into the picture as new ideas began to take hold. The picaresque worldview was very appealing. It was materialistic, deterministic, foreshadowing social Darwinism. It dealt with survival, isolation, and loneliness. The first French picaresque novel, *Gil Blas de Santillane* by Lesage, had appeared, as well as the first psychological novel, *The Princess of Clèves* by Mme. de Lafayette.

The eighteenth-century English writers looked to Cervantes as a source of both narrative technique and ideas. The picaresque worldview, the parody of contemporary values and beliefs, and the presence of the author in his work characterized the works of many leading writers. They also understood the appeal of both the picaresque and romance novels for the reading public. One can easily see how they, like Cervantes, navigate a middle course between these two opposing currents of narrative, accepting them in part. Eighteenth-century writers inherited these tools through Cervantes's work, just as he had inherited them from a previous epoch, and they adapted them to their circumstances just as he had done.

Charles-Antoine Coypel (1694–1752), *Don Quixote at the Ball of Don Antonio*. Oil on canvas, 163 × 283 cm. Chateau, Compiègne, France. Photo: Réunion des Musées Nationaux / Art Resource, NY.

From La Mancha to Westphalia:
Don Quixote and *Candide*

Given the popularity of Cervantes in the centuries after his death and the cultural climate of the eighteenth century, it is not surprising that we find evidence of his imprint on the French and English narrative. By the time Voltaire (1691–1775) started writing *Candide,* his major work, Cervantes's *Don Quixote* had gained an undisputed place of honor in Western letters. *Candide* appeared in 1759, approximately a century and a half after the publication of *Don Quixote,* part 1. A hurried reading of Voltaire's witty account may not reveal any resemblance to *Don Quixote:* both structure and style differ, and so do the main characters. Voltaire's satire has a compact, lineal structure. It is much shorter than Cervantes's novel. It offers few or no obstacles to our comprehension. It is simply a short, brilliant masterpiece, a sort of Fabergé egg, whereas *Don Quixote* is more like a huge country house, full of corridors, secret passages, locked rooms, spacious halls, and turrets, with many stories and new wings attached to an older edifice. The rhythm of action differs. Cervantes gives us a novel that unfolds at a steady, deliberate, and even slow pace. In part 1, various loosely attached tales interrupt the main body of the novel. Voltaire's text has only one chapter, chapter 11, "The Old Woman's Story," that digresses from the main body of the work. If we place both books on a table, look at the tables of contents, open the texts at random, and compare the number of pages and chapters, we realize how different one is from the other.

Cervantes's novel is not only much longer, but it is made of different parts or sections. It was not written as a sequence. The first section contains short stories. It is quite possible that Cervantes was unsure of the success of his novel and as insurance included these short stories in the narrative. At times these stories are flimsily related to the rest of the book. When part 2 was written several years later, the author knew that the knight and his squire could hold the attention of readers without the help of extraneous material. With respect to thematic insights, part 2 is more fine-tuned and on the whole superior to part 1. The novel has two prefaces and two endings, the first one provisional and open, since Cervantes does not want to preclude a sequel. The second one is definitive and closed; Don Quixote dies so there is no danger of a sequel by another author.

While Cervantes's novel is long and does not have the linear structure of *Candide*, it has clusters of chapters that stand out and give the whole a sense of unity. Also, although each adventure is unique and complete, it is thematically linked to the whole. As we continue our examination of the text in the two books, we note that in Cervantes's novel there are two places that provide a nucleus for a series of adventures. In part 1, some of the salient adventures take place in the inn where Don Quixote is dubbed a knight. In part 2, the palace of the duke and duchess is the setting of many chapters dedicated to the ways in which Don Quixote and Sancho cope with difficult ordeals. Here, for the first time they go their separate ways: Sancho leaves his master behind in order to carry out his duties as governor. In both parts, Don Quixote and Sancho come home at the end; in part 1 to rest and recover, and in part 2 Don Quixote comes home to die, having recovered his old personality as Alonso Quijano. He renounces his madness only to give up his dreams of love and glory, and at the same time he gives up his life. Voltaire's work, on the other hand, is seamless, as if written effortlessly in a single session; as soon as poor Candide is booted out of the baron's castle he is unable to stop anywhere for long. On the last page of the book, Pangloss summarizes in a nutshell Candide's adventures: "'All events are linked together in the best of all possible worlds; for, after all, had you not been kicked out of a fine castle for your love of Ms. Cunégonde, had you not been put into the Inquisition, had you not traveled across America on foot, had you not stabbed the Baron with your sword, and had you not lost all your sheep which you brought from the good old country of El Dorado, then you wouldn't be here eating preserved citrons and pistachio-nuts.'"[1]

Similarities and Differences between
Don Quixote and *Candide*

One salient trait that *Candide* and *Don Quixote* share is that they are both "travel books" in two ways: in the physical sense because they travel through many landscapes, and in the spiritual sense because there is a transformation that takes place as they "travel" through life's experiences. The main characters are often on the move. This is especially true of Candide and his companions: they visit the land of the Bulgars (probably Prussia), Lisbon (during an earthquake), Cádiz, Paraguay with its Jesuit missions, the land of El Dorado somewhere in South America, Surinam, France, and Constantinople. The chapters are very short; many are only two or two and a half pages long. Events happen suddenly; we have the impression that we are watching a speeded-up movie. The text is clear and consistent, always light and witty. Aside from being a travelogue, *Candide* is a work of apprenticeship, or as the French novelist and critic André Maurois puts it, "the shaping of an adolescent's ideas by rude contact with the universe. Candide learned to know armies and the Jesuits of Paraguay; murder, theft, and rape; France, England, and the Grand Turk. Everywhere his observations show him that man is a rather wicked animal. Optimist philosophy was personified in Pangloss; pessimism, in Martin, who thinks that man is born to live either in the convulsions of distress or the lethargy of boredom."[2] Candide is ruled by Dr. Pangloss's optimism during most of the novel, reacting in a healthy way only at the end. "The author accepted neither Martin's pessimism nor Pangloss' optimism at their face value. Their last words of the book were: 'We must cultivate our garden'; that is to say: the world is mad and cruel; the earth trembles and the sky hurls thunderbolts; kings fight and Churches rend each other. Let us limit our activity and try to do as well as we can the small task that seems to be within our powers."[3]

Critics have pointed out several sources of inspiration for Voltaire's work, among them the *Arabian Nights* in Galland's translation and Jonathan Swift: "Voltaire had read much of Swift, and was fond of him; and from the Dean he had learned how to tell an absurd story in the most natural manner."[4] There is much in Candide's life and adventures that is inherently absurd, and when we think about Cervantes's possible influence on Voltaire's satire we can easily come to the conclusion that Cervantes's novel is equally absurd. How can an impoverished and old *hidalgo* think he is to become a knight-errant? Knights were young, vigorous, in excellent physical and mental health, and rich enough to be able to afford a good warhorse and solid steel armor and weapons. As his niece points out, Don Quixote fails in every point. Even more absurd was his belief that he could change the world for the better as a single individual. Although less effort is demanded of him, Candide is prey to a similar irrational and utopian trend of thought. According to Pangloss, who is essentially a caricature of the German philosopher Leibniz, we live in the best of all possible worlds, and it is hard to think of ways to make this world better. Leibniz's ideas were complex and abstract, and his system did not envisage an interpretation of everyday life in its social and ethical dimensions. Nevertheless, throughout the eighteenth century, many of his followers interpreted them in the most positive and optimistic sense. They proclaimed that we live, indeed, in a perfect world where constant progress will take place thanks to a benevolent God and to the perfectibility of human beings, helped by science, art, and philanthropy. This utopian and naive attitude, as utopian and naive as Don Quixote's ideas about the excellence of knights errant and the myth of the Golden Age, moved Voltaire to write his powerful and witty refutation.

Voltaire found Leibniz's vocabulary too abstract and at times incomprehensible. For him, the ideas of the German philosopher were not clearly expressed and out of touch with the knowledge gained from daily experience. Voltaire's stay in Prussia ended with a quarrel with the Prussian king, Frederic II, which irritated him and led him to despise everything Teutonic. The problem of the existence of evil could not be solved through naive formulas. A tragic earthquake that devastated Lisbon in 1755 reinforced in Voltaire the idea that neither divine providence nor nature itself could be considered benevolent toward human beings and that it was counterproductive to have illusions on this point. In fact, optimism was a form of fatalism that prevented change and evolution.

We approach Voltaire's text without forgetting that the French writer read *Don Quixote*. He refers to it several times in his writings, and in Voltaire's library two copies of Cervantes's novel could be found, one in Spanish and one in French translation.[5] Hence, we discover several links between the two books. To begin with, both Cervantes and Voltaire pretend not to be the authors of their work. Cervantes creates a more elaborate and complex stratagem than Voltaire. After the title, *Candide ou l'Optimisme,* Voltaire added simply, "Translated from the German of Doctor Ralph." This is what we read in the first edition. In 1761, a second edition appeared in which Voltaire made a long addition to chapter 22. The title became, *Candide or Optimism. Translated from the German of Dr. Ralph. With the additions found in the Doctor's pocket when he died at Minden, in the Year of Grace 1759.* It is difficult to attribute this disguise to a fear of censorship when several of his signed works, such as his *Philosophical Dictionary* and his comments on the Bible, are actually more defiant than *Candide.*

Geography as Destiny

The geographical frame chosen by our authors is another curious coincidence. Cervantes begins his narrative "Somewhere in La Mancha, in a place whose name I do not care to remember, a gentleman lived not long ago" (Gr., 19). La Mancha was, and still is, one of the poorest regions of Spain, not only poor but also not very interesting, lacking beautiful castles, picturesque landscapes, and prosperous cities. This setting presents an ironic contrast to the exotic and spectacular landscapes where most chivalry romances took place. Cervantes chose an area where Don Quixote's imagination had to work very hard in order to create castles and palaces, starting practically from nothing. Any Spanish reader of Cervantes's novel who has traveled to La Mancha or has heard about its desolate plains and mountains can appreciate fully the distance between the *hidalgo*'s creative inner life and an external reality stubbornly resisting a poetic interpretation. Something very similar takes place in Voltaire's work, which starts thus: "In the country of Westphalia, in the castle of the most noble baron of Thunder-ten-Tronckh, lived a youth whom nature had endowed with a most sweet disposition."[6] In this work Westphalia plays the same role as La Mancha in Cervantes's book. When Voltaire traveled through it, Westphalia was a region not worthy of a visit, a place where it could be assumed everybody was bored and no one was wealthy. Voltaire crossed these lands in western Germany in 1750 when he was going to Berlin, answering an invitation from Frederic II. He was impressed most unfavorably and commented in one of his letters, "I have crossed the vast, sad, sterile, detestable plains of Westphalia." And then, "Westphalia: what a miserable country!"[7] A few lines into the novel we find out that "the baron was one of the most powerful lords in Westphalia, for his castle had not only a gate, but even windows, and his great hall was hung with tapestry."[8]

Another link between these two books is the fact that both authors give special importance to the beginning and to the end of their works. We are also dealing with works in which the main character determines the rhythm of action and the consequences of his decisions. The first chapter in Cervantes's novel allows us to witness the "birth" of Don Quixote, from the imagination of the good *hidalgo* Alonso Quijano. Similarly, in the first chapter of his book Voltaire introduces the reader to a candid and innocent young man, the natural son of the baron's sister, who refused to marry the gentleman who fathered Candide because "he could produce no more than seventy-one quarterings in his arms, the rest of the genealogical tree belonging to the family having been lost through the injuries of time."⁹ Thus begins Voltaire's satire against the social prejudices of his time. Candide resembles Don Quixote in some essential traits but not all. Both are credulous and naïve; let us remember Don Quixote's reaction when he meets the "ladies of easy virtue" at the door of the inn in chapter 2 of part 1. In both cases a whole intellectual system of ethical, aesthetic, and metaphysical ideas acts as blinkers, preventing our heroes from interpreting correctly the everyday reality around them. The Spanish hero sees the world through the lens of an ethical and aesthetic system created by the romances of chivalry and courtly love. The French hero follows closely the teachings of his tutor Dr. Pangloss, "the greatest philosopher of the whole province, and consequently of the whole world."¹⁰ Voltaire continues:

> Pangloss taught metaphysico-theologo-cosmonignology. He proved admirably that in this best of all possible worlds, His Lordship's castle was the most beautiful of castles, and Her Ladyship the best of all possible baronesses.
>
> "It is demonstrable," said he, "that things cannot be otherwise than they are; for as all things have been created for some end, they must necessarily be created for the best end. Observe, for instance, the nose is formed for spectacles; therefore we wear spectacles. The legs are visibly designed for stockings; accordingly we wear stockings. Stones were made to be hewn and to construct castles; therefore my lord has a magnificent castle; for the greatest baron in the province ought to be the best lodged. Swine were intended to be eaten; therefore we eat pork all year round. And they who assert that every-

thing is *right,* do not express themselves correctly; they should say that everything is *best.*"[11]

In many ways, this tunnel vision is similar to Don Quixote's determination to interpret every detail received by his senses from a single viewpoint firmly anchored in the romances of chivalry and their aesthetic and ethical focus. For Pangloss and Candide, if the world is good and has been made to serve us, then we should not complain about anything that happens to us. Bad news is an illusion, and in any case our situation cannot but improve soon. This naive, sophomoric, and passive optimism dominates Candide and Pangloss throughout the novel, which can be irritating to the reader. And yet little by little, as happens to Don Quixote toward the end of part 2, Candide opens his eyes and realizes he has been mistaken for a long time. The final chapter is decisive in both texts. Don Quixote recovers his common sense and his original identity before dying. Candide and his friends arrive at the conclusion that common sense and work, both individual and collective, are the best defense when facing a difficult and hostile world. Thus the passive and silly Candide of his young years dies, opening the way for a totally new Candide.

Both heroes interpret sensory data through a filter that distorts them, thus influencing their behavior. Don Quixote's filter is more aesthetic and ethical than metaphysical. Candide's is metaphysical, conditioned by an interpretation of supernatural and divine forces that are supposed to make things in the universe proceed in a favorable way to human beings, given God's benevolence and infinite power, yet a whirlwind of adventures puts him in touch with cruelty, intolerance, oppression, lack of intellectual freedom, hypocrisy, and greed.

Over time our comparison of these two books reveals many hidden points of contact. Both books recount a journey. We learn a great deal about the geography of the regions visited by our heroes—and geography in this case includes customs, social organization, and systems of values. It is precisely this contact with human geography and everyday reality that slowly erodes the preconceived ideas with which Don Quixote and Candide approach their surroundings. Time and time again, Don Quixote tries in vain to superimpose the beautiful ideals learned from the romances of chivalry on the limited and mundane existence of the novel's secondary characters. When he does not manage to do so, he has to take shelter in the subterfuge of imagining that some malicious enchanter is changing reality. Don Quixote needs to imagine a wizard like the one mentioned by Descartes, the "evil geni" capable of distorting and changing what we see and hear, intent on depriving him of glory and victory. As for Voltaire, his characters imagine that beyond unpleasant and even tragic appearances one can find a secret harmony that unites human experiences and divine projects, a harmony that becomes manifest sooner or later. Patience is required, and confidence in a happy ending is indispensable. But Voltaire insinuates ironically that good intentions and optimistic thoughts can lead to passivity and ultimately to disaster. The evil forces will crush naive, passive characters trusting their future to divine providence. Both works, therefore, announce the triumph of a pragmatic attitude, finally free from idealization. Physical laws exist. Don Quixote's helmet breaks or malfunctions. Nobody can fly without wings. Sancho jumps in the air, propelled by his tormenters, and falls down again and again according to the laws of physics, not magic.

Voltaire's outpouring of wit is above all a critical insight into his society and the world of his times. But is Cervantes's novel less critical of Cervantes's country and his epoch? From the very first chapters, when Don Quixote tries to save young Andrés from being whipped by his master and only makes the situation worse, *Don Quixote* offers many examples of social criticism as pointed out in the previous chapter. These examples are not as obvious as the ones in Voltaire's book, but they are neither less telling nor less compelling. Let us think of chapters 19 and 20, part 2: a rich old man is about to marry a young girl against her will. This situation may have happened thousands or tens of thousands of times in Cervantes's Spain, and certainly also in other countries. Cervantes underlines the desperate situation of the young girl and her young lover, and thanks to Don Quixote, this adventure has a happy ending. But no doubt his readers were aware that parents often sold their young daughters to the highest bidder.

Other incidents in Cervantes's novel that comment on social problems and injustice can be found in the chapters about the galley slaves, many of them probably innocent or not deserving of such harsh punishment. Chapter 52, part 2, tells the sad story of Ricote, the Spaniard of Moorish descent expelled like all the other "Moriscos" by order of the king: "No matter where we are we weep for Spain, for, after all, we were born here and it is our native country; nowhere do we find the haven our misfortune longs for. . . . [A]nd the greatest desire in almost all of us is to return to Spain; most of those, and there are many of them, who know the language as well as I do, abandon their wives and children and return, so great is the love they have for Spain; and now I know and feel the truth of the saying that it is sweet to love one's country" (Gr., 813). Ricote has returned in disguise, but his future does not look bright; once more, "ethnic cleansing" is destroying lives and impoverishing both the exiles and the country they leave behind. Fanaticism and racism go hand in hand in Cervantes's Spain.

We do not have to wait long to find social criticism in Cervantes's novel. For example, in chapter 6, part 1, "Regarding the beguiling and careful examination carried out by the priest and the barber of the library of our ingenious gentleman," we find an exercise in literary criticism. The books in the library of Alonso Quijano–Don Quixote are examined one by one, with many discarded but a few saved after the curate and the barber comment on their literary merit. Yet in the next chapter we find out all the books are burned: "That night, the housekeeper burned and consigned to the flames all the books that were in the corral and in the house, and some must have been in the fire that should have been preserved in perpetual archives; but their destiny, and the sloth of the examiner, did not permit this, and so, as the proverb says, at times the just must pay for sinners" (Gr., 54). Censorship and book burning were not uncommon in Cervantes's Spain. The libraries in the palace of Alhambra in Granada were burned after that part of Spain fell to the armies of King Ferdinand and Queen Isabella. The collections on magic and Judaica of the University of Salamanca were also burned in a public ceremony. Cervantes was aware of these events when he wrote these chapters. His mind was ironic and subtle. He did not want to draw attention to the parallel between what happened to Don Quixote and what had happened to the Jewish and Moorish minorities in Spain, yet he must have thought that sooner or later some of his readers would understand. Voltaire is more explicit in his criticism. Yet the more we look at both Cervantes and Voltaire, the more we find they have in common. Voltaire, cruelly beaten by the lackeys of a nobleman and then unjustly imprisoned in the Bastille for eleven months, was even more an outsider than Cervantes. Both felt that justice was absent from their society. Perhaps the first writer to notice the affinity between Cervantes and Voltaire was Anatole France, who in his *Le jardin d'Épicure* observed that both *Don Quixote* and *Candide* were "manuals of indulgence and compassion, bibles of benevolence."[12]

In his novel Cervantes describes a poor, sad Spain, a place where Don Quixote's ideals find no echo in his fellow citizens and where the duke and the duchess, in part 2, amuse themselves with a frivolous and silly game of artificial illusions where neither Don Quixote nor Sancho are appreciated; they become the butt of constant jokes manipulated by the aristocrats. Sancho's intelligent and ethical behavior as governor of his ínsula place him far above what we see in the "nobles," who basically do not deserve their privileges and do not know how to make good use of their power and assumed intelligence. There can be no doubt that Sancho deserves to be governor of the ínsula. However, as we know, everything has been prepared and manipulated by the duke and the duchess and everything will revert back to their hands when Sancho and Don Quixote go on traveling. Once more mediocrity, injustice, and corruption will be enthroned. Once more Don Quixote, loyal to his ideals, and Sancho, a free spirit willing to learn and spurred by ambition, surpass all the other characters in the novel.

Voltaire's Cardboard Characters

Cervantes manages a feat that other writers will find inspiring: he creates situations and characters that ring true and express deep human emotions, and moreover they develop and change throughout the novel. If we compare to these characters the ones created by Voltaire, we may notice that the characters created by the French writer are somewhat pale and cardboard-like. We know nothing, or next to nothing, about the intimate life of a character as important as Pangloss. He is a mouthpiece for certain philosophical ideas, but his true identity is not revealed to us. Don Quixote's evolution in part 2, the changes in Sancho, who grows in importance as the novel develops, and the interaction between the knight and his squire are essential traits of Cervantes's novel.

In contrast, Voltaire creates comic effects by underlining the opposite: his characters, especially Pangloss, do not change in spite of all the changes in their lives. Thus in chapter 28, Candide asks Pangloss if, after having suffered so many adversities, after having been hanged by the Inquisition (but we know the rope was wet, the hanging knot poorly made, which allowed him to survive), then dissected by a Portuguese surgeon (who luckily did not finish his task), beaten many times and compelled to row in a galley, he still thinks that everything is for the best in this world: " 'I have always abided by my first opinion,' answered Pangloss, 'for, after all, I am a philosopher, and it would not become me to retract my sentiments, especially since Leibniz could not be wrong.' "[13] As an aside, note also how Pangloss quite often makes use of philosophical and technical words that his traveling companions do not understand, just as Don Quixote's vocabulary is often unclear to Sancho.

Another Parallel

Another interesting parallel in these two novels is that Voltaire's Cunégonde, "the enchanted Cunégonde" of chapter 29, reminds us of the enchanted Dulcinea in part 2 of Cervantes's novel. Candide's servant, Cacambo, had warned his master about the physical changes in Cunégonde, who had been raped and beaten many times. Nevertheless, Candide is surprised and dismayed: "Even the tender Candide, that affectionate lover, upon seeing his fair Cunégonde all sun-burnt, with bloodshot eyes, a withered neck, her face wrinkled, and her arms red and scaly, started back with horror."[14] We know Don Quixote had a similar reaction when he saw the enchanted Dulcinea, but the parallel stops here because Don Quixote becomes obsessed by the need to find a way to disenchant Dulcinea, whereas Candide, who had promised to marry Cunégonde, finally had to be faithful to his word. The situation worsens: "his wife, every day growing more and more ugly, became headstrong and insupportable."[15]

Let us consider also that in both masterpieces the authors announce or suggest a goal, a purpose that is only partly their real goal, and this purpose hides a more radical one. Cervantes declares that he wrote his novel in order to "move the melancholy to laughter, increase the joy of the cheerful, not irritate the simple, fill the clever with admiration for its invention, not give the serious reason to scorn it, and allow the prudent to praise it. In short, keep your eye on the goal of demolishing the ill-founded apparatus of these chivalric books, despised by many and praised by so many more, and if you accomplish this, you will have accomplished no small thing" (Gr., 8). Yet what Cervantes accomplishes is much more. He may well have started his book with the intent of writing a parody of the romances of chivalry, and there can be no doubt that his book was and is funny and that it is a parody. But this aspect of the novel has paled with the passing of time simply because a parody implies a caricature of a given subject, and the subject must be known by the public if the parody is to be enjoyed fully—and the subject, the chivalry romances, is not known by today's readers. Even in his own time they had passed their prime and would have vanished without Cervantes's help. A parody evokes the image of comedians and of clowns. He creates instead a novel in which characters are well developed, interact, evolve, and react to events, establishing the foundations of realism in literature, a realism that is large enough to accommodate fantasy and dreams along with everyday events, trivia, ridiculous mistakes, and misunderstandings.

Voltaire also announces a goal for his work: to expose and reject the easy optimism of Leibniz-Pangloss and their followers, but this is only part of a much more daring and far-reaching program. During a period when French culture was influential in vast sections of Western Europe, he criticized the social customs of his own country as well as those of several other countries. He was fighting the system of values of the ancien régime, its mixture of hypocrisy, frivolity, fanaticism, and injustice and preparing for the radical changes that later lead to the French Revolution of 1789. Voltaire was relatively moderate and would not approve of every aspect of the revolution, but there is no doubt that the gradual changes he proposed would have had similar results, if perhaps less dramatic but more enduring than the extreme Jacobin measures inspired by Rousseau.

When comparing these two books and placing them face to face, it is possible to find a sort of "mirror symmetry": in the Spanish novel the hero, a madman, faces a society that is "sane" but mediocre; in the French work the hero, sane but mediocre, faces a society, or rather several societies, maddened by fanaticism, ignorance, greed, and vice.

Beginnings and Endings

There are formal similarities between *Don Quixote* and *Candide*. For instance, both books begin with a radical act. In the first novel, the elderly *hidalgo* obliterates his past in order to become another being, a knight, Don Quixote. In the French work, the hero, who is more passive, finds his life redirected, projected into more and more exotic spaces by his violent expulsion from his modest Garden of Eden; he is booted out of the castle and away from the desirable Cunégonde. In both books the final chapter is important. The Spanish novel ends with the sad acceptance that Don Quixote's dreams have been in vain and cannot be sustained. Wisdom brings nostalgia, even sadness. But perhaps not everything is lost. As Don Quixote is about to die he says, "'There are no birds today in yesterday's nests'" (Gr., 937). Yet the idea of the word "quixotic" is about to be born and more Quixotes will be spawned. One can only conjecture where Sancho and his progeny would have taken us, but it is his master who inspired future writers.

Candide does not die a physical death at the end of the book, yet he changes so completely that one may conclude that the "old Candide" is dead. His life had been guided by his love for Cunégonde and his confidence that Pangloss's philosophy guaranteed a good world, a world where ultimately happiness would be found, for in a certain way this was an inescapable consequence. A kind God had made the world: how could He fail to make it the best of all possible worlds? At the end of the tale, Candide's doubts are troubling, and not only for him but for all of his readers. The problem of the existence of evil, of "bad things happening to good people," is old; it would not go away for Voltaire and Candide. At the end of *Candide,* most of the characters have found an antidote against anguish and despair: "that we must cultivate our garden." The Turk says that "'our labour keeps us from three great evils—boredom, vice, and want.'"[16] "'Let's work, then, without disputing,' says Martin. 'It's the only way to make life bearable.'"[17] Voltaire implies that perhaps metaphysical questions are unanswerable, and therefore we should not try to answer them. The group of characters around Candide and Pangloss live in the vicinity of a famous dervish who is known as the best philosopher in Turkey; they go to consult him. Acting as their spokesman, Pangloss says to the dervish: "'Master, we've come to beg you to tell us why so strange an animal as man has been created.' 'Why do you trouble your head about it?' said the dervish; 'is it any business of yours?' 'But my reverend father,' said Candide, 'there is a horrible deal of evil on the earth.' 'What does it matter,' says the dervish 'whether there is evil or good? When His Highness sends a ship to Egypt, does he worry whether the rats in the vessel are at their ease or not?'"[18] The tale ends on a serene note: "We must cultivate our garden." And yet the main characters renounce thinking about many important problems and philosophical subjects. Wisdom has been acquired at the expense of adventurous intellectual thinking. It is possible to detect a tinge of melancholy and sadness in the midst of bourgeois satisfaction with industry and hard work.

In many ways the final messages of both books are similar. In both cases the flights of the imagination are renounced. In their place we find concern about the real world. The authors seem to say, "Let us not fly too high; let us come back to earth."

From now on some of the most acclaimed novels and short stories will be the result of careful, precise observation of time, place, and character. Background details, psychological motivations, and reactions to everyday life become part of the essence of the novel. The characters are subject to all manner of influences. It is almost as if we see the characters as stars and satellites, turning around each other, all part of a galaxy, all influenced by laws of gravitation and by the space around them, as well as by the solar wind, cosmic rays, meteorites, and comets. This does not mean that these novels (we are now thinking of Dickens and Tolstoy, Flaubert and Hemingway, among many others) exclude fantasy and dreams, but when these appear, they will be labeled as such and justified.

The word "quixotic" was created by Cervantes's novel and its success. "Panglossian" or "Pangloss-like" are expressions inspired by Voltaire's satire. These concepts have helped define a part of the eighteenth-century thought.

IMITATIONS AND TRANSFORMATIONS:
THE ENGLISH EIGHTEENTH CENTURY:
DEFOE, FIELDING, STERNE, AND OTHERS

Daniel Defoe: The Picaresque via Cervantes

Two works written by Daniel Defoe (1660–1731) in the early eighteenth century remind us of Cervantes's assimilation of the picaresque mode in *Don Quixote* most likely because the Spanish master's novel was better known in England than any other picaresque novel written in Spain. Cervantes incorporated elements of this literary model but went beyond its limited horizon, creating a more complex and sophisticated work. Defoe, too, presents his own variation using some picaresque elements in *Robinson Crusoe* (1719) and even more in *Moll Flanders* (1722).

In the first book, although the main character comes from a financially comfortable family, he feels the call of the sea, breaks with his kin, goes through a series of voyages from London, is captured by Turkish pirates and taken to a Moroccan prison, escapes, and boards a ship to Brazil where he is quite successful but bored. He finds occasion to board a ship to Africa with the purpose of buying slaves and then selling them to other plantation owners in Brazil. A storm blows up; the ship is wrecked and he is the sole survivor. He finds himself on an island where he will live for many years. Desperate and deprived, he has to fend for himself in the jungle of an island and is expected to succeed by his efforts alone, aided only by his Man Friday, whom he meets after living on the island for many years. He does succeed, as he does not have to deal with a corrupt society. Ian Watt remarks: "Robinson Crusoe can be seen as an articulate spokesman of the new economic, religious, and social attitudes that succeeded the Counter-Reformation."[19] Karl Marx, who read this novel, "attacks Crusoe as a hermit who produces only for himself, and who cannot therefore, be a true representative of the process of production which Marx sees as essentially social."[20] Here, quite obviously, we are not dealing with the elementary naive Spanish picaroon; however, his adventures, living by his wits, survival, and his isolation and loneliness all point in the direction of the picaresque model.

In the second book, *Moll Flanders,* the heroine is born in the squalid, sinister Newgate jail. Her mother "pleaded her belly" because she was pregnant with Moll, and avoided execution. She was transported to the New World, leaving the child, a defense-less orphan half a year old, to the mercy of some gypsies. In both works, the hero and heroine, respectively, must live by their wits, struggling against all odds. The material world is emphasized: food, shelter, clothing, health, and money. Moll Flanders knows by heart the prices of all of the merchandise to be found in the London markets and shops to the point that Defoe's novel was studied by Marx as the perfect introduction to the life of the lower classes in eighteenth-century England. Her adventures are so varied and her life changes so quickly that her loneliness is sometimes held at bay.

Defoe could find in Cervantes all that he needed to create picaresque situations and characters. His own life was close to the picaresque existence depicted in his novels; as a pamphleteer, it was full of uncertainty and chaos. Paid by politicians, he was ready to betray them if their rivals offered him more money. The English author follows the pattern of the Spanish picaresque novels. In his preface to *Moll Flanders* he offers a tantalizing few words that remind us of Cervantes's *Don Quixote,* more specifi-cally of the galley slave Ginés de Pasamonte, who states that he cannot write his autobiography because he is still living. Simi-larly Defoe writes: "We cannot say, indeed, that this history is carried on quite to the end of this famous Moll Flanders, as she calls herself, for nobody can write their own life to the full end of it, unless they can write it after they are dead."[21]

Henry Fielding's Parody

Cervantes's effect becomes more obvious when we turn to other English novelists of the eighteenth century. The presence of an author in his or her work is a novelty, a challenge to the reader, and a sign that the work itself is becoming self-conscious. Cervantes's device of appearing in his own novel was imitated by writers from Fielding (1707-54) to Laurence Sterne (1713-68), especially in *Tristram Shandy*, and finally to Walter Scott (1771-1832). Sometimes an author even helps the critic and the historian of literature by indicating clearly an influence. This is the case with Henry Fielding's novel *The History of the Adventures of Joseph Andrews, and His Friend, Mr. Abraham Adams: Written in Imitation of the Manner of Cervantes, Author of Don Quixote* (1742).

So distinctly declared from the very beginning, Cervantes's influence can be first detected in the general tone of the novel, which is basically a parody of *Pamela*, written by Samuel Richardson (1689-1761). Joseph Andrews is a male version of Pamela, and like her he will defend his chastity against all odds, especially against the attempts at seduction by his employer, Lady Booby, and her irrepressibly amorous friend, Mrs. Slipslop.

Fielding is a master of parody, and his "hero" turns out to be as ridiculous as he is prudish. The novel is hijacked by a new character, Parson Adams. Joseph is traveling to the village where his fiancée, Fanny, lives, but he is attacked and robbed by bandits who finally take him to an inn, where he meets Parson Adams. Adams is whimsical, imaginative, unpredictable, and ultimately as crazy as his Spanish prototype, Don Quixote. Joseph then becomes Sancho to Adams's Don Quixote, and their travels and misadventures become the most intriguing part of the novel.

Fielding borrows two ideas from Cervantes that become dominant in this novel: parody and a mad main character. The idea of parody is apparent because the novel itself makes little sense if we have not read Richardson's *Pamela* or at least have a general idea about *Pamela*. In Richardson's novel we can enjoy the triumph of a young girl, whose virtue is assailed by men who have more power, more money, and more social status than she, and at the same time we take a certain voyeuristic interest in the boudoir scenes where we suspect that her courageous defense will be overwhelmed. Many readers of the Fielding novel had read *Pamela,* for it was one of the most popular publications of that time. As for Cervantes's novel, even if we have not read any romance of chivalry, the novel itself gives partial descriptions of such romances, sufficient for the reader to have a clear image of their contents.

Of the two ideas—parody and a mad main character—both contribute important elements to Fielding's novel but parody is the more essential one. Many critics and readers have thought in the past that parody is a secondary artistic mode, coming at the end of a period of high achievement and marking its decline. Parody is close to comedy and close to laughter, the laughter engendered by derision and by mockery; it cannot compare with an epic poem or a great tragedy. This hierarchy of literary modes is outdated when we realize that parody can be subtle and enlightening in a way that is different from other literary modes, neither better nor worse. Parody can signal a beginning as well as an end. Cervantes's novel, in part a parody, marks the beginning of the modern novel. In England, too, Fielding's parodies mark a beginning.

Let us not forget that one year before *Joseph Andrews* appeared, Fielding had published another parody, *Shamela,* a short story or a novelette, in which the heroine shamelessly deceives her employer, the country squire Booby. In both Cervantes and Fielding, the presence of parody is a strong stimulant: it forces the authors to examine the precarious relation between reality and fiction by creating a complex filter, the text to be parodied, that comes between the two, blurring the distinction between them. Parody is therefore not an end but rather a beginning of a new literary era. Fielding is also clever in his use of the "self-conscious narrator," an authorial voice that reassures the reader that no harm will come to the character who has been chosen as a favorite. No matter how bleak the situation, we know, or guess, that the end will be happy for the author's favorite character. The edge is thus taken from tragic, or potentially tragic, events. We may enjoy vicariously the ultimate triumph of the "good" characters. This device will be picked up by Sterne, and it is in itself typical of an era that was struggling to banish unpleasant facts or ideas. Both tragedy and the epic spirit diminish and almost disappear from eighteenth-century literature. The "happy ending" is not an invention of Hollywood moviemakers but rather the consequence of an era where satire, laughter, and the comic spirit in general is slowly gaining the upper hand.

Tristram Shandy: A New Ginés de Pasamonte

Laurence Sterne is perhaps the most self-conscious writer to follow in Cervantes's footsteps. Tristram Shandy, his hero, is halfway between a real person and an artificial construction of paper and ink. Tristram's efforts to delve into his early days, just after he was born, are intriguing, but at the same time we can find them contrived and self-conscious. How can a character know everything about himself, to the point that he can watch every second of his real life, without becoming paralyzed by this heroic effort? Let us recall that in part 1, chapter 22, Don Quixote is told that Ginés de Pasamonte, a galley slave, has written a book about his own life. It is so good that although he pawned it for two hundred *reales,* he would redeem it for two hundred *ducados,* a coin of much higher value. "'Is it that good?' said Don Quixote. 'It's so good,' responded Ginés, 'that it's too bad for *Lazarillo de Tormes* and all the other books of that genre that have been or will be written.' . . . 'And is it finished?' asked Don Quixote. 'How can it be finished,' he responded, 'if my life isn't finished yet?'" (Gr., 168–69). Ginés is alive and well, and many adventures are to come. This projection into the future makes him one of the most interesting and troubling characters in Cervantes's novel because Ginés's life and the book about it are tightly interwoven in the chapter.

During a period when critical analysis of literature, especially contemporary literature, was either nonexistent or barely beginning, parody was perhaps the only way to show the weaknesses of a particular work. It was a cleansing function and showed many readers that *Pamela* was psychologically unbelievable, lacking in depth, and ideologically driven to the point of being blinded by sentimentality and prudishness. Thus the novels of Fielding and Sterne carry out two important missions: they purify the literary atmosphere through their parodies, and they establish a narrative voice that permeates these books, providing the reader with a trustworthy guide. Ultimately, we know that no harm will come to the characters, the very characters that the authors have made likable to us, and that all will end well. Similarly, Voltaire guarantees us in *Candide* that in spite of Candide's misadventures and the sufferings of poor Cunégonde, we are dealing with a satire, not with life-threatening situations. All will be well at the end provided we do not stop cultivating our garden.

Fielding's *The History of Tom Jones, a Foundling,* appeared in 1749 in six volumes, divided into eighteen sections, each one prefaced by an essay more or less connected to the plot. Through these prefaces Fielding maintains his control of events and connects them to his ethical and philosophical thoughts. Equally important is the sense soon conveyed to the reader that the author is in command of the events, not the other way around. Tom, a foundling, has been adopted by a wealthy philanthropist, Mr. Allworthy, and is educated side by side with Blifil, a hateful character, selfish and hypocritical, the reverse of Tom Jones. The main sections of the novel are organized around Tom leaving his original home, his various love affairs, the betrayal by Blifil, and Tom's arrest and impending execution. It is a precise clock-work series of intense emotional scenes, with increasing anguish toward the end when we realize that Tom's life is about to end on the gallows. At the same time there is a subtle yet convincing subtext: the author of this novel is still in charge, he is, no doubt, our friend and also, most importantly, Tom's friend. The happy ending comes as a relief but not as a complete surprise. Fielding has taken care all along to tell us where the creative powers re-side, who is in charge, and ultimately how to make the positive characters win the final battle.

Eighteenth Century Thinkers and
Laurence Sterne's *Tristram Shandy*

Literary historians tell us that there is probably an unbroken line from one writer to the next. Fielding influenced Laurence Sterne, who in turn influenced Stendhal, who influenced both Balzac and Flaubert and through these writers Tolstoy and Dos-toyevsky, all of whom most probably influenced Vladimir Nabo-kov and many other fiction writers of the twentieth century. This continuity now places Sterne in a privileged position in the field of the modern narrative. He understands fully the message of Cervantes transmitted to him by Fielding and tries to develop it as far as possible.

At the time Cervantes wrote his novel, Europe was emerging from the medieval culture, a time when a figure like the brave knight in a famous engraving by Albert Dürer had marched through a narrow path while on the right and left lurked mon-sters, the Devil, and Death. Positive forces like God and di-vine providence were pitted against malevolent forces, such as witches, wizards, enchanters, black magic, and devils. Don Qui-xote had walked the same path as the knight of the German artist. But by the middle of the eighteenth century, after an earthquake devastated the city of Lisbon, even Voltaire had begun to doubt the benevolence of divine providence and the forces of good and evil. Perhaps other more complex causes had to be taken into account. The English philosopher John Locke (1632–1704), at the beginning of his *Second Treatise,* envisaged primitive men and women living peaceably in a "state of nature," an updated version of the Golden Age that haunted Don Quixote's mind, except in Locke's world private property rights were acknowledged. Men in Locke's natural state were not wholly selfish. They cooperated with each other and they worked sometimes in an altruistic, disinterested way. Yet life in this idyllic state, where there were no organized institutions, was not without difficulties. People had to join together to form a social contract and establish the original institutions for their society. Experience had taught them that they needed a social framework to survive in peace.

The intellectual and artistic landscape is changing significantly and dramatically. What Locke tells us is amplified by the Irish philosopher George Berkeley (1685–1753) and the Scottish philosopher and historian David Hume (1711–76). Man learns through his senses, but Berkeley claims that anything that is real takes place in our minds, and Hume explains that cause and effect are impossible to define or disentangle. Behind every cause there is another one, and thus to infinity. In France, the thoughts of Voltaire and Diderot are working along parallel lines. The new thinkers are disentangling their interpretations from traditional religious views. The new trends are present even within the English establishment. For instance, Berkeley happens to be a bishop. The influence of the shift in emphasis away from God and divine providence soon becomes obvious in such writers as Laurence Sterne (and later, Dickens). Without a fixed line of reference between our existence and divine providence, we are enmeshed in a rather chaotic ambience. Hume, who was a Calvinist, is especially hard on the basic traditional assumption that every event must have a cause. His belief is that the link between cause and effect is grounded in habits of thinking rather than related to the external world. When the center of knowledge and perfection has retreated to human consciousness, literature will react by giving new powers of perception to the inner man and as a consequence, to the author of a novel, whether it be Sterne or Diderot or their followers, Walter Scott, Stendhal, Honoré Balzac, and Fyodor Dostoyevsky. All will be newly empowered.

In the midst of a rational age, writers slowly begin to understand that Cartesian precision and geometric lines cannot reveal everyday reality. We are bombarded from all sides by perceptions that we cannot fully assimilate. Later on, in what we could call the Dickensian Age, Mr. Pickwick will complain that we are all victims of circumstances, and he is the first victim. In France, Stendhal will depict the encounter between his hero in *The Charterhouse of Parma* and "circumstances," in this case the incredibly confused battle of Waterloo, as a struggle between the mind of Fabizio and the external events that cannot be reduced to clear logical lines of reasoning, of cause and effect. Because the external world is so chaotic, primacy must be given to the mind of the hero and behind him to the mind of the writer who creates the hero.

The Life and Opinions of Tristram Shandy, Gentlemen, by Laurence Sterne, appeared in nine volumes between 1760 and 1767. Cervantes's influence is undeniable and *Don Quixote* is quoted a number of times. Also quoted are Rabelais and Montaigne; Diderot thought Sterne's work was "the English Rabelais." Sterne's novel reminds us of Cervantes's masterpiece more for its structure than for its main characters. It is a book that unfolds before us without a clear goal and without a plan, almost by a private, subjective association of ideas beginning and ending in the mind of the writer.

The idea of the novel as a travel book could apply also to

Tristram Shandy, since geography, roads, and inns play a significant role in it. Compared to Cervantes, however, Sterne is not a model of organization and purpose. In any case, the role of the author in *Tristram Shandy* is more important and relevant than the role of Tristram, who is born midway through the novel and is still a mere child at the end of it. It can be said that Sterne himself is the main character of his novel, giving on each page an elaborate literary shape to his consciousness. His fiction leads us into a strange no-man's-land between art and life. Ultimately, there is no reality but consciousness.

The affinity between Tobias, Tristram's uncle, and Don Quixote becomes more and more obvious as the novel progresses. Tobias is candid, naive, quirky, eccentric, obsessed by war architecture, and unpredictable. Trim, his servant, is partially modeled on Sancho Panza. Yet perhaps the main point of contact between the two novels is the way in which the authors insinuate themselves in the narrative, guiding it from beginning to end. Cervantes does it in a subtle way, through his prefaces, through his personal intervention when he finds the missing pages of the novel, through the insertion of tales, and finally in the conclusion of part 2. Sterne carries the authorial intervention to extremes, making the text zigzag through innumerable digressions flimsily attached to the main action: digressions on psychological time, on precocious children, on love, on the character of old Romans, and on a trip to France. Suddenly we find a blank page, a paragraph ending with a long line of asterisks, and all sorts of extravagances that disconcert the reader and make us smile or laugh. Sterne is both a sentimentalist and a humorist, and the novelty of his style and ideas achieved instant success both in England and abroad. Yet, as new chapters appeared, the public grew tired of such a total lack of organization and lost interest. The book was never properly finished—it just petered out without a real conclusion. What in Cervantes's novel is subtle and original becomes in Sterne almost a caricature, chaotically lacking in tension and structure. Readers in Sterne's day expected to find real characters who would live and develop. They found instead a complex ping-pong game played inside the head of the author, a game fascinating at first but incapable, finally, of holding their attention in the long run. Sterne's novel would gain new readers today if it were reprinted as an anthology of its most interesting and original pages.

Charles Dickens and Cervantes

There is another line carrying on Cervantes's influence: from Fielding to Oliver Goldsmith (*The Vicar of Wakefield*) to Charles Dickens (*The Pickwick Papers*). Fielding's *Joseph Andrews* provides a partial model for Goldsmith's vicar, and Goldsmith's main character may have inspired Dickens's Mr. Pickwick. These novels establish eccentricity as a national characteristic, both English and Scottish, by the sort of eccentricity that can be endearing one moment and profoundly overbearing the next; in many cases it borders on madness. Dickens (1812–70) may have been inspired by Fielding and Goldsmith (1728–74), but he did not explicitly recognize Cervantes as a model. Yet after Dickens's death "his friend and biographer John Forster could casually write that 'Sam Weller and Mr. Pickwick are the Sancho and Don Quixote of Londoners' as if all understood this right along."[22] It is significant that, especially in the case of Goldsmith's vicar and Dickens's Mr. Pickwick, the fight for justice and the complaints about unjust institutions of justice mirror Don Quixote's behavior and motives when he frees the galley slaves.

The Posthumous Papers of the Pickwick Club appeared between 1836 and 1837 in installments accompanying a series of drawings but soon became popular in its own right, as soon as Mr. Pick-wick, a new Don Quixote, found his Sancho, his servant Sam Weller. The charm of this novel is due to the fact that readers feel Dickens is improvising every page and every sentence without a proper plan or purpose. Mr. Pickwick was supposed to be the leader of a group of friends interested in hunting, fishing, and traveling. They turn out to be inept at everything they attempt, and then Mr. Pickwick is embroiled in a lawsuit that may damage his reputation and his financial resources. Whether he did so consciously or not, Dickens assembles bits and pieces of the picaresque tradition and of Cervantes's novel into a fast-moving narrative that seems to be going nowhere and at the same time excites our attention because of the variety of curious characters and their incredibly silly, crazy, and stupid activities. It is important to underline that the novel only takes off after Pickwick-Don Quixote finds the witty Sam Weller–Sancho in the fifth installment of the novel.

In his first novel, Dickens experiments with all the resources of imagination and style that he will develop during his successful literary career. His flair for caricature, his witty descriptions, and his intuition for creating suspense are already fully developed in his first literary attempt, and he achieves instant success. There is no doubt that Dickens was a keen observer of his own times, yet he owes much to a literary tradition that was not only English (Smollett, Fielding) but also Spanish (the picaresque, Cervantes). In a few well-chosen words he can portray a character and make us guess how he or she will react to the events. Everything happens fast, much faster than his literary ancestors could anticipate. Dickens is thus the bridge between the classical tradition of the picaresque and Cervantes and a modern literature that on the whole has acquired a faster tempo in the description of events and motivations. What is perhaps outstanding in this new saga is that the physical misadventures of the whole group of adventurers is less painful than those we find in Cervantes's novel, in part because the whole group shares the discomforts of their incompetence and stupidity, and also because the modern world is less harsh and more comfortable than the baroque society in which Don Quixote traveled, though English jails could be starkly cruel, as Dickens knew well.

One adventure follows another, as they do in *Don Quixote*, to the point that some critics have concluded that Dickens's novel lacks a plot. This is not totally true; there is a center of gravity, an outstanding episode, and it is related to the fight for justice, which is also essential for Don Quixote. Pickwick's housekeeper, Mrs. Bardell, sues him for breach of promise. Her unscrupulous lawyers are relentless. Pickwick loses the case and then, scorning the advice of his lawyer and his friends and as a matter of principle and as a protest against an unjust system, refuses to pay the damages awarded to the plaintiff and lands in jail. "Pickwick and principle!" becomes the slogan of his servant, who deliberately breaks the law so he can join his master in prison.

There can be no doubt that Dickens is one of the key interpreters of English modern culture, and further, he contributed more than any other writer in his century to making English society aware of itself, of both its imperfections and its possibilities for improvement. His social and historical role cannot be underestimated, and his flair for caricature in some ways surpasses Cervantes's since it involves a much larger number of characters. Through the *Pickwick Papers* Dickens attempts a definition of English society that is as valid today as it was in his time. As we read the first chapters of the novel, it is worth noting that Mr. Pickwick was pale and undefined before he found his counterpart in the modern Sancho, Sam Weller, whose felicitous sentences were an inspiration to the whole group. As Alexander Welsh remarks, "wise in the ways of the world where his high-minded master is naive, Sam measures out some of that wisdom in Wellerisms—the Cockney equivalent of Sancho's proverbs. A Wellerism typically evokes the materiality or violence within cultural commonplaces, as in 'It's over, and can't be helped, and that's one consolation, as they always say in Turkey, ven they cuts the wrong man's head off.'"[23] On a more frivolous note, could Dickens's Mr. Pickwick be a bridge between the Spanish novel and typical English vaudeville skits?

It is remarkable that Pickwick and Weller are surrounded by a group. Spanish individualism has been superseded by a new social order, a more collective endeavor; however, it is restricted to a few individuals who have common goals and, as the reader soon perceives, common weaknesses and shortcomings. Mr. Pickwick is typical of the English society of his times, but in another way he does not totally fit his historical era: he is too much a caricature to typify a Romantic hero.

The Missing Link: Sir Walter Scott

Much neglected today, Sir Walter Scott was very influential in the nineteenth century. His great accomplishment was to create Romantic heroes by placing them in the context of other periods. In this way, he conceived one of the most influential and durable subgenres of fiction, the historical novel.

Scott, a lawyer who studied at the University of Edinburgh, had apprenticed to his father. As a child, he was sickly and suffered from lameness due to a feverish attack when he was a toddler. He was an avid reader during his young years, submersing himself in books like romances and history, even learning Italian in order to read Dante and Ariosto. During his teenage years he read *Don Quixote*, from which he would draw inspiration. Later, while holding many legal positions, he wrote ballads, folklore, and poetry. Soon these became a more important part of his life than his inclination for the law.

He was already a popular poet when he started his long series of historical novels, such as *Waverley* (1814) and *Ivanhoe* (1819). Cervantes's mark is evident in *Waverley*. The plot tells of old Edward Waverley who has lost his will to live; life for him stopped at the death of Queen Anne and the accession of the Elector of Hanover; he dreams of going back to a Golden Age at odds with the present iron age, that is, the Industrial Revolution. He is a self-educated man who has read a great deal of poetry, history, and chivalric and romance tales while at Waverley Manor.

Like Don Quixote, we are presented with a man whose imagination is filled with the past, roaming through the roads and frequenting the inns; in this way, Scott introduces us to a variety of viewpoints as his main character meets other people. But the author's device of including in the story the finding of a manuscript, and a historical one at that, brings to mind Cervantes's device and the questions it posed concerning the veracity of history and who is writing it. Again, the reader is puzzled by the concepts of reality and truth. Another telling detail that points to Cervantes is that the author does not hesitate to introduce himself in the novel, acting sometimes as a tourist guide and letting us know what facts or events are worthy of our notice.

History, myth, romance, and a realistic attitude toward everyday events are tightly woven into Scott's novels, which met with great success in the first half of the nineteenth century, inspiring many other writers to draw plots, themes, and characters from national histories. Alexander Dumas, author of the *The Three Musketeers*, uses the history of France as background for his action, just as Benito Pérez Galdós in his *Episodios Nacionales* (*National Episodes*) offers vivid portraits of Spanish history from the Napoleonic Wars to the end of the nineteenth century.

6

An Abbreviated Look
at Cervantes in Nineteenth-Century
France, Russia, and Spain

In the nineteenth century there were several literary movements, each one a reaction to the previous one. In the early part of the century, there was a shift away from the Enlightenment's reasoned approach to life to a more subjective, individualistic, and sentimental stance, the mark of the Romantic writers. The next significant movements are realism and naturalism, which depend, respectively, on close observation of life and an explanation of human destiny as the result of genetic inheritance and environment. For example, Zola took a notebook with him to write down descriptions of people and places he saw, comparable to photojournalists today. Naturalism became known as biological and social determinism. Novelists nurtured in these cultural and intellectual currents were attracted to the Cervantine novel. What more Romantic hero in the age of factories and its effects—smoke, overcrowding of cities, poor sanitation—than Don Quixote, who attacked windmills, a symbol of technology? Who more individualistic a man than Don Quixote, who flaunted the ways of his age to create his own reality? Novelists throughout Europe began to forge a new novel in response to the ideas spreading in literary circles, but the distinguished novelists of France and Russia are particularly noteworthy and deserve our attention. These two countries are privileged to have a rich, high-quality literary production. In France, Stendhal, Balzac, Flaubert, Daudet, Zola, and finally Proust make up a glorious dynasty. The map of Russian literature is perhaps more complex, but certainly a line of descent can be established there aloor Gogol, Turgenev, Tolstoy, Dostoyevsky, and Chekhov. In this chapter we will also include Spain, for the works of its foremost novelist, Benito Pérez Galdós, are saturated with references and allusions to the sixteenth-century master's novel. Although our overview is brief, we propose to show the literary debt that these authors owe to Cervantes by examining how they render their Don Quixotes and how they use Cervantes's literary devices.

All of the above authors wrote novels where realistic details were described with great care. They knew how to create an authentic atmosphere through the accumulation of believable details. They also probed the minds of their main characters in an attempt to explore and explain actions and emotions as Cervantes had done. We can almost see in these novels the misunderstandings and confusion that characterized Don Quixote's mind as well as Sancho's reaction to his master. French and Russian novelists used Cervantes's template for interaction and the step-by-step evolution of the main characters as well as dialogue, and his narrative techniques became increasingly important in the nineteenth century.

STENDHAL AND CERVANTES:
NEW APPROACHES TO REALISM

Consciously or not, heroes wearing the Romantic halo found a double inspiration in Don Quixote and Napoleon. This is true for Stendhal's heroes, Julien Sorel in *The Red and the Black* and Fabrizio del Dongo in *The Charterhouse of Parma*. In writing his novels, Stendhal (born Marie Henri Beyle, 1783–1842) drew on his life experiences, which had several interesting parallels with

José Jimenez Aranda (1837–1903), *Don Quixote and Sancho Panza Returning to Battle,* c. 1900. Private Collection. Photo: Art Resource, NY.

those of Cervantes that may help to explain their main characters and the connection between their works.

Both writers started their adult life by choosing military careers. In both cases, their paths to glory were interrupted, and they had to find another profession. Both adored the military and felt more vital in this calling. In earlier chapters we discussed Cervantes's bravery in Lepanto, his imprisonment in Algiers, his return to Spain, and his struggle to eke out a meager living in bureaucratic positions. Stendhal grew up in Grenoble, fought in Napoleon's army, and took part in the invasion of Italy and the disastrous Russian campaign. His military and administrative career under Napoleon was promising, even brilliant; after Waterloo, his fortune changed.

Both writers created heroes who were dissatisfied with their lives and times, men who were trying to change themselves and perhaps the world around them. From this deep disagreement between the main characters and the society around them comes a double vision: the novel's hero sees in his society things that the people around him do not see.

Cervantes's realism comes from the contrast of Don Quixote and Sancho. What Don Quixote sees, Sancho does not, and vice versa, but Sancho's common sense dominates his master's subjective interpretation. Nonetheless, Don Quixote has chosen the high road. He pursues love, beauty, courage, and the vision of a Golden Age, a road far different from that traveled by his contemporaries.

Stendhal's realism in *The Red and the Black* and in *The Charterhouse of Parma* comes from the clear descriptions of how the main characters cope with outside stimuli and how these affect their inner plans. Julien Sorel feels the attraction of military life, symbolized in the color red, but after Waterloo, in a Europe almost anesthetized by the peace imposed by Metternich and the conservatives, a military career seems meaningless. The church, symbolized by the color black, still means power and real influence. But Sorel is not a true believer, alternating between hypocrisy, outbursts of sincerity, and a dangerous love affair that leads to disaster. The world outside ultimately proves to be too powerful to sustain Sorel's plan, which is also what happens to Don Quixote's even more ambitious projects. As for Fabrizio, the hero of the later novel, Stendhal traces his trajectory from Waterloo to the Carthusian monastery. He is both an action hero with many adventures and an intellectual trying to make sense of the many impressions gathered by his senses. A typical section is the long description of the battle of Waterloo. Fabrizio arrives late and tries to join the French army, but nobody can tell him what is happening; confusion and chaos reign everywhere. Stendhal seems to tell us that we can find reality only if we reorganize the stimuli of our senses, which is much harder than we may think, almost impossible in certain cases. Similarly, Don Quixote has difficulty aligning his inner perception of the noble deeds he wishes to accomplish in the outer world with external everyday reality.

Both writers wrote their masterpieces rather late in life. In both we can assume the presence of a nostalgic look toward their personal past and also the immediate past of their countries as a source of their literary inspiration. For Cervantes, the Spain of Charles V was a period of freedom and glory. The Spain of Philip II and Philip III, however, was a period when bureaucrats succeeded heroes. For Stendhal, the collapse of Napoleon's empire meant the end of his career, a mediocre Restoration, and a timid and greedy bourgeois society.

BALZAC, THE NOVELIST FOR A BOURGEOIS SOCIETY

It is true that Stendhal had very few readers during his lifetime, yet he had a reader and admirer who more than made up for the rest: Honoré de Balzac (1799–1850), a keen observer of his time. Society was changing, Romanticism was slowly receding, and a political revolution gave increasing power to the bourgeoisie. Both Balzac and Gustave Flaubert witnessed significant social changes and reflect them in what would be called "realism." It is difficult to call this trend "new" since it had already been fully developed by Cervantes in *Don Quixote*. Nevertheless, it seemed new to nineteenth-century readers and critics, and Balzac, together with Flaubert, was proclaimed as its main inventor or discoverer. As Douglas W. Alden points out:

> After 1830, a critical year of social revolution, the situation changed abruptly and the novel became the main literary genre. In keeping with the bour-

geois spirit of the age, the new novel was realistic and its inventor was the bourgeois Balzac. Trained in the Romantic historical novel in its worst forms and in its best (after doing romantic pot-boilers he managed one of the best historical novels in *Les Chouans* [1829]), he knew the value of plot and description but, unlike the Romantics, he also knew the value of character; he struck upon the original device of making description reveal character and he returned to the primordial principle of French classical tragedy by making the characters responsible for the plot.[1]

We should not forget that the nineteenth century witnesses the development not only of Romanticism and the bourgeoisie, but also, and perhaps more significantly, of nationalism. French critics, as well as their allies in other countries, are often nationalistic, even chauvinistic. They tend to underplay the influence of non-French writers upon French literature, and specifically when dealing with Balzac, they ignore the fact that Cervantes already knew full well how description of physical appearance could reveal character and character could in turn advance the plot.

After Balzac and Flaubert, the French novel veers toward determinism: individual actions are channeled and defined by external forces, ruled by the iron hand of biology and economics. An attempt is made by Zola and his followers to establish a scientific foundation under this new trend. Industrial bourgeois society is described by the Naturalists, as these novelists are called, yet the results are very similar to what we find in the Spanish picaresque novels: individuals fighting to overcome their desperate circumstances are predetermined to lose the battle. The picaresque elements in Spanish novels had been infiltrating Western literature for centuries. They certainly exist in Cervantes's works, including *Don Quixote,* and since Cervantes's masterpiece was much better known than other Spanish novels, it is probably through *Don Quixote* that the picaresque determinism influenced Zola either directly or secondhand. As Douglas Alden observes, "Zola and his contemporaries, especially Maupassant and Daudet, practiced their novelistic trade so methodically that it was evident that the realistic-psychological novel . . . had become a kind of stereotype. The subsequent history of the novel in France is an attempt to break this stalemate."[2]

A Female Don Quixote: Madame Bovary

In a chronology of Gustave Flaubert's life established by the critic Albert Thibaudet, we are told that young Flaubert (1831–81) was introduced to *Don Quixote* by his neighbor and classmate, Mignot.[3] Flaubert was then eleven years old. He was already beginning to write fiction. His first works were passionate, personal, brilliant, and romantic. When *Madame Bovary* appeared in 1857, his style had morphed and matured in its apparent simplicity and directness becoming impersonal yet effective, even overpowering. The novel is a portrait of contemporary French bourgeois society, more specifically middle-class provincial life, and reveals a stifling dreariness, a general mediocrity, boredom, and monotony that lead the main character, Emma Bovary, to despair, adultery, and finally suicide.

From school, young Emma carries under her cloak books forbidden to girls, novels that resemble the chivalry romances that obsessed and deranged Don Quixote's mind. She also borrows books from the libraries: "They were invariably about love affairs, lovers, mistresses, harassed ladies swooning in remote pavilions. Couriers were killed at every relay, horses ridden to death on every page; there were gloomy forests, broken hearts, vows, sobs, tears and kisses, skiffs in the moonlight, nightingales in thickets; the noblemen were all brave as lions, gentle as lambs, incredibly virtuous, always beautifully dressed, and wept copiously on every occasion. For six months, when she was fifteen, Emma begrimed her hands with this dust from old lending libraries."[4]

In the first chapter, she is restless, frustrated, and determined to leave behind her immediate surroundings, very much like Don Quixote. Again, life penetrates literature and literature penetrates life. She is trapped in a loveless marriage to a dull and insensitive man and dreams of escaping her monotonous life: "Deep down, all the while, she was waiting for something to happen. Like a sailor in distress, she kept casting desperate glances over the solitary waste of her life, seeking some white sail in the distant mists of the horizon. She had no idea by what wind it would reach her, toward what shore it would bear her, or what kind of craft it would be—tiny boat or towering vessel laden with heartbreaks or filled to the gunwales with rapture."[5]

Also reminiscent of our knight with his friends and relatives who are preoccupied with his favorite pastime is Emma's mother-in-law, who advises that she do some physical activity, house errands, rather than spend endless hours reading. A married woman in provincial nineteenth-century France was almost powerless. The Napoleonic Code of Law gave so much power to the husband that, in fact, the wife was a ward. Don Quixote was a bachelor; he was a man in charge of his own life. Emma had only her willpower, her desire to be happy, and her sexuality. She became ensnared in unsatisfactory adulterous affairs and she was deeply in debt. At the end, despair pushes her to suicide, which Flaubert describes in gruesome detail. Remember that Don Quixote in his despair, depressed and bitter as Emma after being defeated by Sansón Carrasco, asks Sansón to end his life. This does not happen. Instead when Don Quixote dies, he is in bed, has made his will, has confessed, and is surrounded by family and friends. Flaubert details Emma's suffering from the arsenic poisoning and the black vomit that pours from her contorted mouth.

We ponder the deaths of these two main characters and the feelings of Cervantes and Flaubert toward Don Quixote and Emma, respectively. The Don, whose ventures lead him on a noble path to do good, dies a gentle death, although during the novel he is beaten, often harmed physically, even run over by pigs. The last days of Emma's life may have been more full of suffering than Don Quixote's full tenure as a knight-errant; further, her last weeks, when she realizes what being deeply in debt entails, may be comparable to the anguish that Don Quixote experiences when he faces an enchanted Dulcinea.

Perhaps the conclusion can be that both writers feel a deep ambivalence toward their main character. Inasmuch as Don Quixote is a frustrated hero, he may have embodied in part what Cervantes thought about his own life of economic penury and lack of literary success. As for Flaubert, he makes abundantly clear why Emma found her married life unbearable, therefore justifying psychologically, if not morally, her infidelities. Her agony seems unwarranted and excessive. Could it be a punishment for her infidelities? Not, we think, from the pen of an agnostic. Perhaps once again Flaubert identified with his heroine who rebelled against the bourgeois society of provincial France during the Louis Philippe period, which Flaubert despised but from which he could not totally escape, hence the need for a harsh, violent punishment.

ALPHONSE DAUDET:
A QUIXOTE FROM SOUTHERN FRANCE

In passing we make mention of Alphonse Daudet (1848–97), who wrote *Tartarin de Tarascon* (1872), a very popular novel in his time. Daudet has been called the French Dickens, and in this novel he creates the main character Tartarin, as contradictory, quirky, and eccentric as any invented by Dickens. His passion for reading about adventures and his wild imagination recall Don Quixote, as is seen early in the novel:

> In the middle of the study was an occasional table, and on this table a decanter of rum, a Turkish tobacco pouch, the novels of Fenimore Cooper and Gustave Aimard, sportsmen's tales of bear hunts, falconry, elephant shooting, etc. Lastly at this table sat a small, fat, thick-set and red-faced man of between forty and forty-five with a short beard and flashing eyes. He was in his shirtsleeves and flannel breeches. In one hand he held a book, and with the other brandished a huge pipe with an iron stopper. And as he read some blood-curdling tale of scalp-hunters, he pushed out his lower lip in a terrifying grimace, which lent the honest face of this small-town rentier the same look of harmless ferocity that reigned throughout the house.
>
> This was Tartarin, Tartarin of Tarascon, the great, bold and incomparable Tartarin of Tarascon.[6]

Hence we find Tartarin, a middle-aged gentleman physically resembling Sancho Panza, bombastic and cowardly, with the ambition and desire to accomplish great deeds, much in the spirit of Don Quixote. Reality and the limitation of his deeds decree otherwise. The modern world is bourgeois and basically anti-heroic. Even a sport like hunting, which can bring to mind the prowess of ancient men battling saber-tooth tigers and mast-odons, is now in decline. There is nothing to hunt near his home-town, Tarascon. Yet his imagination is boundless and he lives to tell tales about past exploits. After reading many adventure novels and exotic descriptions of hunting expeditions, he imagines himself to be a great explorer and superb hunter. He plants exotic shrubs and trees in his backyard—his baobab tree never grows higher than a meter—and he starts a collection of weapons from every corner of the globe. He regales his friends with invented heroic tales, and finally his friends begin to demand concrete proof of his heroic adventures, compelling him to travel to North Africa and try his luck at hunting a lion or two. He travels to Algiers carrying enormous luggage full of weapons, and he dresses like a Muslim pasha. Disappointed at finding the area too civilized, he is ensnared by the charms of a young Arab woman. He finally manages to kill an old blind lion led on a leash by a beggar who made a living by showing the beast to passersby. He is taken to court and fined. He returns to France, followed by a camel that he had bought, which will not be separated from his master no matter how hard Tartarin tries. Daudet leaves his novel open-ended, like the first part of *Don Quixote.* Two sequels follow, *Tartarin in the Alps* and *Port-Tarascon;* however, they are less humorous.

Cervantes and Proust in Search of Time

Let us recall Cervantes's use of Time, the "invisible character" always present, side by side with Don Quixote and Sancho and guiding even the secondary characters. It makes its presence felt through a complex system of actions and reactions, dialogue and exchanges of viewpoints. Claudio Guillén perceptively remarks, "a dialogue in Cervantes is a joining of critical perspectives."[7]

Time also plays a prominent part in Marcel Proust's *Remembrance of Things Past* (1913). Marcel is the main character in this mostly autobiographical novel, and he recounts recollections from his childhood and of society through the three families he introduces. The plot is the pouring out of his life as a stream of consciousness, and in so doing memory becomes the Time frame. The past blurs with the present. The main character at the end of the work begins to write the work that already has been narrated. Proust (1871–1922) establishes a dialogue between different layers of his memory, slowly advancing from the past toward the present and finally toward a disenchantment with the myths, illusions, snobbish prejudices of his own past, a disenchantment that presages and preludes his own death. The recognition of the tragic futility of all human relations and all hopes and dreams, aside from artistic and literary creation, is strangely similar to the lost illusions and acceptance of death in the last pages of Cervantes's masterpiece.

As we will discover, the flawed French heroes and heroines are not nearly as complex as their Russian counterparts. Both, however, look to Cervantes in terms of character development and technique, framing their lives within a historical context.

The Spanish Connection: From Pushkin to Gogol

The famous Russian poet Alexander Pushkin, idol and mentor of Nicolai Gogol (1808–52), gave him the idea of writing *Dead Souls*. It was also at Pushkin's urging that Gogol read *Don Quixote*, at the time available in Russia only in French. Pushkin probably advised Gogol to pattern his novel on *Don Quixote*, and we can be fairly certain about his influence. No doubt Cervantes's creative work was offered as a possible example to emulate.

A few of Gogol's comments about the gestation of *Dead Souls* are noteworthy: "For some time Pushkin had been urging me to undertake something bigger: at last, after I had read him one short story which appealed to him more than the rest, he said to me: 'Why, when you have the gift of seeing into a man and painting his whole portrait in a few strokes, making him as though he were alive, don't you begin some really big piece of work? It is really a sin!' He cited the example of Cervantes, who, although he had written some admirable short stories, would never have held his present rank among writers if he had not embarked upon *Don Quixote*."[8] A friend of Gogol, Alexandra Smirnov, wrote in her diary: "Pushkin spent four hours at Gogol's place and gave him the subject for a novel which, like *Don Quixote*, will be divided into cantos. The hero will travel all over the provinces. Gogol will use his own travel notes."[9] On October 7, 1835, Gogol wrote to Pushkin: "I have begun *Dead Souls*. The subject is expanding into a very long novel, which I think will be very funny. In this novel I should like to portray all of Russia, if only from one point of view."[10]

The basic idea that Gogol developed was to write a comic epic. In *Dead Souls*, the "hero" Chichikov is very different from Don Quixote. He is an ambitious, smooth-talking scoundrel who has found a way of deceiving the Russian income tax system by buying names of deceased serfs from their owners for a nominal price, "settling" them on a piece of land, and obtaining a big mortgage for them at the State Landlords' Bank. The atmosphere is picaresque, a series of adventures through which is portrayed the whole range of society. In *Don Quixote*, Cervantes offers a cross section of Spanish society, from the muleteers and prostitutes of Palomeque's inn in part 1 to the aristocratic duke and duchess and their entourage in part 2. Geographically, Don Quixote's travels encompass a huge expanse of Spain, from La Mancha and lower Castile to Andalusia and then to Barcelona in Catalonia. Gogol knew Russia from the Ukraine to Moscow and Saint Petersburg as well as Cervantes knew Spain, and in his portraits of country squires drawn with infinite care, he displays and analyzes the whole of the Russian social fabric, not with a jaundiced critical eye but with affection.

Don Quixote, naive and noble in righting the wrongs of the world, pits his fantasies and dream world against the constant erosion of everyday life. He is at once a fool, a madman, and a visionary who upholds high ideals. Chichikov is acting out his dreams too, only his have a profit motive. Both are extravagant figures. Gogol strived to perceive the fantastic side of everyday life. He was apt to see how eccentric people act and was drawn to caricature them whether he knew them in person or not, or he simply imagined them by combining traits of people he met, perhaps reminiscent of some of Dickens's characters. There is a warmth and muted admiration in Gogol's caricatures of society of which his characters are a part. He seems to be telling us that we are all irrational survivors and human frailty is everywhere.

Like Cervantes, Gogol has baffled his critics, who have tried in vain to make sense of the many contradictory and complex features of his works and his life. A relentless critic of the many shortcomings of Russian society and of the country's political system, and an admirer of Western literature who felt at home in Italy, Gogol fell prey to a Rasputin-like monk toward the end of his life, became a "born-again" Orthodox Christian, and stopped writing, fasting himself to death.

The Ever-Present Quixote in Turgenev's Life and Works

Ivan Turgenev (1818–83) was born into a wealthy family on a large estate in what was then the Ukraine region of Russia. To escape his strict and domineering mother, he left the family manor and went to study at universities in St Petersburg and Berlin. For a short period he worked for the Russian civil service but soon turned to writing full time. His first book, *A Sportsman's Sketches* (1852), was a set of short stories recounting the views of an upper-class person about the lives of the peasants on his estate. It is believed to have helped Tsar Alexander II in his decision to free the serfs, but some opinions expressed in the book earned Turgenev detention and house arrest.

During the next ten years, Turgenev wrote a series of six novels. In the first, *Rudin* (1856), the eminently intelligent main character visits an estate and opines on beauty and truth but suffers a frustrated love, unable to reconcile matters of the head and heart in the same manner that the Russian writer's own life unfolded; the novel also exhibits weakness in the main character's convictions. In chapter 11 of this novel when Rudin leaves the estate of the overbearing Darya Mikhaylovna, although he is desperately in love with her daughter Natalya, he says to Basistov, a disciple, (his Sancho Panza): "'Do you remember what Don Quixote said to Sancho Panza after leaving the Duchess's court? "Freedom," he said, "my friend Sancho, is one of a man's most precious possessions, and happy is he to whom heaven has given a crust of bread, who has no need to be obliged to another man for it!" What Don Quixote felt then, I feel now.'"[11]

These works set the tone of the novelist's life and writings, and the spirit of Don Quixote looms large in both. The great passion of his life, his Dulcinea, was Pauline García Viardot, a married opera singer with whom Turgenev had a child. For a number of years, he lived with or near Madame Pauline and her husband, Louis (who produced a bad French translation of *Don Quixote*).

In the year that Turgenev completed writing *Rudin,* he wrote in a letter of June 10: "When I cast an eye over my life thus far I observe that absolutely all I have done, or so it seems to me, is to carry on a wild goose chase. At least Don Quixote believed in the beauty of his Dulcinea; whereas our modern Quixotes clearly see that their Dulcineas are plain as pikestaffs, and still they chase after them."[12] Here Turgenev saw himself as a modern reincarnation of Don Quixote although somewhat diminished from the model

In 1860 he delivered his celebrated lecture "Hamlet and Don Quixote," in which he claims that mankind can be classified into two basic types, the Hamlets and the Don Quixotes. The first is full of reflection, doubt, and hesitation and makes the essential decisions when it is already too late, the second rushes into action before the dust has settled. Both are tragic and dramatic, each in his own way. Intention and purpose are paramount. Turgenev points this up in the concluding lines of his essay:

> Don Quixote's death fills one's heart with unspoken tenderness. In that moment, the whole enormous significance of the man becomes clear to everyone. When, intending to console him, his ex-squire says that soon they will again set out on adventures of knight-errantry, the dying man replies:
>
> > "Let us go gently, gentlemen," said Don Quixote, "for there are no birds this year in last year's nests. I was mad, but I am sane now. I was Don Quixote de la Mancha, but to-day, as I have said, I am Alonso Quixano the Good. May my sincere repentance restore your former esteem for me."
>
> This is surprising. First and final reference to the new nickname astonishes the reader. Certainly, in the face of death any words carry greater meaning: all things pass, all things vanish—the highest rank, power, universal genius—all things crumble to dust—

Everything earthly great
Dissipates like smoke . . .

But good deeds do not vanish into thin air like
smoke. They outlast the most radiant beauty. "All
things pass," said the Apostle, "only love remains."[13]

The Russian novelist's interpretation brings us back to the old
ethical problem of ends versus means. If we are aiming toward
a good goal, are we entitled to make endless mistakes and, more
specifically, to hurt other people or commit crimes in the pursuit
of such a good goal? A notable link can be made between the
lecture and his undisputed masterpiece *Fathers and Sons* (1862),
a novel full of well-crafted characters that deals with essential
ethical and political problems. The young generation is fierce,
stubborn, and rebellious. It is idealistic and wishes to change
and reform the world right away. The older generation is confused, hesitant, slow, and reluctant to make changes. Its members want to make peace with their sons and daughters but they
meet only with contempt and rejection. "And yet they feel that
there was a time when they too fought fervently for an ideal of
justice. They remain loyal to their passion for art and poetry.
They timidly try to get the young men to share their tastes, but
the young men will have nothing to do with a literature that
does not fight, is not effective, committed. All that matters to
them is direct politics. They do not even condemn violence as a
means to their ends."[14] The main character, Bazarov, a medical
student, shows the decisiveness and courage of a modern Don
Quixote. He may be doctrinaire, a nihilist (Turgenev coined the
word), a man who recognizes no authority, but he is also a man
of flesh and blood, capable of falling madly in love. "Turgenev
has felt affection for his rebel-hero and had to fight back the
tears when relating his death. 'With the exception of his views

on art, I share almost all Bazarov's other convictions,' he said a few years later." [15]

Turgenev's novel was, in turn, misunderstood by most readers. Left-leaning readers rejected it as too harsh a portrait of the new generation and accused him of having sold out to the Slavofile, conservative party. To his dismay, conservative readers congratulated him. Perhaps unconsciously, he had projected the Romantic version of Don Quixote over the face of his young hero, while the shadow of an indecisive Hamlet had obscured the virtues of the older characters.

Tolstoy's Two Quixotes and One Dulcinea

Leo Tolstoy (1828–1910) wrote *War and Peace*, the greatest of all historical novels, from 1865 to 1869. It is a whole literature and world unto itself. Set against the backdrop of the Napoleonic Wars between France and Russia (1799–1815), the story relates the lives of five families and includes more than five hundred characters. It is set in a period in history when changes are in the air. The radical ideas of the French Revolution are slowly filtering everywhere. External signs that the French revolutionaries thought that they were starting from the bottom in the political and social structure may be seen in their design to change the calendar (the names of the months and the number of the years), and the way things were measured (meters and kilometers instead of yards and miles, etc.), weighed, and practically every other way of gauging the space and matter around us.

Tolstoy's main characters, especially the questioning, intellectual Prince Andrey and the eager but irresolute Pierre Bezuhkov, also want to change the world. The former imagines himself Napoleon, hence again, the Romantic halo of the hero finding inspiration in both Don Quixote and Napoleon. He plans to reform the Russian army by creating a new military code. A new powerful army will allow him to change countless destinies. (Tolstoy knew that around 1820 a coalition or conspiracy of army officers was planning to change Russia, and even the world, by taking over the authoritarian and corrupt tsarist government). Pierre Bezuhkov, more quixotic and certainly more naive, blunders constantly. At first, he is seduced by the nebulous beliefs of the Freemasons, also intent upon changing the world. He seems foolish to others and with abandon spends the fortune left to him by his biological father, reminding us of the way Don Quixote sells his lands to buy books. Alexander Welsh explains:

> Tolstoy's two heroes are linked by friendship and by a single Dulcinea: Natasha Rostova, who before her aborted elopement from the one and eventual marriage to the other represents something like life itself to both men. In the same historical novel, Tolstoy plays again and again the Cervantes game of mocking an existing narrative in order to validate his own. When it comes to public events—that is, the Napoleonic wars—and their ostensible causes, he never tires of telling the reader that they did not happen the way historians want us to believe but the way they are described here. In this way *War and Peace* is like *Joseph Andrews* and *Tristram Shandy* in seizing hold of both branches of Cervantes's endowment of the novel, the hero and the method.[16]

Tolstoy, whose personal life was not devoid of anguish and remorse, finally abandoned wife and home at the end of his life. He is gentle in his treatment of his main characters' outcome. Pierre and Natasha marry and will lead a placid bourgeois life.

Natasha will grow fat. Prince Andrey dies a hero. Here, Tolstoy like Cervantes spares his main characters from a brutal or unsavory end in recounting their deaths.

DON QUIXOTE AS JESUS'S BROTHER

Dostoyevsky (1821–80) wrote *The Idiot* in 1868–69, at approximately the same time that Tolstoy wrote *War and Peace.* In his novel, Dostoyevsky takes on the complex question of the clash between principles and ideals, on one side, and practical, unyielding reality, on the other, a thread that unites *Don Quixote, The Idiot, War and Peace,* and, as we saw earlier in the discussion of Dickens, *The Pickwick Papers.* In the darkness and misery of his prison, Mr. Pickwick wants to change the world just as Don Quixote does, but perhaps in a humbler, more limited way. So does Prince Myshkin, who submits to blackmail even when he knows the blackmailer is an imposter. Similarly, Tolstoy's Prince Andrey and Pierre Bezuhkov entertain aspirations of changing the world both politically and ideologically.

Fyodor Dostoyevsky's writings are powerful, thought provoking, and often deeply upsetting. He wrote in a letter to his niece: "The main idea of the novel is to portray a positively good man. . . . There is only one positively good figure in the world—Christ —so that the phenomenon of that boundlessly, infinite, good figure is already in itself an infinite miracle . . . of the figures in Christian literature, the most complete is Don Quixote. But he is good only because at the same time he is ridiculous . . . and that's the only reason it succeeds. Compassion for the good man who is ridiculed and is unaware of his own worth generates sympathy in the reader. And this ability to arouse compassion is the very secret of humor."[17]

In the same letter he makes mention of Mr. Pickwick but suggests that his stature is not quite on the same level as Don Quixote's, although noteworthy. Prince Myshkin like Don Quixote chooses to ignore reality, lacks practical common sense, and possesses naive foolishness. As Alexander Welsh points out: "Prince Myshkin [the hero of Dostoyevsky's novel] is the one memorable hero who is mentally unstable since Don Quixote himself. Dostoyevsky dramatizes the idea of wisdom in folly, however, by confining the action of the *The Idiot* to Myshkin's window of sanity between bouts of illness in a Swiss asylum."[18] Where does folly end and wisdom begin? The Romantic interpretation of *Don Quixote* has asked this basic question. Answers are not easy.

In *The Brothers Karamazov* (1880), Dostoyevsky increases the tension to an unbearable point in the episode of "the Grand Inquisitor." Jesus has come back to our world. He is seen to disturb the peace and is now in jail. The Grand Inquisitor visits him and explains to him that Jesus's message is not what the world needs. Power and riches are sought and Jesus made a mistake coming back. No doubt he will be executed a second time. The Grand Inquisitor prepares to leave. Jesus kisses him, a sign that Jesus forgives the Grand Inquisitor. The scene is dramatic and powerful. It makes us think, but reaching an unshakable solution is not easy. Is Jesus being foolish? If Don Quixote is both a fool and a wise man, can it be said that Jesus is both supremely wise but foolish in the ways of the world? Suddenly the shadow of Don Quixote acquires a philosophical, ethical, and theological dimension. We recall the numerous times Don Quixote has acted foolishly, immaturely, and unaware of the way society works.

Prince Myshkin finds children pure and wise. His behavior is often childish. The Spanish critic Arturo Serrano Plaja explains that "here too—as in Don Quixote—the complete description of the character demands a kind of double perspective. From the outside, with the insufficient and hurried vocabulary that circumstances and 'society' impose, the character will appear to be an 'idiot'—Don Quixote's 'madness'; but, from within, we see that we are confronting a 'pure soul' or 'a truly beautiful soul.'"[19]

Perhaps words from the Gospels make the dichotomy of mad (foolish)–good (pure) soul clearer and enable us to see the parallel between Prince Myshkin and Don Quixote more distinctly: "At the same time came the disciples unto Jesus, saying, 'Who is the greatest in the kingdom of Heaven?' And Jesus called a little child unto him, and set him in the midst of them, and said, 'Verily I say unto you, Except ye be converted, and become as little children, ye shall not enter the kingdom of Heaven. Whosoever therefore shall humble himself as this little child, the same is greatest in the kingdom of Heaven. And whosoever shall receive one such little child in my name receiveth me'" (Matthew 18:1–5).

This esteemed group of Russian writers all valued Cervantes. Anton Chekhov, another Russian and a voracious reader, best underlines their admiration when he encourages his younger brother Mikhail, who had just discovered the joy of reading the European and American authors: "Have a look at . . . *Don Quixote* (complete in all seven or eight parts.) It's a fine work written by Cervantes, who is just about on the level of Shakespeare."[20]

THE SPANISH LEGACY: BENITO PÉREZ GALDÓS

During the Golden Age, Spain made major contributions to the modern novel. But the didactic nature of eighteenth-century literature and the Romantic movement of the first part of the nineteenth, with its focus on poetry and theater, were a setback for the cultivation of the novel. The Spanish novel had to be reinvented, partly through foreign models. No one was more prolific, authoring a substantial number of first-rate novels, than Benito Pérez Galdós (1843–1920), who was inspired not only by Dickens and Balzac but also by Cervantes.

Like Turgenev, young Galdós sought to escape his domineering and fanatical mother by leaving the Canary Islands and traveling. He studied law in Madrid, although he failed his courses
for lack of attendance. He was more interested in journalism
and literature, and he spent most of his time going to elegant
parties and exploring the Madrid underworld, making mental
sketches of hundreds, perhaps thousands of people. They represented every nook and cranny of Spanish society that, once
transformed by his imagination, would populate the (literally)
more than a hundred novels he wrote and published during his
long life.

Of this indisputable giant of Spanish letters in the nineteenth
century, one critic writes: "If the reader wishes to get a rough
idea of Galdós, let him take one of the better works of Balzac,
add the warmth and color and melodramatic sense of Dickens,
the grave and ironic tone of Cervantes, and he will have something which approximates the picture. Psychologist, moralist,
philosopher, Christian, in the final analysis Galdós was the only
novelist of his time who truly sought to amalgamate the old
and the new, to understand all Spaniards and humanity, to inte-
grate modern philosophy and science with social justice and the
spiritual and religious needs of man. Galdós sought not only the
meaning of human nature, but in his eternal quest the meaning
of life itself."[21]

Galdós is Cervantes's true heir in the Hispanic world. Sometimes Cervantes's presence in Galdós's novels is specific; at other
times, it is general and diffuse. We refer to a few specific examples of Cervantes's distinct influence that Michael Nimetz
points up in his comprehensive study *Humor in Galdós*. First, in
El Doctor Centeno, the geography, the well-crafted description
of the main character, and Galdós's use of the Cervantine technique of merging literature and reality are unmistakable: "Alejandro is an inveterate dreamer, given to a very dangerous use of

the imagination. He comes from La Mancha, the seat of Don Quixote. His aunt, doña Isabel de Godoy, is also from La Mancha and is as mad as can be. . . . . For Alejandro as for Don Quixote, literature is more vivid than life. Fiction encroaches upon reality and effaces the line between the two."[22] Another case in point appears in *La desheredada* (*The Disinherited Woman*) in the form of a letter written to his niece Isadora by her uncle "from el Tomelloso," a town in La Mancha. "The letter with its archaic, moralizing flavor and its mixture of good sense and *disparate* [folly] is an adaptation of Don Quixote's advice to Sancho Panza before Sancho goes off to govern his island."[23] The critic goes on to say that Galdós was proud to acknowledge his debt to Cervantes, noting how close to the original the text of the letter was. A third instance that Nimetz comments upon, in Galdós's work *Nazarín,* is his use of the "fictitious authorship device . . . unquestionably a hand-me down from *Don Quixote*" and of the main character's erratic behavior, which varies between being Christlike and mad and reminds us of Don Quixote: "The reader, from beginning to end, is so conscious that Cervantes' novel lurks behind the scenes that he tends to compare Nazarín with Don Quixote instead of with Christ."[24]

In terms of a more general and diffuse presence of Cervantes, we offer, for instance, in Galdós's portrait of the humble and downtrodden, the servant Benina in *Misericordia,* at bottom more generous and morally superior to her snobbish mistress. Let us remember how Cervantes makes Sancho smarter and more sympathetic than the duke and the duchess, who are mired in petty practical jokes. Galdós, like Cervantes, is interested in mental diseases, and several of his characters (a good example would be Maxi in *Fortunata y Jacinta*) are truly clinical studies of the progress of mania, obsession, and bipolar disease. Finally, in *Miau,* a novel about Spanish bureaucracy, we find sharp social criticism (incompetence, corruption), megalomania (one of the bureaucrats has a plan to change the world by improving the bureaucratic machinery), and humor. (It turns out that the plan includes four levels of action, and the acronym for these essential steps spells "Miau," a cat's voice in Spanish, exposing the plan to laughter and derision.) Here Galdós paints a harsh view of nineteenth-century Spain, evokes sympathy for the unfortunate, and penetrates the inner thoughts of his characters, all reminiscent of Cervantes in his novel. As these examples illustrate, and a closer scrutiny of Galdós will show, the focus of his lens, the themes, the literary technique, and his humor all point to Cervantes.

7

Don Quixote and the New World

TWO AMERICAN PERSPECTIVES

MELVILLE'S FASCINATION WITH CERVANTES'S WORK

The Romantic movement was not exclusively a European literary and intellectual phenomenon. In the Americas, writers responded to the same stimuli. Although lacking the experience of the Middle Ages with its castles, knights, and fabled dragons, America possessed parallel spiritual affinities: an individualistic spirit, a love of liberty, and an admiration of nature. The vast frontier awakened in many people a sense of adventure and the potential for discovery of new places and encouraged the freedom they needed to develop their individualism. The Americas were ripe for the Romantic movement in literature and the arts.

One example is Herman Melville (1819–91) whose famous *Moby Dick* introduces us to Captain Ahab, a flawed hero like Don Quixote, who devotes his life to the pursuit of a whale much like our Manchegan knight pursued his dream. The comparison is not without foundation, although the portrayal of the two main characters and Melville's motivation will reveal significant differences. Nevertheless, we know that Melville was an admirer of Cervantes. Harry Levin points out that Melville's copy of *Don Quixote* is full of penciled notes, remarks, and underlined sentences: "The object and inspiration of his quest, the fair Dulcinea, is often signalized by Melville's pencil. Her knight's defense of courtly love prompts Melville to append his most revealing note: 'I have already often said it, and now repeat it, that a knight-errant without a mistress is like a tree without leaves, a building without cement, a shadow without a body that causes it.'"[1] We know that Melville mentions Cervantes's *Don Quixote* in entries in his diary that coincide with his writing *Moby Dick*. In Levin's opinion:

> The profoundest tribute to Cervantes is that which other writers have paid him by imitation and emulation. It goes too deep to be altogether reducible in terms of conscious literary influence; it springs from the almost Homeric circumstances that made him the first to master a genre which— through that very process of mastery—has come to predominate in modern literature. Don Quixote is thus an archetype as well as an example, the exemplary novel of all time. . . . No American author, however, can more fitly be compared with Cervantes than Herman Melville. The harsh schools in which the two men educated themselves were immeasurably far apart: a whaling ship, Melville boasted, was both Yale and Harvard to him. Yet a sailor in the South Sea Islands may learn, even as a soldier in Algerian captivity, to make life itself a commentary on book-learning.[2]

An important difference separates his novel from Voltaire's and Cervantes's masterpieces. In Melville's novel there is hardly a trace of humor, whereas the works of Cervantes and Voltaire are full of humor and satire. For Cervantes, slapstick is an essential element of parody, satire, and humor, but he fuses these elements with the more serious levels of social and literary criticism. Voltaire's text offers abundant social and philosophical criticism, always wrapped in satire and wit. Nothing similar can be found in Melville's work. We must conclude that there was a deep change in the literary climate following Voltaire and the Enlightenment. This change has come to be known as the Romantic movement.

Pablo Picasso (1881–1973), *Don Quixote,* 1955. Musée d'Art et d'Histoire, St. Denis, France. Photo: Scala / Art Resource, NY. © 2005 Estate of Pablo Picasso / Artists Rights Society (ARS), New York.

The Mad Romantic Hero

The most striking difference is the way in which the hero is conceived by the author. Both Don Quixote and Captain Ahab are mad, yet they are mad in very different ways. Don Quixote is mad in a clumsy way; we always expect him to make a mistake that will induce laughter. Ahab, in contrast, is prey to a serious, intense madness that increases dramatically toward the end of the novel, a madness that inspires awe, not laughter. The Romantic hero is, in this case, a flawed hero but not a laughable one.

As Isaiah Berlin explained in *The Crooked Timber of Mankind*, around 1820 one finds poets and philosophers, particularly in Germany, saying that the noblest thing a man can do is to serve his own inner ideal, no matter at what cost. "This ideal may be confined to the solitary individual to whom it is revealed, it may appear false or absurd to all others, it may be in conflict with the lives and outlook of the society to which he belongs, but he is obliged to fight for it, and, if there is no other way, die for it."[3] Moreover, the question of whether an ideal is true or false is no longer thought to be important. "The ideal presents itself in the form of a categorical imperative: serve the inner light within you because it burns within you, for that reason alone."[4] The true and only goal of a man is to realize the personal vision within him at whatever cost. His worst crime is to be untrue to this inner goal, which is his and his alone. Given the strength of this new definition of a true hero and its rapid acceptance by most Western European thinkers, writers, and philosophers, its impact was incalculable and would persist for several generations. It is very probable that Melville did not find this new definition of a hero in German sources. Thomas Carlyle, the Scottish historian, philosopher, and essayist was his guide in this respect, and Carlyle was a strong influence on Melville's writings.

It is difficult to reason with Don Quixote, yet Sancho tries to do so repeatedly with limited success. It is impossible to reason with Captain Ahab. Passion, revenge, and hatred push Ahab relentlessly. We understand from the very beginning that he is a hero, but one who will not be easy to admire. There is much that is theatrical and even flamboyant about him. Only after the ship has been at sea for several days does Captain Ahab appear on deck. He is a tall, powerful man who seems "made of solid bronze," and though seemingly healthy and strong, he displays two deformities: an ivory leg replacing the one he lost in his fight with Moby Dick and a livid scar running all across his face. Thus, Melville displays visibly a portrait of a flawed hero. We do not laugh at him. We are overpowered by fear and anguish because we have already guessed the novel will have a tragic ending. The moving force behind the action is a man out of control, propelled only by anger. Toward the end, his madness compels him to see a kind of kinship between himself and little Pip, the Negro boy who has been driven mad by fright. Ahab's protective instinct is aroused. All men are brothers, he concludes, and at this point there is a chance he may yet escape his obsession. He begins to identify with the rest of mankind. Starbuck, always sensible, urges him to think of home and family; he is about to put an end to his quest and go home (chapter 132). "At this point in the story Ahab reaches to the very edge of the pit into which he has fallen and is ready to pull himself up to salvation, but long habit (or fate) prevents it. On the following day the distinctive odor of whale, wafted across the waves to his quick nostrils, finally overpowers all his favorable resolutions. His wild hatred revives; forgetting all else, he commands full sail in the direction of the White Whale."[5]

The final chapters of Melville's novel are a model of tense, dramatic crescendo that ends with the destruction of the ship, attacked by the whale, and the death of Ahab. When we compare the structure of the book with that of Cervantes's, we see immediately remarkable similarities and also clear differences. Melville's novel starts slowly; it is interrupted several times by digressions related to whaling and hunting for whales until we learn everything we want to learn, and much beyond, about the subject. The end of the story, in contrast, is tense and dramatic, unsurpassed as a source of suspense and emotion. Melville's work is driven by the quest of a flawed hero, a madman, and yet we do not see Ahab's faults as clearly as we see Don Quixote's mistakes. The new conception of the hero created by the Romantic movement has changed the rules of the game. We stand in awe of Ahab. We hardly have the time or the inclination to criticize him, although his madness grows much more dangerous than Don Quixote's and ultimately brings doom and death to himself, the ship, and all the crew aboard the ship.

As Tyros Hillway comments, "the appealing thing about Ahab is his courage—though perhaps foolhardiness would be a more accurate word—in playing for high stakes with a stacked deck. In his courage to disobey he resembles Prometheus. . . . Melville certainly means to convey in *Moby-Dick* the conviction —forced upon him by his own philosophical inquiries—that, on the one hand, pursuit of the Absolute leads to frustration and madness; on the other, arrogance in the search is inherently self-destructive."[6]

Ahab's attitude is heroic, yet in its failure to accept human limitations and in its assumption of finding the possibility of learning the definitive truth, he places himself upon such a lofty pedestal that he may be said to rival God. In his declaration of man's freedom to control his destiny and delve into all the secrets of the universe, Captain Ahab, as created by Melville, foreshadows some of the central ideas of Nietzsche's Superman. "Thus the most famous voyage in American literature ends in overwhelming tragedy—the 'total wreck' that Ahab consciously preferred over submission to human fate."[7]

It is significant that Melville felt the need to distance himself from his novel. He confesses to his friend Hawthorne, "I have written a wicked book and feel spotless as the lamb."[8] Yet today's average reader probably feels a mixture of admiration and reproach about Ahab. First we must come to terms with the meaning of the White Whale. What was Melville trying to tell us through this monster? A huge white whale may be terrifying, yet our senses can tell us that it is possibly real, a real being. Fighting it is somehow acceptable—it is a monster out of control, one that has already shown itself to be vicious and dangerous. It is easier to react to a visual target, a white whale, than to abstract ideas. Both Don Quixote and Candide were fighting abstract ideas: the first fought injustice and cruelty, sometimes personified and made visible—at least visible to him—in the shape of giants and monsters; Candide had to fight and dispel a series of misadventures and disasters, and the idea that God and divine providence were protecting human beings, even when events proved that they had turned their back on humans or, even worse, were deliberately hostile. In his case, his faith in a benevolent Presence does not take a concrete visual shape. It could be argued that religious symbols or images might have been useful to Candide in his struggle to explain away the dark side of life, but Voltaire probably thought it prudent to avoid them since their presence in the novel would have complicated the situation and have exposed its author to vicious attacks. Blasphemy would have been suspected by his many enemies.

The greatest contrast between *Don Quixote* and *Moby Dick* is what at first hand appears to be their major link: the strange, powerful, eccentric personalities of the two heroes. Needless to say, Don Quixote and Ahab are unique individuals, and yet each is conditioned by his historic time. Don Quixote has made a conscious effort to identify himself with medieval heroes; at bottom, however, we see him as a Renaissance man, easier to understand and appreciate after reading such descriptions of the ideal Renaissance man as *The Courtier* by Baldassare di Castiglione. Don Quixote is a warrior, certainly, but also a sophisticated man of letters, capable of quoting poets in Spanish, Italian, and Latin, inspired by ideals of feminine beauty, and in tune with the glory and the suffering inspired by Platonic love as interpreted through a Petrarchan sonnet. In traditional Japan it was normal for a Samurai or a Ronin to be familiar with refined calligraphy and the haiku of Matsuo Basho. Weapons and literature were not enemies; they complemented each other. As for Captain Ahab, he is also a powerful and strange man, knowledgeable about ships and navigation, devoted to whaling, and a perfect example of a nineteenth-century entrepreneur, not unfamiliar with accounting and banking, although his obsession about Moby Dick transforms him into an idealist hunter, almost, one could say, a philosophical hunter, yearning to find the Absolute Whale and conquer it at last. We should not forget the important role of whaling in nineteenth-century industrial societies. It closely paralleled what is today the petroleum industry, so vital to our present needs. Once more, the contrast between these two heroes depends not only on their social role, but also on the fact that Romanticism makes it imperative that a real hero must be, in principle, a tragic hero, while during the Renaissance writers were less strict about the role of their literary characters. There was no doubt that Don Quixote could inspire laughter and tears. At the same time, the ideals he tried to bring back to life were part of the cultural background of most educated readers and were worthy of admiration and respect.

Juvenile Literature?

An obvious but no less interesting point that Cervantes's and Melville's novels have in common is that both have often been classified as juvenile literature, children's books. As Leo Spitzer explains, "The average European meets the ingenious hidalgo Don Quijote for the first time as a child. This is not so of the average American; in America the *Don Quijote*, along with other things Spanish, became a victim of the philosophy of the Enlightenment; but in Europe the *Don Quijote* is first of all a children's book. . . . Several great books of world literature, not purposely written for children, have reached this consecration as books able to form the sensitivity of man in the making: *Don Quijote, Robinson Crusoe, Gulliver's Travels, Moby Dick, Gil Blas,* and *Tartarin* (that French pocket-edition of the *Quijote*)."[9] To this list, without hesitation, Mark Twain's *Huckleberry Finn* can be added.

Cervantes was conscious that his book could be read at different levels and would appeal to a vast reading public. Cervantes's novel appeals to a young audience because it is possible to identify with Don Quixote. His bravery is unquestionable, his tenacity and resourcefulness are enviable. No matter how much he suffers and falls down, he always picks himself up and continues his quest. His resilience and his energy allow him to surmount every obstacle and regain confidence in himself. At certain moments, today's young readers may be reminded of another courageous character, also familiar with adversity and misadventure, Wily E. Coyote of cartoon fame.

Moreover, almost every young reader has fantasized, perhaps more than once, about the possibility of leaving home and all the familiar faces and going off to explore the world. By his example, Don Quixote shows the young readers that it is possible to do so and also that it is possible, after all, to come back home. A vast world is out there waiting for us, beckoning us to face danger and show everybody how brave we are. Even failure can be accepted as a way of learning more about the world and acquiring wisdom. Don Quixote may not be the ideal, perfect hero, but this makes him more sympathetic to young readers, who may well think that they can learn from Don Quixote's mistakes and thus succeed where the Spanish knight fails. A young reader may also learn patience and perseverance by reading such a long novel.

The variety of situations and adventures makes the book easy to read, and even when reading it as an adventure story, the young reader may intuit that there are messages hidden in the text that will be revealed later, when as a mature individual he or she reads the novel for a second time.

As for *Moby Dick,* it is also a magnificent travel and adventure book, full of surprises and with an exciting climax, and once more some of the most important messages of the book may have to wait until a second mature reading takes place. Compared to the Cervantes novel, Melville offers a crescendo of excitement toward the end, and yet some of the more technical chapters devoted to the hunting of whales, the tools of the trade, and the details of every step of the complex operations of a whaling ship may be tedious for a young reader—and often have been deemed boring for mature readers as well.

The new conception of heroes and heroism in the Romantic era was bound to have retroactive consequences for the nineteenth-century interpretation of a heroic Don Quixote. Obviously the Romantic hero could not be an object of laughter or derision. The stakes of the game had been raised: the Romantic hero had become a tragic hero, and for a while no other kind of hero would be acceptable. If it was true that Don Quixote suffered innumerable defeats throughout the novel, it was equally true that after each mishap, our knight was able to recover his balance and sally forth in search of new adventures. Courage was a virtue he possessed in abundance and that, together with the ability to endure suffering, endeared him to readers like Miguel de Unamuno, who saw him as a model for a Christian hero, perhaps even a saint.

We are now beginning to see how flexible and protean Don Quixote has become in the years since his creation. He is capable of inspiring such a hero of the Enlightenment as Candide, who finally learns that only teamwork offers us the possibility of a better future. Was Voltaire thinking of the heroic efforts of his friend Diderot and his band of writers, scientists, and artists who produced the *Encyclopédie* against all odds? The character of Don Quixote can also suggest to Melville a hero such as Ahab, who in his furious obsession destroys himself and all, or almost all, those who accompany him in his quest. Most Romantic heroes have tragic endings. In the meantime, literature has come to a fork in the road: Romanticism will continue to produce tragic heroes until the end of the nineteenth century and beyond, but realism will slowly gain the upper hand in the field of the novel—and realism will also find an important source of inspiration in *Don Quixote*.

Traveling Down the Mississippi with Don Quixote: Twain's Version

The picaresque worldview that had persisted in European literature resonates in the works of Mark Twain (1832–1910), where we find the familiar themes of cruelty, lies, and hypocrisy, and a critical attitude toward society. The just and lasting fame that both Cervantes and Mark Twain enjoyed originated in their initial success with the public. Neither writer convinced the most illustrious critics of his day that his works would endure and continue to attract the attention of great numbers of educated readers and be included in studies compiled by the best literary critics. In other words, the victory of both writers was difficult for very similar reasons. As a literary genre, the novel was not appreciated in Cervantes's time. The greatest author, poet, and creator in those years, Lope de Vega, likewise disparaged *Don Quixote*, and his opinion was shared by other critics of that epoch. Similarly, the work of the southern humorist Mark Twain, who was almost as famous for his dramatic lectures as he was for his literary output, and whose books, articles, stories, and essays were entertaining but according to some critics and readers a bit superficial, was little appreciated by serious critics during his lifetime.

Cervantes and Mark Twain, however, are united from the beginning by the immediate acclaim of their readers, the unjustified reserve of the official critics of their eras, and their unquestionable glory in the present and the future. In a certain way, each of these authors is an iconic symbol of his era and also of his culture, and for this reason the ties that unite their works are of great value when we attempt to appreciate Spain's cultural contribution to the United States. On the vast screen of world literature, Cervantes is Spain just as, to a great extent, Mark Twain is the United States.

When Mark Twain published his first story, "The Celebrated Jumping Frog of Calaveras County," which appeared in 1865, *Don Quixote* had reached a level of critical attention and appreciation among educated readers that was unsurpassable. It had been translated into numerous languages, continuously reprinted, and subjected to constant in-depth examination by Spanish, English, French, German (above all), and American critics and intellectuals. Mark Twain read and admired Cervantes's masterpiece. It is not certain and is most likely doubtful that he was familiar with other aspects of Cervantes's work. *Don Quixote* was a star of the highest magnitude in the literary sky that Mark Twain contemplated. And the novel by Mark Twain that received the greatest recognition, contemplation, and readership was also the novel that contemporary critics consider to be the decisive work within his oeuvre, *The Adventures of Huckleberry Finn*. As the critic Steward Ross points out: "By 1913, H. L. Mencken was calling *Huckleberry Finn* 'one of the greatest master-pieces of the world.' Ernest Hemingway believed 'all modern literature comes from one book by Mark Twain called *Huckleberry Finn*. . . . It's the best book we've had. All American writing comes from that. There was nothing before. There has been nothing as good since.'"[10]

The Quixotization of Tom Sawyer

Similarities with Cervantes's style can be seen in, for example, chapter 3, entitled "The Ambuscade of the Arabs," in which Twain describes a heroic and fantastic project thought up by Tom Sawyer: an ambush organized by a band of boys and teenagers and led by Tom Sawyer, naturally, against a caravan made up of rich Arabs and Spaniards, with camels and elephants, who are transporting diamonds and precious stones. Huck Finn doubts that this enterprise will be viable, but he is very eager to see camels and elephants:

> so I was on hand next day, Saturday, in the ambuscade. . . . But there warn't no Spaniards and Arabs, and there warn't no camels nor no elephants. . . . It warn't anything but a Sunday-school picnic. . . . We busted it up, and chased the children up the hollow; but we never got anything but some doughnuts and jam. . . . I didn't see no di'monds, and I told Tom Sawyer so. He said there was loads of them, anyway; and he said there was Arabs there, too, and elephants and things. I said, why couldn't we see them, then? He said if I warn't so ignorant, but had read a book called Don Quixote, I would know without asking. He said there was hundreds of soldiers there, and elephants and treasure, and so on, but we had enemies which he called magicians, and they had turned the whole thing into an infant Sunday-school, just out of spite.[11]

The quixotization of Tom Sawyer is complete, and in a certain way that transfers the role of Sancho to Huck Finn, who follows his friend and boss in his crazy adventures without being totally convinced that what he imagines has occurred. To reinforce the parallels between Twain's two characters and the heroes of Cervantes's work, we should recall that Tom Sawyer is relatively rich and educated. His family must have had a good library, where he not only read adventure books—stories of pirates, noble bandits (such as Robin Hood), and explorers—but also, and most especially, *Don Quixote*. Huck Finn, on the other hand, is very poor, almost never goes to school, and is extremely ignorant and humble. His only treasure is his common sense, just like Sancho Panza; from this treasure some of the best chapters in both *Don Quixote* and *Huck Finn* emerge.

The quixotization of Tom Sawyer began in Twain's earlier novel, *The Adventures of Tom Sawyer,* which appeared in 1876. Tom Sawyer, dissatisfied with the ordinary life of his family, his neighbors, and his small community finds models of the heroic life in books and legends from the Anglo-Saxon tradition, and very specifically in the epic legends of the bandit and benefactor of the poor, Robin Hood. Like Alonso Quijano in the first chapters of the Cervantine novel, Tom is transformed into a legendary hero. Luckier than Don Quixote, Tom Sawyer has already managed to attract a friend so that his transformation can find an echo and response in that of the other teenager. They are both at the edge of a great forest:

> Just here the blast of a toy tin trumpet came faintly down the green aisles of the forest. Tom flung off his jacket and trousers, turned a suspender into a belt, raked away some brush behind the rotten log, disclosing a rude bow and arrow, a lath sword and a tin trumpet, and in a moment had seized these things and bounded away, bare legged, with flutter-

ing shirt. . . . Now appeared Joe Harper, as airily clad and elaborately armed as Tom. Tom called:

"Hold! Who comes here into Sherwood Forest without my pass?"

"Guy of Guisborne wants no man's pass. Who art thou that—that—"

"Dares to hold such language," said Tom, prompting—for they were talking "by the book," from memory.

"Who art thou that dares to hold such language?"

"I, indeed! I am Robin Hood, as thy caitiff carcase soon shall know."

"Then art thou indeed that famous outlaw? Right gladly will I dispute with thee the passes of the merry wood. Have at thee!"

They took their lath swords, dumped their other traps on the ground, struck a fencing attitude, foot to foot, and began a grave, careful combat.[12]

The parallels with the first chapters of the Cervantine novel are very clear. They include the heroic and mythic transformation of the main character (in this case, the two main characters), the improvised weapons, the archaic language, and a ritual challenge, although in the case of Mark Twain's text, the awareness of imitating a literary text is clearer, as Tom helps his friend Joe finish a sentence taken from a text that Joe has half-forgotten.

It is worthwhile to point out as well that in the earlier pages of the novel the young Tom Sawyer has found his Dulcinea. She is Becky Thatcher, who must be about ten or eleven years old. And he has made friends with Huck Finn, who plays an essential role in the second novel, *The Adventures of Huckleberry Finn*. If we compare these two novels by Mark Twain with the first and second part of Cervantes's novel we can see that modern critics find the second parts much more interesting than the first, that is, the second part of *Don Quixote* and the novel centered on Huck Finn. In both of these works, the character who was previously subordinate, that is, Sancho in one case and Huck Finn in the other, finds his own voice, dominates center stage, and assumes full awareness of himself, a triumph of common sense over imagination.

Friendship

The parallels between *The Adventures of Huckleberry Finn* and *Don Quixote* are stronger and more decisive than those between *The Adventures of Tom Sawyer* and *Don Quixote*. The novel by Cervantes is, among many other things, the story of a friendship, the friendship that unites Don Quixote and Sancho, and the story of a journey, interrupted for a few days and resumed in the second part of the novel. During this journey the friendship of the two main characters flourishes. The author emphasizes the dialogue between the two and transforms the passing of time into the essential spring. Only the flow of time and the experiences that time carries permit him to explore the characters more deeply, see them from inside, and appreciate the ways in which they change. Don Quixote is no longer the same after he sees his Dulcinea enchanted. He appears dejected, tired, and melancholic. Sancho is not, and cannot be, the same after his adventures in the palace of the duke and duchess and after his triumph and also his failure as governor of Barataria Island. It is the passing of time that makes or breaks the characters, and when the end of the novel is reached, and the Manchegan knight understands that in the nests of the present day one cannot find the birds of days gone by, he recovers his awareness of being Alonso Quijano the Good and prepares himself for death.

In his second novel, Mark Twain allows us to witness the internal transformation of Huck Finn, who in the first novel is presented as a marginal adolescent, despised by almost everyone, the son of a drunk, who little by little becomes aware that society is unjust and cruel in its way of treating slaves. Mark Twain knew this situation well: his father owned three slaves. Huck Finn feels that he has to save and protect Jim, the fugitive slave. In his conscience two value systems are battling: one that corresponds to society, which forces him to report on Jim, and the other to his friendship and solidarity with the slave who is fighting for his freedom.

At this culminating moment in the novel, the influence of Jean Jacques Rousseau, direct or indirect, has to be added to the influence of Cervantes, as Huck Finn closely approaches what we can call the child who is born good and is about to be corrupted by society. Luckily, Huck Finn has grown up like a wild plant, like a naturally good being, despite his appearance and deplorable manners. Sancho is also an ignorant man with no formal education, though he gives evidence of possessing exceptional wisdom and common sense while serving as governor. Sancho is a precursor, in a certain way, to Rousseau's theories on the individual and society.

Again the Picaresque

Another aspect of the Cervantes-Twain relationship springs from the presence of a picaresque atmosphere in the work of both writers. In chapter 2 we referred to the relationship between Cervantes and his use of picaresque literature. It is undeniable that there are aspects, subtleties, and situations in Cervantes's work that clearly remind us of picaresque literature: a few scenes in Don Quixote (the inn, the innkeeper, Maritornes) offer a certain picaresque aspect. With respect to the two novels by Mark Twain, particularly the second, there is contact with the picaresque. "Everyone lies," is the cynical conclusion reached by

Huck Finn. The two characters who are swindlers, the king of France and the dramatic swindler who accompanies him, occupy several central chapters of the novel. Even the way they swindle and deceive the public that is attracted by their so-called theater spectacles can easily remind us of a Cervantine *entremés*, "El retablo de las maravillas" ("The Show of Marvels").[13]

We cannot rule out completely a possible Cervantine influence in this case. Nevertheless, it seems doubtful for various reasons. On one hand, the picaresque occupies a relatively modest place in the total work of Cervantes, and as a whole it is counterbalanced and even surpassed by the Platonizing idealism of the Renaissance that is the polar opposite of the picaresque. And on the other hand, Mark Twain's experiences as a young adult, both on the steamboats that traveled the Mississippi and in the places he visited in the Far West and San Francisco, must have included dozens, perhaps hundreds, of picaresque situations. In other words, Mark Twain lived the picaresque, and for that reason he needed no literary model to approach it. As for the *Exemplary Novels* and the *Entremeses*, it is not very likely that Mark Twain read them because they were not well known by American readers.

Mark Twain ended his days distrusting Christianity and all other religions. The death of his wife and favorite daughter brought on a physical and spiritual depression that inspired his most negative and bitter pages. His daughters, friends, relatives, and editors conspired to keep those comments from being published. They succeeded, and it was only in recent years that they were rediscovered and brought to light for the first time.

Two Critical Views of Society

Another very important parallel between Cervantes's novel and *Huckleberry Finn* is the presentation of the everyday reality surrounding the characters, that is, the realistic description of a society we could call normal. The Spanish master's novel offers us two focuses: one, in part 1, which is described by the Knight of the Green Coat, his house, and his family; the other, in part 2, develops in the several chapters about the duke and duchess, their palace, and their varied residences. Don Quixote's reaction to the tranquil but prosaic life of the Knight of the Green Coat is negative. The horizon that he sees, and that we see, is restricted. It lacks depth and a clear goal; in a word, the Knight of the Green Coat lives a restricted life of limited range because he lacks ideals. Don Quixote cannot spend much time under the roof of that house. As for the palace of the duke and duchess and the aristocrats who live there, Cervantes shows us superficial lives, without love and without ideals, empty lives as stagnant and mechanical as the wooden horse Clavileño, which they use in their attempt to impress Don Quixote and Sancho. Idleness dominates. All seems artificial, especially the taunts with which the duke and duchess receive Don Quixote and Sancho.

Cervantes paints for us a cruel society, with gloomy traits inspired by the picaresque. Examples of this are found in part 1 in the various chapters where the innkeeper and several characters at the inn appear, and also in chapter 4, where the youth Andrés is cruelly whipped by his master, who refuses to pay him for his work, thus pointing up social injustice and the exploitation of the poor.

Mark Twain's *Huck Finn* clearly describes the cruelty of a slave society in which slaves who fled were ferociously pursued and when captured suffered the most severe punishment. The so-called duke of Bridgewater and the so-called king of France spend hours planning to trick and exploit their victims. After listening attentively to a sermon praising the virtues of neighborly love and the brotherhood of all human beings, the members of the Grangeford family spring against an enemy family, the Sheperdsons, in a series of ambushes and fights in which dozens of youths from both sides are killed. Hypocrisy, lying, and cruelty prevail throughout the novel as characteristics typical of society in the American south. Let us not forget that in *The Gilded Age*, published in 1873, Twain had lashed out against venality, corruption, and hypocrisy in other regions and social classes, above all against bankers, businessmen, and politicians when he affirmed that "the only completely criminal class in the country was the members of Congress."

Cervantes's criticism of his society is, of course, more cautious, as we have noted, but one must read between the lines. For example, in the interlude "El retablo de las maravillas" ("The Show of Marvels"), Cervantes attacks and ridicules the obsession with "purity of blood," that is, the pride one has for not having Jewish or Moorish ancestors. In his sonnet "To the Duke of Medina on His Entrance into Cádiz,"[14] Cervantes makes fun of the false pride of one of Spain's haughtiest aristocrats because he "enters triumphantly" into Cádiz only after the English troops have evacuated the city, which they had occupied and sacked for twenty-five days. Yet we should not forget that Cervantes makes fun of all the social classes. In the interlude "La elección de los alcaldes de Daganzo" ("The Selection of the Mayors of Daganzo"), we find a peasant who takes pride in his ignorance and proclaims that the ability to read is dangerous:

> BACHILLER: Do you know how to read, Humillos?
> HUMILLOS: No, certainly not
> and I can't show that in my lineage
> there's one person with such little sense
> that he would learn such chimera,
> that lead men to flames
> and women to the brothel.
> I can't read, but I can do other things
> that are far better than reading.
> BACHILLER: And what things are they?

HUMILLOS: I know by heart
   four complete prayers, and I say them
   each week four and five times.
RANA: And with that you're thinking of becoming
   mayor?
HUMILLOS: With that, and the fact I'm an Old
   Christian, I'd dare be a Roman senator.[15]

The message here is that because Humillos is illiterate he is qualified to become mayor since being illiterate means that he is a Christian of long standing as opposed to the cultured city people who are suspected of being new Christians (converts) and of having divided loyalties.

Cervantes had to be much more mindful of his criticism than Mark Twain. The person of the king was untouchable, both physically and figuratively. This sort of situation was not limited to Spain alone. In the works of Shakespeare, we find no criticism of Queen Elizabeth I, direct or indirect. The same occurs in the plays of Molière with respect to Louis XVI. Mark Twain, however, wrote at a time when freedom of the press was protected by the Constitution, and so he could make the strong assertion he did in *The Gilded Age* calling congressmen criminals.

Humor and Beyond

Both Cervantes and Mark Twain were fully aware of the high literary and moral value that humor can attain. Laughter is born of the absurd, from surprises, and from the shock that the unexpected produces. It is also born of the subconscious, the hidden desire we have to see someone make a mistake, so that we, who do not make a mistake, feel superior. Like the Aztec gods, humor frequently requires victims. The most difficult part for us, even for a professional humorist, is to be able to laugh at ourselves. When we do so, we reveal and see ourselves from the inside and outside at the same time, which increases our self-awareness, without which there can be no true wisdom. In effect, laughter is a source of knowledge and wisdom. If humor shows us a disorderly, chaotic world in which there is an abundance of foolishness, stupidity, and madness, sooner or later we feel the need to seek the source of the mistake, and if such a thing is possible, to correct it where it is found—in individuals, in society, or in our own selves.

Neither Cervantes nor Twain was merely and exclusively a humorist. The great novel by Cervantes quickly met with international fame and success and, quite possibly through a misunderstanding, it seemed to be a highly comical novel. This explains, in part, why some critics and literary figures in Spain during the time of Cervantes did not give Cervantes's work the attention and credit it deserved. We should keep in mind a cultural factor that may seem slightly absurd to us today: the great literary tradition, starting with Homer, had always been one of epic or lyrical poetry and theater. The novel was a relatively new genre. It was customary to read stories after dinner in the inns where travelers stayed the night. For this reason, many early novels were divided into episodes. An example is *Lazarillo de Tormes*. As with any new idea, the novel did not have the same respect and admiration as the theater had. In Cervantes's time, poets like Lope de Vega wrote poetry and plays, and the latter were always or almost always in verse. Dazzled by Lope de Vega, the reading public neither knew how to appreciate Cervantes nor understood that his message was more universal and coincided much more with a vision of the modern world, one in which it is not easy to bend the forces of nature. The characters in *Don Quixote* obey the rules of the physical and material world of the *nuova scienza* as the Italians said, which is physics. Sancho, tossed in a blanket into the air, launched upwards, keeps falling again and again;

for each action there is a corresponding and opposite reaction, as Newton would discover two generations later. Our illusions and those of Don Quixote are exposed; they erode, wear down, weaken, and disappear to the degree that events contradict them and the world keeps changing. It is a double-edged sword: a source of knowledge and joy for certain spectators and an intimate tragedy for those who are losing their illusions. This happens to Don Quixote in part 2 when he discovers the enchanted Dulcinea and above all at the end of the novel itself when he is beaten by the bachelor Sansón Carrasco in chapter 64 of part 2.

The greatness of a literary work becomes more and more visible as we become aware that the work gives rise to various interpretations, to divergent readings, just as a diamond with its many facets casts its glitter in different directions. Next to a comical Don Quixote we find a tragic Quixote, discovered and especially valued by German Romantic critics in the nineteenth century and then exalted and almost venerated by Unamuno, who turns him into a hero and nearly a saint. The Manchegan knight becomes a symbol of the highest hopes and the most exalted moral values and of the frustration that follows when one is not able to achieve them. In this respect, he is also a symbol of a Spain where it was not possible to achieve all the goals that one pursued.

It is worth noting that there is an entire aspect to the work of Mark Twain, most especially in the novel *The Adventures of Huckleberry Finn*, that goes beyond the strict limits of a humorous novel or a novel for adolescents and turns the book into a work of universal appeal. It is also worth keeping in mind that his novels were not fully appreciated when they were first published. The reason, in part, is that these novels were written for an adolescent public, which restricted his subject matter. In Victorian times some themes, such as sexual experiences, were deemed too daring and consequently were not acceptable for young people. Twain gave very popular public lectures in which he turned into a comic actor, almost a clown. It was difficult, then, for official and academic critics to take him seriously. But Twain himself knew well that the reach and depth of some of his works far surpassed the level of the purely comical. In his autobiography, he denies having been a pure and simple humorist, pointing out that throughout his life many other humorists — and he gives a list of seventy-eight names — captured the attention of the public for a time and then were quickly forgotten simply because they were humorists and nothing more. Naked humor is only a perfume or a decoration, but sometimes a message is concealed behind the humor. Then the text gains eternal life. Mark Twain's message is that one must fight every day against hypocrisy, stupidity, and evil, and the work in which this message appears most clearly is *The Adventures of Huckleberry Finn*.

Constructing the Novels

The central part in *The Adventures of Huckleberry Finn* is the long and slow journey of Huck and Jim sailing on a boat down the Mississippi, a journey that is at the same time an intensive education and a rite of passage to maturity for Huck. It is a series of lessons about the true character of individuals and society. In the course of the novel Twain introduces us to swindlers, charlatans, liars, cruel racists, and hardened criminals, among whom Huck maintains his integrity and affirms himself as a youth — almost a man — who is capable of risking his life to protect the freedom of the slave, Jim, who is in constant danger of being betrayed and returned to his owner. Indeed, Jim is recognized and captured, but he will be saved and given his freedom thanks to the efforts of Huck and his partner and friend Tom Sawyer.

Each novel contains some chapters that are more significant and dramatic than others, chapters that we could call the centers of gravity of the story. *Don Quixote* is much longer than *Huckleberry Finn,* and the inexhaustible imagination of Cervantes offers us a great number of chapters, each of which might seem to be the central, essential one. The earliest chapters are decisive, as in them we see the transformation of Alonso Quijano into Don Quixote de la Mancha. But others stand out as well—the adventure of the windmills, and the episodes with the lion, the wineskins in the inn, the show of Master Pedro, the enchanted Dulcinea, the Cave of Montesinos . . . the list can go on, and every reader can make his or her own list.

The decisive chapter in *Huckleberry Finn,* the axis of the novel, is chapter 16, in which Huck lies for the first time (he will have to lie many times more) so that no one will discover that Jim is a fugitive slave. Huck Finn is asked if there is anyone accompanying him (Jim is hidden), and he replies yes, a white man is accompanying him. Before and after the lie there is a heroic fight in Huck's mind and heart; all that he has heard and learned from his society and culture—a slave society and a culture that in great part is hypocritical—requires that he turn in the slave, but his heart tells him to save Jim. Nevertheless, this heroic act is followed by regret. It was difficult to oppose the norms of a society like that of the southern United States in those years, when the law, customs, and public opinion decisively supported the institution of slavery. In this way, the novel becomes a symbol and code for the doubts, the regrets, the passions, and the rebellious acts that would culminate in the Civil War with Lincoln, Lee, Grant, and the emancipation of the slaves. It is, then, a novel and history at the same time, or rather, a novel that contains at its core elements that would shape history.

Similarly, *Don Quixote* contains elements of heroism, madness, and wretchedness as well as the Platonic ideals and picaresque degradation of the Renaissance. These factors not only shaped Spanish society in Cervantes's era, but they also were the key to the greatest triumphs and the saddest defeats of Spain in the Golden Age. We should add that on another level, the two novels are organized around two journeys: the journey through central and southern Spain, from la Mancha to upper Andalucía, with a long trip to Barcelona, which Cervantes praised lavishly as the cradle of courtesy and culture, and in Mark Twain's novel, the journey down the mighty Mississippi, which is almost like the sea, with picturesque towns lining its shores, steamboats with high smokestacks and great paddlewheels on each side, and on the horizon, the fields cultivated by slaves like Jim who dream of freedom.

It is also important to emphasize that in both novels we witness the development of a friendship between characters who at the beginning seem to have little in common. There are great social, cultural, physical, and intellectual disparities between Don Quixote and Sancho. Huck Finn, a white boy, resembles the black Jim only in his ignorance. This is more evident when Huck is with Tom Sawyer, who seems to have read all the books in the world, or at least all the adventure books.

Literature turns into a labyrinth of mirrors. This is an audacious experiment, and yet it suggests the idea that language may suddenly bite its own tail like a strange serpent. Mark Twain offers us: "All generalizations are false, including this one." Cervantes plays with this labyrinth of mirrors in part 2 of his novel, in chapters 2, 4, and 5, when Sancho announces to Don Quixote that his adventures have been registered and printed. Don Quixote becomes alarmed but curious and wishes to read his own adventures, his own life as a character in a novel, and the story of this interaction is then influential in part 2 of the novel. Mark Twain offers us a very similar experiment. In *The Adventures of Tom Sawyer*, Tom and his friends Joe and Huck have run away from home looking for adventures. The entire town believes them dead, most likely drowned. Gathered in the church as the bells ring, dressed in mourning, the congregation listens to the funeral rites as the Protestant minister reviews the lives of the three boys, emphasizing the positive aspects and forgetting the negative, between the sobs of the congregation, while the three boys listen to a retelling of their lives from a hiding place in the upper gallery. Suddenly they make a dramatic, triumphant appearance at the end of the eulogy. Literature within literature, as the eulogy has been a literary genre ever since the times of the great church orators of the Spanish Golden Age and Bossuet in France. In Twain's telling, two kinds of lives face each other: the "real" life of the boys meets the virtuous, corrected, and ennobled life of the minister's sermon.

We see that the similarity between Cervantes and Mark Twain increases as we penetrate into the life experience of their main characters and analyze the stylistic resources of both writers. They are also united by the fact that both were professional writers. The two were deeply familiar with their societies and portrayed them faithfully and honestly. Humor was for both of them a double-edged sword, a luminous blade that provides us with the joy of laughter and a sharp and tragic blade that reveals the meanness and cruelty of human life. In their main works, the two take their characters, step by step, to universality and eternal fame through provincial places that are difficult to find on a map: a town on the banks of a great river and, on the other side of the Atlantic, the plains of La Mancha, the poorest, the least beckoning, and the least picturesque part of the arid Spanish plateau.

8

Sightings of Cervantes and His Knight in the Twentieth Century

The twentieth century has introduced new ways of telling a story through film, television, and the Internet, which break with traditional forms. Now books are made into films or television series or seen as DVDs. Technology has provided us with new visual means to communicate a tale. In spite of these innovations, Don Quixote, a character born as the Renaissance faded, and Cervantes's literary devices continue to play an important role with contemporary writers.

Don Quixote was influential in the twentieth century in his own country. At the turn of the century he came to symbolize Spain, which had reached a low point in its history in 1898 when it lost the last of its colonies. The political and economic decline was acute. In 1895, Miguel de Unamuno (1864–1936), philosopher, essayist, and rector of the University of Salamanca published a collection of his essays under the title *Vida de Don Quijote y Sancho* (*The Life of Don Quixote and Sancho with Related Essays*).[1]

In these essays, Unamuno interprets Cervantes's novel chapter by chapter. His interpretation is subjective and reveals a Romantic viewpoint that shows his preference for individualism and action. He was a spiritual rebel at odds with the Spanish attitudes of his day regarding politics, religion, and culture. Unamuno identifies with Don Quixote's passion and anguish because he, too, had a dream for the rebirth of Spain. For him, Don Quixote symbolizes "the eternal essence of Spain," and he believes that only through a renewal of its spiritual qualities and reaffirmation of the heroic ideals of the Manchegan knight can the Spaniards of his day save their national pride and integrity. While praising Don Quixote's heroic qualities, Unamuno complains that Cervantes does not fully understand the essence of his character. In saying this, Unamuno is suggesting that Don Quixote is so authentic that he lives as an autonomous being outside the confines of Cervantes's novel. Unamuno totally ignores the humor in the novel and chooses to focus on the tragic situation that Don Quixote finds himself in. Given Unamuno's preoccupation with Spain's decline and his personal tragic sense of life, one is not surprised that his interpretation is sober and moving. One feels his passion and anguish, too, as he comments on Don Quixote's attempts to realize his noble goals and on his repeated failures.

UNAMUNO'S *NIEBLA:* AN EXPERIMENTAL NOVEL

In 1914, Unamuno published his novel, *Niebla (Mist)*. This is an experimental work that he hesitated to call a novel, and in fact the subtitle is "Nivola," a made-up word that suggests that the book should be deemed an experiment. Although the first chapters tell a conventional story, the end of the book makes us think of Cervantes's technique of playing reality against fiction and vice versa. The plot involves a young wealthy man, Augusto Pérez, who falls in love with a woman who at first rejects him in favor of a young man with Bohemian tastes. Finally, she accepts Augusto and marries him only to abandon him later. She goes back to her first love. Augusto, who is heartbroken, contemplates suicide. He decides to travel to Salamanca, where Unamuno lives. Augusto has read his essay on suicide, and he hopes to receive his advice. Augusto soon realizes that he is not "real" but instead a character in a novel, born from a writer's imagina-

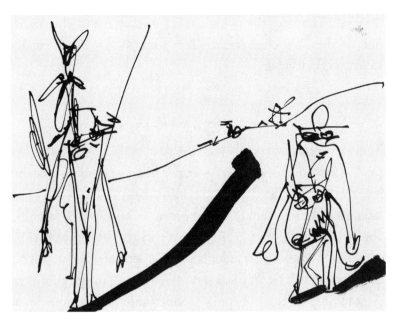

Antonio Saura, *Todo eso no me descontenta*, 1987. Indian ink on paper. © 2005 Artists Rights Society (ARS), New York / ADAGP, Paris.

tion. When he declares his intention to kill himself, Unamuno objects. Augusto has no will of his own and cannot commit suicide without the permission of his creator. Back home, he over-eats and soon falls ill. He still has time to send Unamuno a short telegram: "You win. I am dead."

This device of the character having an independent life outside of the fictional work and at the same time having the role of the main character in the work recalls Cervantes's literary ingenuity. As we remember, the characters in part 2 have read part 1 and consider Don Quixote and Sancho as characters in the novel. The knight and the squire step out of the pages of the novel in part 2 and discuss their former life, the events depicted in part 1, with the duke and duchess although Don Quixote and Sancho are part of the fictional work. Cervantes does not dwell on this, and part 2 develops smoothly, in a natural, logical way that we do not question. Unamuno, however, focuses his attention on the main character's escape from the novel and creates something artificial.

THE GREAT GATSBY: A SELF-CREATING HERO

Many cosmologists claim that the first milliseconds following the Big Bang are of great importance if we want to understand how the universe developed from its birth until the present. The same could be said about the first pages of *Don Quixote*. It would not be difficult to find in them incidents that have given birth to similar themes and incidents in twentieth-century novels. A case in point is F. Scott Fitzgerald's *The Great Gatsby*, published in 1925, in particular chapter 5, which resembles chapter 1 of part 1 of Cervantes's novel.

Both heroes require a dress code: Don Quixote wears his old armor; Jay Gatsby has "his massed suits and dressing gowns and ties, and his shirts piled like bricks in stacks a dozen high."[2] Gatsby is propelled by ambition and love. He wants to forget his rather humble origins: "His parents were shiftless and unsuccessful farm people—his imagination had never really accepted them as his parents at all. The truth was that Jay Gatsby of West Egg, Long Island, sprang from his Platonic conception of himself... so he invented just the sort of Jay Gatsby that a seventeen year old boy would be likely to invent, and to this conception he was faithful to the end."[3]

Fitzgerald (1896–1940) describes the inner process of the creation of the future Jay Gatsby. We are present at his nightly musings as he conjures up a new reality for himself. Although a well-hewn exterior was forming, his mind and soul were troubled:

> For over a year he had been beating his way along the
> south shore of Lake Superior as a clam-digger and a
> salmon-fisher or in any other capacity that brought

him food and bed. His brown, hardening body lived naturally through the half-fierce, half-lazy work of the bracing days. . . . But his heart was in a constant, turbulent riot. The most grotesque and fantastic conceits haunted him in his bed at night. A universe of ineffable gaudiness spun itself out in his brain while the clock ticked on the washstand and the moon soaked with wet light his tangled clothes upon the floor. Each night he added to the pattern of his fancies until drowsiness closed down upon some vivid scene with an oblivious embrace. For a while these reveries provided an outlet for his imagination; they were a satisfactory hint of the unreality of reality, a promise that the rock of the world was founded securely on a fairy's wing.[4]

Daisy is as elusive as Dulcinea. Jay Gatsby's beloved is of flesh and blood unlike Dulcinea, but both take shape as a figment of their admirer's imagination. Daisy tells Jay that she does not love him in the same way that he loves her. Both Don Quixote and Jay Gatsby are in love with love. Jay, however, is more notably driven in his quest for success. Not even the presence of the woman he loves, Daisy, makes him forget completely his dreams of wealth and glory and his fantasy of being superior to others, almost invincible: "There must have been moments even that afternoon when Daisy tumbled short of his dreams—not through her own fault, but because of the colossal vitality of his illusion. It had gone beyond her, beyond everything. He had thrown himself into it with a creative passion, adding to it all the time, decking it out with every bright feather that drifted his way. No amount of fire or freshness can challenge what a man will store up in his ghostly heart."[5]

Just as Alonso Quijano requires a new name for his new personality, James Gatz will morph into Jay Gatsby. "James Gatz—

that was really, or at least legally, his name. He had changed it at the age of seventeen and at the specific moment that witnessed the beginning of his career—when he saw Dan Cody's yacht drop anchor over the most insidious flat on Lake Superior. It was James Gatz who had been loafing along the beach that afternoon in a torn jersey and a pair of canvas pants, but it was already Jay Gatsby who borrowed a rowboat, pulled out to the *Tuolomee,* and informed Cody that a wind might catch him and break him up in half an hour."[6] Cody is fifty years old and many times a millionaire. Gatsby becomes "in turn steward, mate, skipper, secretary, and even jailor, for Dan Cody sober knew what lavish doings Dan Cody drunk might soon be about, and he provided for such contingencies by reposing more and more trust in Gatsby."[7]

The novel has introduced us to a Gatsby who is now rich and famous, and, like Don Quixote in part 2, is the subject of speculation and gossip: "Gatsby's notoriety, spread about by the hundreds who had accepted his hospitality and so become authorities about his past, had increased all summer until he fell just short of being news. Contemporary legends such as 'the underground pipe-line to Canada' attached themselves to him, and there was one persistent story that he didn't live in a house at all, but in a boat that looked like a house and was moved secretly up and down the Long Island shore."[8]

Further parallels appear when we read on. Both Don Quixote and Gatsby are self-absorbed narcissists who are deeply attached to an idealized self, incapable of criticizing their own faults and not above manipulating their friends, their allies, and their servants. Gatsby's fantasy world overpowers his troubled, conflicted inner world, whereas Don Quixote presses on guided by his code of chivalry. He is purer and more naive: his world does not include carnal love, passion for money, bootlegging, contact with dubious individuals who may turn out to be gangsters, and the acquisition of drugstores where most of the profits will come from the illegal sale of alcohol. Gatsby's message to the reader is: "Welcome to the modern world." As Cervantes, Voltaire, and Flaubert had done before, Fitzgerald is critical of his society and his times, the so-called Jazz Age. In spite of his faults, Gatsby outshines the other characters (except the narrator). They are callous, greedy, and ungrateful. They forget about him after he dies and do not attend his funeral.

GRAHAM GREENE AND THE
ECCLESIASTIC DON QUIXOTE

The English novelist Graham Greene (1904–91) has written very successful thrillers that he called "entertainments" and also serious novels concerned with the moral, social, and religious problems of our times. He converted to Catholicism in 1926. One of his main subjects is the presence of evil in our midst, often combined with moral doubts, suspense, and fear. In *Monsignor Quixote* (1982), he borrows from Cervantes the concept of the duality of viewpoints through the dialogue of two friends in order to present the opposing dogmas of Catholicism and communism. One of them is a priest, whose family name is Quixote. He calls his decrepit old car Rocinante and roams through present-day Spain in the company of a communist mayor, who has just lost his position and needs a vacation. Their conversation is lively, witty, but never bitter. Like two good fencers, they attack and parry without either one being seriously wounded. Quixote calls his friend Sancho who often makes fun of religious subjects and religious books, and Quixote complains: "'You can mock *me* as much as you like, Sancho. What makes me sad is when you mock my books, for they mean more to me than myself. They are all the faith I have and all the hope.'" And also: "'I know I am a poor priest errant, traveling God knows where. I know that there are absurdities in some of my books as there were in the books of chivalry my ancestor collected. That didn't mean that all chivalry was absurd. Whatever absurdities you can dig out of my books, I still have faith.'"[9]

The parallels with Cervantes's novel are obvious, and at the same time striking differences appear. Sancho, the communist ex-mayor, is much more intellectual than Cervantes's character. Also, Greene's Sancho is in possession of his own sacred books, around which he has organized his thoughts and even his life. He carries some of these books with him, among them the *Communist Manifesto* and some of Lenin's writings. He prefers Marx's *Manifesto* to his *Das Kapital,* which he finds too abstruse and dry. St. Theresa of Lisieux, who takes the role of Quixote's Dulcinea, is a dead woman, a saint instead of the earthy farm girl and idealized lady. Another difference is the sexual theme, which Greene's two main characters discuss freely.

In Greene's novel, misunderstandings propel the action. After a while, Monsignor Quixote is held to be mad. His bishop forbids him to say Mass. A road accident kills him, but in his agony his faith is reborn. Delirious, he says a truncated Mass, and both human and divine love seem reborn for a few seconds. Graham Greene's interpretation is like Unamuno's basically Romantic vision, underlining the noblest feelings associated with Cervantes's hero—faith, kindness, and courage.

FRANZ KAFKA AND A TWIST: DON QUIXOTE AS SANCHO, SANCHO AS DON QUIXOTE

Kafka's novels and short stories are often brooding, disturbing, and troubling. They remind the reader of a familiar face seen in a distorting mirror. It is worth underlining that Kafka mentions in his works only two classical authors, Homer and Cervantes.

What Kafka (1883–1924) has to say about Don Quixote and

Sancho is puzzling and confusing. In the short story, "The Truth About Sancho Panza," Kafka describes Sancho as follows: "Without making any boast of it Sancho Panza succeeded in the course of years, by feeding him a great number of romances of chivalry and adventure in the evening and night hours, in so diverting from himself his demon, whom he later called Don Quixote, that this demon thereupon set out, uninhibited, on the maddest exploits, which, however, for the lack of a preordained object, which should have been Sancho Panza himself, harmed nobody. A free man, Sancho Panza philosophically followed Don Quixote on his crusades, perhaps out of a sense of responsibility, and had of them a great and edifying entertainment to the end of his days."[10]

In this short story, which has overtones of a parable, we notice the importance of Sancho. Don Quixote's role has changed. He is only an emanation of Sancho, a product of Sancho's ambition or longings. He has become a part of Sancho, a demon, tamed and cast off by Sancho's willpower, who then goes forth in search of adventure. Sancho follows Don Quixote out of a sense of responsibility. If Don Quixote is but an emanation of Sancho's mind, he is almost like a rebellious, unpredictable son who has to be watched by his father. We know that in part 2 of Cervantes's novel, Sancho grows self-assured and more independent than his master. He becomes governor of Barataria, and at the end of the novel he seems to have more energy and more projects than his master. Still, as a reflection on Cervantes's novel as a whole, Kafka's text seems to be incomplete, puzzling, and questionable.

Here is a possible interpretation: Kafka wrote his short piece in 1917. The First World War was raging, and the Austro-Hungarian Empire was collapsing. Perhaps it was the right moment to underline the importance of common sense and to exalt Sancho, a man of peace, a pragmatist full of common sense, rather than an idealist like Don Quixote.

PARALLEL UNIVERSES: JORGE LUIS BORGES, PIERRE MÉNARD, AND DON QUIXOTE

Borges (1899–1986) and Kafka have much in common. Both like parables. Kafka's parables tend to be mysterious, dark, and tragic. Borges's parables are more whimsical, sometimes contradictory and ambiguous, often disconcerting, and occasionally irritating. Borges plays games, invents nonexistent literary works, even encyclopedias. He creates fake footnotes; in other words, he has fun and at the same time sends messages for the reader to decipher. This technique is reminiscent of that found in murder mysteries where the reader may eventually guess the identity of the murderer after uncovering clues along the way.

Borges's "Pierre Ménard, Autor del Quijote"("Pierre Ménard, Author of *Don Quixote*") is full of pitfalls and hidden traps where the innocent reader can easily be ensnared. Are we reading an essay, a short story, or an obituary-cum-bibliography? It is obvious from the very beginning that Borges is writing tongue-in-cheek about a nonexistent author whose fake bibliography contains several fabricated items—we soon come to the conclusion that it is entirely fake.

The point of Borges's essay is that the French author Pierre Ménard admires Cervantes's novel, wishes to recreate it, and tries to do so, although his work is unfinished. He makes an effort to think like Cervantes, to learn seventeenth-century Spanish, and ultimately this effort is partially successful: he recreates two chapters of the novel. When the original text is placed side by side with the new text written by Ménard, something extraordinary happens. We are aware that the two paragraphs, placed side by side, are identical, and yet we are told the meaning is not the same. What has happened? Although Borges never says it, the passing of time has altered, however slightly, the meaning of words and sentences and ultimately the meaning of the whole book. The novel written by Cervantes has split, bifurcated (like the garden paths of another tale by Borges), and has become thousands of novels as it has acquired thousands of readers, one of these being Pierre Ménard: "Being, somehow, Cervantes, and arriving thereby at the *Quixote*—that looked to Ménard less challenging (and therefore less interesting) than continuing to be Pierre Ménard and coming to the *Quixote* through the experiences of Pierre Ménard."[11]

Borges has played enough with his readers. It is time to reverse the tables and ask for a real meaning. Possibly he is hinting at the "reception theory" of literary criticism, which is that each reader reacts in a personal, subjective way to the books he or she reads, and this personal reaction constitutes the core of critical understanding for each individual reader. But if we rely exclusively on our own experience, there is much we may miss in the text. Borges does not dwell on the possible weakness of the subjective approach to criticism, an approach that ultimately makes discussion of literary works impossible or fruitless. Borges's approach to criticism is ironic and devastating. We are close to laughter and perhaps also close to understanding the meaning of this "essay," when we read:

> It is a revelation to compare the *Don Quixote* of Pierre Ménard with that of Miguel de Cervantes. Cervantes, for example, wrote the following (Part I, Chapter IX):
>
>> . . . truth, whose mother is history, rival of time, depository of deeds, witness of the past, exemplar and adviser to the present, and the future's counselor.
>
> This catalogue of attributes, written in the seventeenth century, and written by the "ingenious layman" Miguel de Cervantes, is mere rhetorical praise of history. Ménard, on the other hand, writes:

... truth, whose mother is history, rival
of time, depository of deeds, witness of
the past, exemplar and adviser to the
present, and the future's counselor.

History, the *mother* of truth!—the idea is stagger-
ing. Ménard, a contemporary of William James, defines history not as a *delving into* reality, but as the
very *fount* of reality. Historical truth, for Ménard,
is not "what happened"; it is what *we believe* happened. The final phrases—exemplar and adviser to
the present, and the future's counselor—are braz-
enly pragmatic.[12]

The words used to define history are the same, but their meaning is not, simply because the cultural horizon has shifted toward
relativity. Starting with the Enlightenment and Kant's philosophy, this fact erodes the belief in an absolute, immutable truth
in the field of history, accessible to true, devoted, scientific historians. Whatever Cervantes may have thought about history,
we are today less confident of reaching a perfect understanding
of the past, and Borges's essay (or is it an obituary?) states this
in an ironic and oblique fashion; there will always be room for
another interpretation of the past. This applies to Cervantes's
novel, which will be the subject of new interpretations as new
generations appear on the historic horizon. Borges himself has
stated again and again that his readers have interpreted whatever he wrote and that basically it is up to them to decide on
the meaning of his work. In "Borges and I," moreover, he sees
himself as having a double personality: "It's Borges, the other
one, that things happen to. . . . Years ago I tried to free myself
from him, and I moved on from the mythologies of the slums
and outskirts of the city to games with time and infinity, but
those games belong to Borges now, and I shall have to think up

other things. So my life is a point-counterpoint, a kind of fugue, and a falling away—and everything winds up being lost to me, and everything falls into oblivion, or into the hands of the other man. I'm not sure which of us it is that's writing this page."[13]

It would not be too difficult to apply Borges's parable to Cervantes and to his writings. The man who wrote *Don Quixote* was perhaps only one of the two faces of Cervantes, and the complexities of *Don Quixote* may have been distant, even alien, to the Cervantes who wrote *Persiles and Sigismunda*.

CERVANTES AND THE THEATER: LUIGI PIRANDELLO AND TENNESSEE WILLIAMS

Cervantes's influence has extended to other literary genres, in particular the theater. We are thinking of the distinguished Italian playwright Luigi Pirandello and the mid-twentieth-century American playwright Tennessee Williams (1911–83). They take on the task of defining what is real and what is fiction, along with raising the questions of identity, free will, and circumstance, much the same as Cervantes did.

Luigi Pirandello (1867–1936), winner of the Nobel Prize for Literature in 1934, would probably be included in any list of the ten most influential dramatists of the twentieth century. His *Six Characters in Search of an Author* premiered in 1921, and it has become a classic of the modern stage. It deals primarily with the interaction between literature and real life, and the Spanish historian and critic Américo Castro was the first to call attention to the similarity between this play and Cervantes's novel in an article published in the Buenos Aires daily *La Nación* (*The Nation*) in 1924, later reprinted in his book *Hacia Cervantes* (*Toward Cervantes*) in 1967.

Pirandello's play begins when a group of actors and a director are rehearsing a new play by Pirandello on an empty stage.

Another group, a fifty-year-old father, an anguished mother, a rebellious stepdaughter, a son, and two young children, interrupt the actors and director. The father explains to the dumfounded director that they have come out of the imagination of an author who created them but never fully developed their characters and their relationships. Now abandoned and incomplete, they are looking for a new author who can turn them into real, finished characters who will be given new life in a play that will be a first-rate work of art. Each character tries to explain his problems and his confused and troubled relationship with the others. A shouting match follows, and the suggestions by the director and the actors are rejected as ridiculous or impossible. The characters' personalities and destinies need control, a control that only art, in the shape of a good play, can give them. Fulfillment has to wait until a good author crafts a good play— but yet both the director and the actors come up with inept suggestions. Humankind's paramount wish, self-knowledge, is cast in doubt.

América Castro underlines the importance and the novelty of having a character become conscious of his own existence within a work of literature. Does Pirandello consciously imitate Cervantes? It is possible but not certain. Once a literary device is published and enters the public consciousness, it becomes part of a culture and may be used again and again without a strict reference to its origins. It can be said that *Six Characters* is not strictly using the device of "a play within a play," as Shakespeare did in *Hamlet*, nor does it make use of short stories within the general narrative, as Cervantes did in *Don Quixote*. It is, rather, "the rehearsal of a play interrupted by the characters of another, unfinished play," and what links it to the Spanish novel is, as Castro points out, the fact that "modern literature owes to Cervantes the art of establishing interferences between what is real and what is imagined. . . . We find in his novel for the first time a character that talks about himself as a character, who claims for himself an existence that is at the same time real and literary, and claims the right of not being treated carelessly."[14] This brings to mind Unamuno's Augusto in *Niebla*, published seven years before.

Pirandello's play pits the main characters against the director and the actors, who are incapable of understanding what is happening and ultimately deny that the characters can take charge of their own destiny. "Is he wounded, is he really wounded?" exclaims the director on hearing the revolver shot and the anguished scream of the mother. The actors deny it: "Don't believe it! It is a fiction, all fiction!" The characters remain isolated and misunderstood. In Cervantes's novel, the two main characters are suspicious when they realize that their adventures have been written down and published by a Moorish historian, who probably has distorted the truth. Their irritation knows no bounds when they also realize they are the subject of another narrative, this time penned by a mysterious writer who uses a false name—Avellaneda—who has completely misunderstood and distorted their personality.

The counterfeit *Quixote* written by the enigmatic Avellaneda describes several secondary characters around the two main ones, Don Quixote and Sancho. One of these minor characters is a certain Don Álvaro Tarfe, scion of a well-known family from Granada. As if by chance, this character seems to come out of the Avellaneda novel and enter the one by Cervantes, just as in Pirandello's play, not the actors but the characters that they are going to portray take on a life of their own and begin to question the author. Cervantes (or is it Cide Hamete Benengeli?) has a surprise in store for this character, for the spurious Avellaneda, and also for the readers of Avellaneda's fake novel. In part 2, chapter 72, Don Quixote and Sancho are guests at an inn. A traveler on horseback arrives, along with his servants, one of whom says to the traveler: "'Señor Don Álvaro Tarfe, your grace can spend the hottest part of the day here: the inn seems clean and cool.' Hearing this, Don Quixote said to Sancho: 'Look, Sancho: when I leafed through that book about the second part of my history [he is talking about the Avellaneda fake version of the novel], it seems to me I happened to run across this name of Don Álvaro Tarfe.'" Sancho concurs and suggests that they question the traveler. Don Quixote asks the traveler about his destination. The answer: "'I, Señor,' responded the gentleman, 'am going to Granada, which is my home.'"

"'A fine home!' replied Don Quixote. 'But would your grace please be so kind as to tell me your name.' . . . 'My name is Don Álvaro Tarfe,' responded the guest at the inn," after which Don Quixote asks him whether he is the Álvaro Tarfe who appears in the novel written "by a modern author," meaning the imposter Avellaneda. "'I am,' responded the gentleman, 'and Don Quixote, the principal subject of this history, was a great friend of mine.'" Don Quixote then asks: "'And, Señor Don Álvaro, can your grace tell me if I resemble in any way the Don Quixote you have mentioned?' 'No, certainly not,' responded the guest, 'not at all'" (Gr., 924–25).

The rebellion of the characters against the author, that is to say, Avellaneda, is complete. Cervantes accomplishes a literary feat. By contrasting his characters with the ones created by Avellaneda, he makes his Don Quixote and Sancho much more real and convincing and at the same time discredits the ones created by Avellaneda. Cervantes's use of a character portraying another fictional character is more enjoyable and more impressive if we read it after seeing or reading Pirandello's play. We realize that every literary character is full of possibilities, perhaps not totally expressed by the author, and we come to believe that, as Unamuno has remarked, Don Quixote is more real and more enduring than thousands of people we have encountered during our life.

Tennessee Williams's play *Camino Real* (*The Royal Way*) went through an elaborate process of rewriting, from its premiere in New Haven in 1948 to its Broadway opening in 1953 to its subsequent publication the same year. With each revision, the role of Don Quixote became more important. His is more than a cameo appearance. The Spanish knight is for Williams a symbol of endurance and hope. In this difficult play, hope is an emotional element in the midst of fear and anguish.

Don Quixote becomes an archetype, a noble human being seeking dignity and love in a contemporary world where dignity and love are fast disappearing. The title *Camino Real* has two meanings, since the Spanish word *real* means both "royal" and "real," thus suggesting both the world of lofty goals and that of banal cravings. Williams tries to explain his purpose in the foreword of his play: "My desire was to give these audiences my own sense of something wild and unrestricted that ran like water in the mountains, or clouds changing shape in a gale, or the continually dissolving and transforming images of a dream. This sort of freedom is not chaos nor anarchy. On the contrary, it is the result of painstaking design, and in this work I have given more conscious attention to form and construction, than I have in any work before. Freedom is not achieved simply by working freely."[15] Neither the public nor the critics understood fully the play's message. In the play, Don Quixote and Sancho, Lord Byron, Casanova, Marguerite Gautier, a Gypsy and her daughter Esmeralda, and Kilroy, among others, are characters traveling a mysterious road going nowhere—and, at the same time, everywhere, starting in a spacious plaza that has been described as "a weigh station for lost souls."

Intimations of death, decay, and anguish are never far away from some of the characters. We see a superannuated Casanova and an aging, lonely Marguerite Gautier. Don Quixote, who is not younger than they are, is being deserted by Sancho Panza who exclaims: "I'm going back to La Mancha!" Don Quixote asks: "Without me?" And Sancho replies: "With you or without you, old tireless and tiresome master." Don Quixote feels very tired: he will sleep for a while and dream. "And my dream will be a pageant, a masque in which old meanings will be remembered and possibly new ones discovered, and when I wake up from this sleep and this disturbing pageant of a dream, I'll choose one among its shadows to take along with me in the place of Sancho."[16]

It can be argued that the rest of the play is a dream within Don Quixote's dream. In it we see familiar and unfamiliar characters come and go. The fountain at the center of the plaza has dried out. Cynicism and sincerity do battle inside of Kilroy, who stands for Everyman. Poetic dialogue follows with rapid-fire adventures where many characters appear and disappear like mirages. Don Quixote wakes up and approaches the fountain. It begins to flow again; he drinks from it and bathes in its basin. He advises Kilroy: "Don't! Pity! Your! Self! . . . The wounds of the vanity, the many offenses our egos have to endure, being housed in bodies that age and hearts that grow tired, are better accepted with a tolerant smile—like *this!* You *see?* . . . Otherwise what you become is a bag full of curdled cream—*leche mala,* we call it!—attractive to nobody, least of all to yourself!" Finally he asks Kilroy whether he has any plans. Kilroy wants to escape. Quixote says: "Good! Come with me." Kilroy asks: "¿Dónde?" To which Don Quixote answers: "¡Quién sabe!" Don Quixote ends the play: he raises his lance in a formal gesture and cries out hoarsely, powerfully: *"The violets in the mountains have broken the rocks!"*[17] answering the anguished question of another character, who thought flowers were weaker than rocks. Don Quixote thus affirms the nobility and endurance of the human spirit. We can conclude that the author has ordered his play around an axis of hope and willpower, Don Quixote, in spite of its apparently chaotic and confusing composition. Don Quixote has only a short appearance in *Camino Real*, yet it is revealing of his enduring presence on the modern stage.

In the musical *Man of La Mancha*, Don Quixote's pessimism and anguish vie with a more courageous and positive view of the future. In Tennessee Williams's play, some of the characters, such as Casanova and Marguerite Gautier, express their anguish about becoming old and less physically attractive, a theme in other plays by the same author. *Man of La Mancha* is a musical, subject to rules that differ from the theatrical vision guiding Tennessee Williams, whose play is much more original and audacious. *Camino Real* is a surrealistic dream, a collage of unconnected, or apparently unconnected, sections and a constant flow of poetic language. On the other hand, *Man of La Mancha* offers attractive, even unforgettable songs, a visual display of sets and choreographed movements, and continuous dramatic tension. Yet the image of Don Quixote, the dreamer of an impossible dream, parallels the one envisioned by Tennessee Williams. Both are closely related to the interpretation made popular by the Romantic era, when it was common to identify Don Quixote with a heroic quest for justice. In canto 13 of Byron's *Don Juan* (1823), the English poet invokes a Don Quixote type to free "the helpless native":

> Revenging injury, redressing wrong,
> To aid the damsel and destroy the caitiff;
> Opposing singly the united strong,
> From foreign yoke to free the helpless native.

And yet, as readers of the Cervantes novel know, the two main attempts to fight for justice by Don Quixote, the episode with the young Andrés and the chapters on the liberation of the galley slaves, had unintended consequences and cannot be counted as true victories, but Byron believes that good intentions should count for something, even when results became elusive. There is no doubt that both Tennessee Williams and the authors of *Man of La Mancha* were aware of Don Quixote's limitations as a fighter for justice, as "a true hero for all ages." For the Romantic individual, the appeal is emotional. A Romantic soul responds to the passion of the flawed hero. It is necessary to place the Williams play and the musical within the intellectual and historical context of the post–World War II years. The cold war and the pessimism of writers like Beckett, Ionesco, the existentialists, and dramatists of the theater of the absurd had created an atmosphere of gloom and doom in which cynicism and despair were mixed in almost equal proportions. This was not the period in which a dramatist or a librettist of a musical could delve into the subtleties of "reality" versus "fantasy" in the Cervantes novel. There was for Tennessee Williams an inescapable need to find an antidote to the doomed anguish of his main female characters in *The Glass Menagerie* and *A Streetcar Named Desire*, as well as assorted other doomed characters in his other plays. A guiding light had to be found for Kilroy, the all-American young man, former boxer, stubborn and confused, and at the same time, vaguely reminiscent of Marlon Brando's character in *On the Waterfront*. This positive, hopeful, heroic individual could be none other than Don Quixote, helping Kilroy to get out of the trap and go forth with him, following him in a "Camino Real" that could become once more "royal" instead of "real."

CERVANTES AND CONTEMPORARY VIEWERS AND READERS

Cervantes and the tale he created found new life in the popular culture of twentieth century. Even among people who have not read *Don Quixote,* it is difficult to find anyone who has not heard of the knight who attacked windmills in La Mancha.

We will circumvent the issue of what constitutes popular culture since today's "pop culture" often becomes tomorrow's "classic." But let us look at the duality of Cervantes's worldview, the comic and the tragic, and ask ourselves if this is not the foundation of vaudeville's "funny man" and "straight man"? Take for instance, Stan Laurel and Oliver Hardy of the early films. The parallel is plausible. Don Quixote is the funny man; he always has the initiative and always makes the most glaring mistakes. The straight man has an important role, too: he witnesses the mistakes, tries sometimes to correct or prevent them, and is often an involuntary victim of the incredible and laughable errors of the funny man. We might find occasional moments in the plays of the Roman Plautus and the French Molière that could resemble the basic situation of this antagonism yet never in the sustained way that we find in *Don Quixote.*

Popular culture plays by its own rules. Even when the inspiration for a contemporary play comes from a classic text, the new version in its tilt toward popular culture will pick and choose certain essential facts and change or ignore others. This is clearly evident in *Man of La Mancha* where facts regarding Cervantes's life are mixed with elements of Don Quixote's story. The source of *Man of La Mancha* was not even the novel. It was a television play by librettist Dale Wasserman who was familiar with the story but had not necessarily read the novel. The curtain opens with the imprisonment of Cervantes "during the Spanish Inquisition." Other inmates, an underworld horde who are in need of entertainment, set upon Cervantes and his faithful servant. They organize an underworld trial in which the new inmates, Cervantes and his servant, will have to defend themselves before "The Governor," a self-appointed leader of the inmates. Because he is a writer, Cervantes wants his defense to take the form of entertainment. Cervantes presents the familiar story in a distorted way to fit the needs of a musical comedy. In real life, Cervantes was a prisoner of war in Algiers whereas Dulcinea was a dream in the head and heart of Don Quixote, and not of Cervantes, as is shown in the play. In the musical, she plays the role of one of the prostitutes at the inn and Don Quixote mistakes her for "a sweet lady and a fair virgin." Sansón Carrasco becomes a doctor intent on healing the knight; however, he is not so much interested in healing his patient as he is in the old man's fortune since he is engaged to the knight's niece and hopes to inherit some of it. This brief synopsis of the first part of the musical should suffice to convince us that in spite of its tuneful songs, *Man of La Mancha* has taken too many liberties with Cervantes's novel to be a sound introduction to the original text. What is memorable is the beautiful song "The Impossible Dream." Perhaps the virtue of this musical is that it has made tens of thousands of theatergoers aware of the existence of the original Spanish creation, and it may even have spurred a few of them to read it.

WOODY ALLEN AND *THE PURPLE ROSE OF CAIRO*

Cervantes's sphere of influence goes beyond literary genres. Don Quixote has been the subject of many artists, among them Honoré Daumier, Gustave Doré, Pablo Picasso, and Salvador Dalí, and an inspiration to composers of music and choreographers of ballet like Richard Strauss, Marius Petipa, Goffredo Petrassi, and more recently, George Balanchine.

It is possible to find a link between Cervantes's novel and a groundbreaking and audaciously experimental film by a famous contemporary director. The title of the movie is *The Purple Rose of Cairo* (1985). Among today's author-directors Woody Allen (1935-) is probably the one who is most familiar with literature, as he has shown in *Love and Death*. A summary of *The Purple Rose of Cairo* brings to mind the questions dealing with the complexity of reality that were raised in *Don Quixote*. The movie is set in the dreary Depression years and tells the story of a young waitress, Cecilia (Mia Farrow), who is trying to escape her meaningless life and her abusive husband. She loses her job and takes refuge in a movie house, watching time and again a film titled *The Purple Rose of Cairo*. Tom Baxter, a dashing young archeologist, is the male lead. Suddenly, much to her surprise, Tom Baxter walks off the screen, approaches her, and talks to her. They start a romance, but there is a drawback: Tom is not real. Meanwhile, producers and theater owners in Hollywood and elsewhere are panicking when they realize that other Tom Baxters are trying to leave the screen in other theaters. We wonder if Tom will go back to the screen and finish the film (inside the film) or perhaps stay in the real world, to which he is not well adapted.

It is easy to draw a parallel between the film and Cervantes's novel. In both the novel and the film, the main character is at once a part of the action within the fictional work and a spectator. Woody Allen's hero and Don Quixote are similar in several ways.

Both act foolishly and are incapable of understanding that the world around them is almost totally different from their intellectual frame of reference: in one case, the script for a Hollywood class B movie of the early thirties, and in the other, the romances of chivalry. In both cases, the two characters are unable to adapt, to change, and to evolve. They are trapped in their own self-definitions. In the film, the dashing young archaeologist becomes a rebel: Tom "breaks the mold" literally by jumping out of the screen, walking away from a prescribed role that limits his actions and robs him of his independence, but at the same time he creates a number of serious problems. First, he hardly understands the other actors' motivations. Second, they think he is a fool out of touch with reality. Allen's creation is also dangerous and defiant: he is out of control; he could create serious financial and juridical problems for his Hollywood producers, for the theater owners, perhaps for the public at large. The archaeologist's actions produce confusion and disarray for the other actors taking part in the film, who suddenly lose an essential actor in the script (a parallel here with Don Quixote's family and friends who feel they have lost him).

Woody Allen's Tom recalls the Manchegan model who, like Tom, is a maladjusted madman for reasons that can be traced to the society in which he lived. As Carroll Johnson has underlined, "Don Quixote's madness, his estrangement from society's norms and expectations, can mean simply an amusing inability to understand the world as it is."[18] Similarly, in the Woody Allen film, there is an allusion to the unbearable tension between the gilded, rosy scripts of innumerable Hollywood movies with their happy endings, their Busby Berkeley displays of pretty girls, their sumptuous interiors and the squalid reality of Depression-era poverty and insecurity. Many contemporary spectators of such films are blissfully unaware of this contrast between screen fiction and everyday life during the Depression, just as Spanish readers of chivalry romances did not see how much they differed from real life.

The Exaggerated Influence of Books

For a number of authors, the question of books and their influence first raised by Cervantes becomes a subject of their works. An early novel by Jean-Paul Sartre, *La Nausée* (1938), tells the story of a character obsessed with an encyclopedia. This novel became truly influential in the middle of the twentieth century and contained the germs of the author's philosophical ideas.

Briefly, the story conveys the tale of Antoine Roquentin, a writer at odds with his own life and with everything that surrounds him. He is at the center of a vortex of anguish where objects become menacing and absorbing, where, for example, the roots of a tree can acquire a monstrous power capable of engulfing a human existence. Yet the novel is not without a quirky sense of humor. One of its secondary characters, the Self-Made Man (L'Autodidacte) has been reading the encyclopedia methodically, has finished digesting several volumes, and still has a long journey until he reaches the letter z and the final pages. His life is both absurd and in some respects heroic, just like Don Quixote's life. Sartre (1905–80) apparently agreed with Cervantes that obsession is always close to the absurd and also close to humor.

One of the most imaginative writers of our time, Ray Bradbury (1920–), describes in *Fahrenheit 451* a world where books are banned and the firefighters' mission is to find them and burn them, another clear reference to the book-burning episode in *Don Quixote* and to the Hitler era. Bradbury is recognized as one of the best and brightest writers in the field of science fiction. This short novel, a small masterpiece published in 1950, elevated him to this stature. A film interpretation of this work, directed by François Truffaut in 1967, contributed to the international fame of Bradbury's work.

Bradbury depicts a somber time, a new dark age where the state demands conformity and ignorance from all its citizens. Guy Montag is a third-generation fireman who is beginning to question the emptiness of his own life and that of his fellow citizens. He wants to break free from ignorance but does not know how to overcome his apathy and is looking desperately for meaning. He meets Professor Faber, a retired English professor who still possesses a few precious books and would like to find more. He alerts Montag to the possibility of finding people in the countryside who still own books. Going out of the city, Montag feels a renewal in his contact with the forces of nature and finally meets a strange group of people, intellectual hobos who have committed their lives to the preservation of literature through the dark ages. Each of them has memorized a book in its entirety and for all practical purposes has become that book, changing his or her name and identity: they are known as "David Copperfield," and so on. Finally Guy breaks free from the bonds of discipline, turns against his superior, Captain Beatty, the head of Montag's fire department, and escapes toward a new life surrounded by his newly found friends.

Bradbury knew that book burning was a symbol of oppression from the beginning of time. In this powerful novelette, Bradbury places books at the crossroads with a monotonous everyday life lacking in meaning, just as Cervantes does at the very beginning of his novel. Book burning is also an important motif that unites these two works. Don Quixote's relatives and friends burn his library because they have come to the conclusion that books have deranged his mind. In contrast, book burning in Bradbury's novel is a more general phenomenon ordered from above by a system afraid of individualism, a government that does not want anybody to think for himself and wants all its citizens to be equally ignorant. Many people have become hostile toward books out of envy since they do not want to feel inferior to those who have read more than they have.

The main difference between the two works is one of tone. Bradbury's novelette is gloomy and somber and clearly separates the characters who yearn for knowledge, renewal, and freedom from those who are obsessed with technology, ignore nature, and want to create equality by bringing down everybody to the lowest common denominator. Cervantes's novel is sunnier. Although the pernicious effect of romances of chivalry is exposed, we are dealing with an individual case, not with a deep social problem, and even when Don Quixote's folly is criticized, Cervantes establishes a subtle contrast between the noble thoughts of Don Quixote and the pettiness of some of the other characters. Was Don Quixote happier before all his misadventures or after his obsession became paramount? Cervantes does not answer this fundamental question. Bradbury clearly applauds the ascent of Montag from blind obedience to personal independence and freedom.

Possibly the most extravagant exploitation of the theme of the influence of books is that of James Thurber (1894–1961), author and cartoonist, who was one of America's greatest twentieth-century humorists. His cartoons, many published in the *New Yorker*, often depicted melancholy-looking animals or oversized wives bedeviling undersized husbands. Thurber, who took the post of staff writer and managing editor of the *New Yorker* in 1927, occupied a position of responsibility and power in a magazine that has long been seen as "the Establishment" of high literary culture in the United States, and yet Thurber was also a bridge to popular culture. His short story "The Secret Life of Walter Mitty" became a film of the same title in the 1950s.

Walter Mitty, played by the famous comedian Danny Kaye in the film version, is a modest proofreader for a vast publishing firm. Subdivisions specialize in cowboy stories, war stories, adventure stories, spy stories, and so on. He has internalized the contents of many pages he has proofread and now, as he drives his car downtown, any suggestion, such as the sight of a cowboy hat, will explode in his mind. His imagination shows him acting heroically in the midst of highly dangerous situations, often saving a damsel in distress (portrayed by Virginia Mayo). In one episode, during a storm that tosses their boat around, she cries, "You are hurt!" "It's nothing," he replies, "just a broken arm." Once more, fiction proves to be more powerful than reality.

We should point out that the film, although loosely based on the Thurber story, accentuates the connection with the Cervantes novel. Like Don Quixote, Walter Mitty is influenced by the written word; in this case, by the several magazines he is proofreading professionally. His imagination does the rest, breaking constantly the barriers between everyday life and a mythical, heroic life of adventure that he longs for. In the short story, the impulse to dream is given by subtle events in a humdrum existence. Thus, at the very end of the story, his wife (as so often in Thurber, he is a henpecked husband married to a critical, sometimes nasty wife) leaves him at the door of a drugstore. She goes into the drugstore and he leans against a wall. It is this apparently innocuous act of leaning against a wall that starts an epic and dramatic daydream:

> They went out through the revolving doors that made a faintly derisive whistling sound when you pushed them. It was two blocks to the parking lot. At the drugstore on the corner she said, "Wait here for me. I forgot something. I won't be a minute." She was more than a minute. Walter Mitty lighted a cigarette. It began to rain, rain with sleet in it. He stood up against the wall of the drugstore, smoking. . . . He put his shoulders back and his heels together. "To hell with the handkerchief," said Walter Mitty scornfully. He took one last drag on his cigarette and snapped it away. Then, with that faint, fleeting smile playing about his lips, he faced the firing squad, erect and motionless, proud and disdainful, Walter Mitty the Undefeated, inscrutable to the last.[19]

Like Thurber, Cervantes was able to express the competing and conflicting nature of mankind, one aspect of which leads us to the loftiest of ideals and the other that tells us that to survive we must face certain realities. Cervantes's genius lies in the fact that he was able to show us the essence of human nature and experience. No one since has been able to do so with his genius, humor, and depth.

This unique mix of insight and genius continues to inspire writers, and Don Quixote refuses to die as an idea, whether in Unamuno's experimental "nivola" (novel) *Mist*, or as a scoundrel in F. Scott Fitzgerald's *The Great Gatsby*, or as a Catholic priest in Graham Greene's *Monsignor Quixote*. The reincarnations are many, with some guises more recognizable than others. The rusty armor can morph into ecclesiastical habit or white flannel suits and silk shirts. Kafka in *The Truth about Sancho Panza* and Borges in *Pierre Ménard* force us to search a little deeper into ourselves to discover the soul of Don Quixote through their worldviews. It is as though these two authors tease and taunt us to come up with renderings of their interpretation. The theater and movies provide fertile ground for investigation of the influence of Cervantes on technique as characters march on and off the stage or screen. For example, in Pirandello's *Six Characters in Search of an Author* or in Woody Allen's *The Purple Rose of Cairo*, the playwright and director blend audience and actor, reader and character, offering limitless dramatic possibilities. Finally, there are a series of works that recall Cervantes's focus on the worthiness and absurdity of books (Sartre), his penchant for men who become books (Bradbury), or his use of fantasy and dreams as an escape to a self-imposed better place (Thurber), much as Don Quixote and his loyal companion do. Today, Cervantes techniques and innovations continue to be recognized and to influence not only the traditional narrative but also different media, be it theater, film, or television.

Conclusion

Don Quixote speaks to us and has inspired so many of the novelists that flourished after its publication because the hopes and doubts expressed in its pages, emblematic of Cervantes's times, are universal. Indeed, today we are still enthralled by the same high hopes and tormented by the same nagging doubts.

Mark Van Doren alleges that *Don Quixote* "enjoys the reputation of being perhaps the best novel in the world. Not that its author ever speaks of it as fiction. He says it is history, or if you like biography; and he does not even claim credit for its composition."[1] Van Doren continues with the very apt observation that "the sign of its mysteriousness is that it can be talked about forever. It has indeed been talked about as no other story ever was. For a strange thing happens to its readers. They do not read the same book. Or if they do, they have different theories about it."[2] No doubt the last part of this statement accounts for the proliferation of interpretations and is the reason why writers across the centuries have found in *Don Quixote* a point of departure for their own creations.

The elusiveness of *Don Quixote* can be explained by a basic fact: Cervantes is helping to create and consolidate a new literary genre—the novel—a genre that breaks with the narrative forms of the past as exemplified by the epic tradition and didactic tales of the Middle Ages. Whether the roots of the novel can be found in epic poetry or not does not alter the fact that the novel will forge a new direction as Octavio Paz, the Mexican poet and essayist, pointed out in his work *El arco y la lira* (*The Bow and the Lyre*).[3]

While Cervantes claims in the preface of part 2 to write a "funny novel," he ended up writing a novel that was also "mysterious," as Van Doren states. We have tried to ascertain how this transformation came about in our portrayal of Cervantes's life and times, as well as his work, and the contribution of his followers that has kept his ideas alive into the twenty-first century, four hundred years after the birth of *Don Quixote*.

An essential feature of Cervantes's masterpiece, one that sets it apart from others, is the popularity of its characters. The novel's main characters are recognizable to millions of people, even those who have not read the book. This is not the case with Flaubert's *Madame Bovary* or Kafka's *The Trial* where even those who have read these novels do not recall the physical appearance of the main characters. The answer lies in the fact that Cervantes has described his main characters with care, has endowed them with clear personalities, and has contrasted their physical appearance by placing the tall, gaunt Don Quixote side by side with the short, portly Sancho. It is precisely this contrast that has made the task of the novel's illustrators easy and almost irresistible. Gustave Doré, Honoré Daumier, Pablo Picasso, and Salvador Dalí have created unforgettable interpretations of their appearance. Furthermore, their appearance has been reinforced in the popular mind by several films, ballets (Minkus, Petrassi, Petipa, and Balanchine), an orchestral suite by Richard Strauss, and by the thousands of statuettes, ceramic tiles, and even life-size statues that have been produced. Here we may add that a windmill usually appears as well, recalling the early episode of Don Quixote jousting with the "giants" cum turning sails, a reminder that we, too, do battle with windmills at one time or another in our lives. Body language and physical activity, including a good amount of slapstick humor, especially in part 1, are also prime ingredients of the novel and an open invitation to illustrators and artists.

Honoré Daumier (1808–1879), *Don Quixote and Sancho Panza.*
Photo: Agnew & Sons, London UK / Bridgeman Art Library.

Surprisingly, scholars, critics, and average readers largely ignored one of the most enduring and influential aspects of Cervantes's creation, what we could call "the comic couple." Some
features of a work of art are just too obvious to be analyzed. The
"comic couple" is hardly found in the classics, not in Aristopha-
nes and only very occasionally in Plautus. It does not appear
in the Italian commedia dell'arte. Only the Spanish playwright
Tomás de Rueda attempted to portray this pair, but without success, in some of his short act plays, with which Cervantes may
have been familiar.

The comical aspect is reinforced by the visual contrast between the two characters. Don Quixote appears taller, more decisive, and more menacing when seen alongside a rotund, fear-
ful, and skeptical Sancho. Contrast becomes exaggeration, and
exaggeration is almost always comical. Moreover, another source
of comedy is the element of surprise. We never know how Don

Quixote may react given a concrete external stimulus. Yet we can count on Sancho to object and dissent when he thinks Don Quixote is going too far. Thus, the contrast is not only physical but also psychological. Both Cervantes and his contemporary readers were right in declaring that *Don Quixote* was a source of mirth and laughter, a true "comic book," although we know, and Cervantes surely must have known, that it was much more than that. Yet in the modern projections, the contemporary descendants of Don Quixote and Sancho in, for example, Neil Simon's play "The Odd Couple," fully validate the comic value of Cervantes's novel.

The presence of two contrasting characters gives way to revealing conversations between them. Dialogue is one of the prominent features of *Don Quixote*. It has become routine in contemporary narrative where writers have at times experimented with advancing the action of the novel. Cervantes's immediate "tools," the romances of chivalry and the picaresque, do not develop dialogue to the extent that he found necessary in order to reveal his characters' inner soul and basic motivations. There is almost no dialogue in the picaresque, flowery, elaborate language in the pastoral, and the dialogue in the romances of chivalry is stilted and appears contrived.

What is most interesting and enduring is that by separating Don Quixote from his friends and neighbors, Cervantes creates a gulf of misunderstanding between him and the rest of the world. Only by dialogue can this be bridged. If all of the characters in Cervantes's novel were afflicted with the same delusions, their conversations would be brief and would end in mutual applause. Dialogue is vital because Don Quixote does not see the world around him in the same way that Sancho, the curate, and Sansón Carrasco do. The transformation of Sancho, a major theme in *Don Quixote*, is made manifest through dialogue. In the first pages of the novel, Don Quixote talks to himself. This situation cannot be sustained too long. Cervantes creates for him a companion who is much humbler in social rank and education yet capable of listening, learning, and giving opinions that are often based upon common sense and are streetwise. Don Quixote and Sancho have more in common than appears at first: Sancho can be moved by the idea, in principle quite preposterous, of becoming the ruler of a small dominion. Don Quixote has explained that often a knight errant may become the ruler of a kingdom and then decide to install his squire as governor of a part of it. It makes sense only in the rarefied atmosphere of romances of chivalry, yet Sancho is seduced by ambition and greed, half-believing and half-disbelieving in such a glorious future for himself and his family. He then comes to believe that he will be governor of an island, an indication of his master's power of persuasion. Sancho learns so much from Don Quixote that in the episode of the enchanted Dulcinea he is capable of reproducing the flowery and precious speech of the chivalry novels when addressing the "enchanted Dulcinea." Consequently, he makes a better foil to Don Quixote than, for instance, Dr. Watson to Sherlock Holmes, for Dr. Watson does not seem to change from one episode to the next, whereas Sancho is evolving from the beginning of the novel until the final chapters when he proposes new adventures, as shepherds or hermits, to his downcast master.

After reading *Don Quixote* we remember the tone as well as the content of the dialogue between the two main characters. It shows us the warm and loving relationship between Don Quixote and Sancho, which is also ironic, sad, critical, angry, and conciliatory. It introduces the reader to the complex nature of friendship and the very human preoccupation with life's contradictions and yearnings. There are other voices in *Don Quixote*, the author's among them. In the book there are the voices of almost six hundred persons who come from all walks of life and who want to be heard. They speak of their lives, thoughts, and feelings, and in the aggregate give an overview of Spain and its people. The seemingly endless chatter is characterized by rich vocabulary, proverbs—some deliberately misquoted for comic effect—slang, and earthy regional expressions as well as elegant, gracious, and aesthetic discourse. Cervantes's manipulation of dialogue to convey ambiguity, for instance, his use of play on words so characteristic also of the theater of his day, often leads to humorous and ironic observations regarding the human condition. It is therefore his inimitable, masterfully crafted dialogue that no doubt accounts for the popularity of the book in his own time and for its appeal to future generations of writers.

Also worthy of reflection is the realistic premise of *Don Quixote*. As he says in the beginning of his tale, he wants to create a novel that resembles real life, that is, possessing verisimilitude. Realism is not as easy to define in literature as it is in the sciences. For instance, when we read Gabriel García Márquez's *One Hundred Years of Solitude*, we know instinctively when the author speaks to us with a realistic voice and when he soars into fantastic heights that are totally devoid of common sense and scientific fact. Thus, it is possible to say that Cervantes established the accepted boundaries of realism. To go beyond them has always been possible, but the blueprint for the modern novel has been to develop within these boundaries.

In *Don Quixote*, Cervantes is, on one hand, inside the novel, guiding our steps, whispering advice, and voicing an opinion as he does in the titles of his chapters; for instance, in the episode of the Cave of Montesinos, he says that it (the episode) may be spurious, whetting our curiosity. This technique was cultivated by such painters as Velazquez, whose portrait appears in the background of *Las Meninas* (*The Ladies in Waiting*). On the other hand, we have also observed that Cervantes disclaims being the novel's author. The technique adds dimension and perspective to the narrative and opens the door to the exploration of ambiguity and irony, additional critical aspects of his work. Opposing but viable ideals energize Don Quixote and Sancho, yet their efforts turn against them regardless. What does this say, then, about "reality"?

Don Quixote is not the traditional hero. Alonso Quijano is a middle-aged, physically weak man, yet he attacks windmills and armies of sheep for his ideals. He creates his image and his role and is therefore a *self-created* hero. What makes him "real" and not a cartoon character is his *flawed* character. He is obsessed like Melville's Captain Ahab or Flaubert's Madame Bovary. The flawed hero who makes fictional characters believable, and more like us, becomes not just another hallmark in the Cervantine novel but also in the novels of today's writers. We have seen how flawed Fitzgerald's Jay Gatsby, another self-created hero, is, and before that Gogol's swindler, Chichikov. Both are inverted versions of Don Quixotes with respect to values.

Throughout the second half of this book we have considered the works of many writers in our endeavor to point up connections between their works and Cervantes's. In some cases, the connections are very obvious; for example, Alphonse Daudet who combines Don Quixote and Sancho into one character or Graham Greene's *Monsignor Quixote*. In others works, like those of the French and Russian writers, there is a clear identification with Don Quixote's soul as in, for example, Tolstoy's Pierre Bezuhkov or Prince Andrey. Another group of writers, including Flaubert and Sir Walter Scott, read the work in their formative years. Here the influence of the novel may be more elusive, but we maintain that there are, in fact, clear-cut connections. Finally, in the twentieth-century, writers like Pirandello, Tennessee Williams, and Ray Bradbury, and a cinematographer like Woody Allen, approach the book from their own unique perspectives. Like a multifaceted diamond sparkling in all directions, *Don Quixote* has inspired and still inspires many writers who may differ in their approach to Cervantes's masterpiece.

As testimony of Cervantes's worth after four hundred years, we offer the words of Simon Jenkins, former editor of the London *Times,* who recently expressed his dismay that the world is celebrating the anniversary of the publication of Einstein's *Special Theory of Relativity* (1905) with a lot of hoopla while the anniversary of the publication of *Don Quixote* (1605) is being largely ignored outside of Spain. In his moving tribute, Jenkins says of Cervantes: "He surveyed the landscape of post-medieval Europe and asked, but where is Man? He grasped at valour, love, loyalty, triumph and mortification and, like his contemporary, Shakespeare, compressed them in a human frame. He told a tale like no other man. If Cervantes had not existed, he could not have been invented. There would be a hole in the tapestry of Europe."[4] And, may we suggest, of the world. How very deprived we would be if we did not have the enjoyment of reading about the unprecedented adventures and memorable conversations of the Knight of the Sorrowful Countenance.

Notes

Introduction

1. Miguel de Cervantes, *Don Quixote,* trans. Edith Grossman (New York: Harper Collins, 2003), 478. We refer to this translation throughout the text as (Gr.).
2. Robert McCrum, "The 100 Greatest Novels of All Time: The List." *Guardian,* The Observer Review. October 12, 2003. http://observer .guardian.co.uk/review/story/0,6903,1061037,00.html (accessed October 13, 2003).
3. Lionel Trilling, "Manners, Morals and the Novel," in *The Liberal Imagination: Essays on Literature and Society* (New York: Harcourt Brace Jovanovich, 1979), 197.
4. José Ortega y Gasset, *Meditations on Quixote* (New York: W. W. Norton, 1961), 162.
5. Thomas Mann, "Voyage with Don Quixote," in *Essays of Three Decades,* trans. H. T. Lowe-Porter (New York: Alfred A. Knopf, 1975), 369.
6. Ivan Turgenev, "Hamlet and Don Quixote," in *Little Russian Classics: Karamzin, Pushkin and Turgenev,* ed. and trans. Rebecca Scott (Amherst, Mass.: Pyncheon House, c. 1993), 41, 55, 43.
7. Vladimir Nabokov, *Lectures on Don Quixote* (San Diego: Harcourt Brace Jovanovich, 1983), 51–52.

ONE
Cervantes

1. Malveena McKendrick, *Cervantes* (Boston: Little, Brown, 1980), 16–17.
2. Ibid., 9.
3. Salvador de Madariaga, *Don Quixote: An Introductory Essay in Psychology* (London: Oxford University Press, 1961), 11–12.
4. Ibid., 17.
5. Robert Alter, *Partial Magic: The Novel as a Self-Conscious Genre* (Berkeley: University of California Press, 1975), 5.

6. Jean Canavaggio, *Cervantes,* trans. J. R. Jones (New York: W. W. Norton, 1990), 245.
7. William Entwistle, "Ocean of Story," in *Cervantes: A Collection of Critical Essays,* ed. Lowry Nelson, Jr. (Englewood Cliffs, N.J.: Prentice-Hall, 1969), 163.
8. J. B. Avalle-Arce, "Cervantes and the Renaissance," in *Cervantes and the Renaissance.* Papers of the Pomona College Cervantes Symposium, ed. Juan de la Cuesta (Easton, Pa., 1980), 5.

TWO
Experimenting with Existing Narrative Tools

1. McKendrick, *Cervantes,* foreword by J. H. Plumb, ix–x.
2. Carlos Blanco Aguinaga, "Cervantes and the Picaresque Mode," in *Cervantes: A Collection of Critical Essays,* ed. Lowry Nelson, Jr. (Englewood Cliffs, N.J.: Prentice-Hall, 1969), 138–39.

THREE
Constructing *Don Quixote*

1. Canavaggio, *Cervantes,* 214.
2. Carroll B. Johnson, *Don Quixote: The Quest for Modern Fiction* (Boston: G. K. Hall, 1990), 91.
3. Ibid., 91–92.
4. Michel Foucault, *The Order of Things: An Archaeology of the Human Sciences* (New York: Vintage Books, 1973), 47.
5. Jean Cassou, "An Introduction to Cervantes," in *Cervantes across the Centuries,* ed. A. Flores and M. J. Bernadete (New York: Dryden Press, 1947), 8.
6. Harry Levin, "The Example of Cervantes," in *Cervantes: A Collection of Critical Essays,* ed. Lowry Nelson, Jr. (Englewood Cliffs, N.J.: Prentice-Hall, 1969), 37.
7. Alter, *Partial Magic,* 5.
8. Gerald Brenan, "Cervantes," in *Cervantes: A Collection of Critical Essays,* ed. Lowry Nelson, Jr. (Englewood Cliffs, N.J.: Prentice-Hall, 1969), 28–29.
9. Ibid., 29.
10. René Descartes, Meditation III, in *Great Books of the Western World* (Chicago: Great Books, University of Chicago, pub. by *Encylopaedia Britannica,* 1952), vol. 28, p. 81.

11. Canavaggio, *Cervantes*, 212.
12. Ibid., 213–14.

FOUR

A Look into Cervantes's Masterpiece

1. Leo Spitzer, "Perspectivism in Don Quijote," in *Linguistics and Literary History: Essays in Stylistics* (Princeton: Princeton University Press), 42–43.
2. Alter, *Partial Magic*, 8.
3. Foucault, *Order of Things*, 46.
4. Levin, "Example of Cervantes," in *Cervantes: A Collection of Critical Essays*, ed. Nelson, 38.
5. Erich Auerbach, "The Enchanted Dulcinea," in *Cervantes: A Collection of Critical Essays*, ed. Lowry Nelson, Jr. (Englewood Cliffs, N.J.: Prentice-Hall, Inc., 1969), 102–3.
6. Cervantes makes use of several names for the purpose of showing different aspects of reality. See also Leo Spitzer's interpretation of the different names of Don Quixote at the beginning of this chapter, note 1.
7. Richard Predmore, *The World of Don Quixote* (Cambridge: Harvard University Press, 1967), 42.
8. Helena Percas de Ponseti, *Cervantes: The Writer and Painter of Don Quijote* (Columbia: University of Missouri Press, 1988), 48.
9. Johnson, *Don Quixote, The Quest for Modern Fiction*, 18.
10. Harry Levin, *Grounds for Comparison* (Cambridge: Harvard University Press, 1972), 227.

FIVE

Cervantine Sallies into Eighteenth-Century France and England

1. Voltaire, *Candide*, trans. Henry Morley (New York: Barnes & Noble, 2003), 130.
2. Voltaire, *Candide*, trans. Lowell Bair, intro. André Maurois (New York: Bantam Books, 1981), 7–8.
3. Ibid., 8.
4. Ibid., 9.
5. Voltaire, *Candide*, intro. George R. Havens (New York: Holt, Rhinehart & Winston, 1969), iv.
6. Voltaire, *Candide*, trans. Morley, 11.
7. Voltaire, *Candide*, trans. Havens, 113–14.
8. Voltaire, *Candide*, trans. Morley, 11.

9. Ibid., 11.
10. Ibid., 12.
11. Ibid., 12.
12. Anatole France, *Le jardin d'épicure* (Paris: Calmann-Lévy, 1895), 31.
13. Voltaire, *Candide,* trans. Morley, 123.
14. Ibid., 124.
15. Ibid., 126.
16. Ibid., 129.
17. Ibid., 129–30.
18. Ibid., 128.
19. Ian Watt, *Myths of Modern Individualism* (Cambridge: Cambridge University Press), xv.
20. Ibid., 178.
21. Daniel Defoe, *Moll Flanders* (New York: Collector's Edition, Pocket Books, 1951), xii.
22. John Forster, *The Life of Charles Dickens,* 2 vols. (London: Dent, 1948), 1:11, quoted by Alexander Welsh in "The Influence of Cervantes," *The Cambridge Companion to Cervantes,* ed. Anthony J. Cascardi (Cambridge: Cambridge University Press, 2002), 87.
23. Alexander Welsh, "The Influence of Cervantes," in *The Cambridge Companion to Cervantes,* ed. Anthony J. Cascardi (Cambridge: Cambridge University Press, 2002), 88.

SIX
An Abbreviated Look at Cervantes in Nineteenth-Century France, Russia, and Spain

1. Douglas W. Alden, *Dictionary of French Literature,* ed. Sidney D. Braun (Greenwich, Conn.: Fawcett Publications, 1958), 321.
2. Ibid., 322.
3. Gustave Flaubert, *Oeuvres,* vol. 1 (Paris: Éditions de la Pléiade, 1951), xiv.
4. Gustave Flaubert, *Madame Bovary,* trans. Francis Steegmuller (New York: Modern Library, 1950), 41.
5. Ibid., 69–70.
6. Alphonse Daudet, *Tartarin of Tarascon,* trans. J. M. Cohen (London: Folio Society, 1968), 14–15.
7. Claudio Guillén, *Literature as System: Essays Towards the Theory of Literary History* (Princeton: Princeton University Press, 1971), 152.
8. Nicolai Gogol, *Avtorskaia ispoved* (*Confession of an Author*), 1847, quoted

by Henri Troyat, *Divided Soul: The Life of Gogol* (New York: Doubleday, 1973), 116.

9. Ibid.
10. Ibid.
11. Ivan Turgenev, *Rudin,* trans. Richard Freeborn (London: Penguin Books, 1975), 142.
12. Henri Troyat, *Turgenev,* trans. Nancy Amphoux (New York: E. P. Dutton, 1988), 54.
13. Ivan Turgenev, "Hamlet and Don Quixote," in *Little Russian Classics: Karamzin, Pushkin and Turgenev,* ed. and trans. Rebecca Scott (Amherst, Mass.: Pyncheon House, c. 1993), 61.
14. Troyat, *Turgenev,* 77.
15. Ibid.
16. Cascardi, ed., *Cambridge Companion to Cervantes,* 92.
17. Fyodor Dostoyevsky, *Selected Letters of Fyodor Dostoyevsky,* ed. Joseph Frank and Daniel I. Goldstein, trans. Andrew R. MacAndrew (New Brunswick: Rutgers University Press, 1987), 269–70.
18. Cascardi, ed., *Cambridge Companion to Cervantes,* 89.
19. A. Serrano Plaja, *"Magic" Realism in Cervantes: Don Quixote as Seen through Tom Sawyer and The Idiot* (Berkeley: University of California Press, 1970), 33.
20. Henri Troyat, *Chekhov* (New York: E. P. Dutton, 1986), 29. Letter written on April 8, 1879, in Anton Chekhov's *Life and Thought: Selected Letters and Commentary,* trans. Michael Henry Heim with Simon Karlinsky (Berkeley: University of California Press, 1975); orig. pub. as *Letters of Anton Chekhov* (New York: Harper and Row, 1973).
21. Richard E. Chandler and Kessel Schwartz, *A New History of Spanish Literature* (Baton Rouge: Louisiana State University Press, 1961), 219.
22. Michael Nimetz, *Humor in Galdós: A Study of the Novelas Contemporáneas* (New Haven: Yale University Press, 1968), 66.
23. Ibid, 119.
24. Ibid., 120.

SEVEN

Don Quixote and the New World

1. Harry Levin, "Don Quixote and Moby Dick," in *Cervantes across the Centuries,* ed. M. J. Bernadete and Angel Flores (New York: Dryden Press, 1948), 220.

2. Ibid., 217–19.
3. I. Berlin, *The Crooked Timber of Mankind: Chapters in the History of Ideas* (Princeton: Princeton University Press, 1990), 187.
4. Ibid., 187.
5. Tyros Hillway, *Herman Mellville,* rev. ed. (Boston: Twayne Publishers, 1979), 105.
6. Ibid., 90–91.
7. Ibid., 106.
8. *The Letters of Herman Melville,* ed. M. R. Davis and W. H. Gilman (New Haven: Yale University Press, 1960), 142.
9. Leo Spitzer, "On the Significance of Don Quijote," in *Cervantes: A Collection of Critical Essays,* ed. Lowry Nelson, Jr. (Englewood Cliffs, N.J.: Prentice-Hall, 1969), 82.
10. Steward Ross, *Mark Twain and Huckleberry Finn* (New York: Viking, 1999), 36.
11. Mark Twain, *The Adventures of Huckleberry Finn* (New York: Bantam Dell, 1981), 13.
12. Mark Twain, *The Adventures of Tom Sawyer* (Berkeley: University of California Press, 1982), 66–67.
13. An *entremés* is an interlude, a short one-act play.
14. Miguel de Cervantes, *Obras completas* (Madrid: Aguilar, 1965), 61. There is no English translation.
15. Ibid., 558–59. This is a line-by-line translation of the interlude.

EIGHT
Sightings of Cervantes and His Knight in the Twentieth Century

1. Miguel de Unamumo, *Vida de Don Quijote y Sancho* (*The Life of Don Quixote and Sancho with Related Essays*), trans. Anthony Kerrigan (Princeton: Princeton University Press, 1976).
2. F. Scott Fitzgerald, *The Great Gatsby* (New York: Charles Scribner's Sons, 1925), 97.
3. Ibid., 104.
4. Ibid., 104–5.
5. Ibid., 101.
6. Ibid., 104.
7. Ibid., 106.
8. Ibid., 103.
9. Graham Greene, *Monsignor Quixote* (London: Vintage, Random House, 2000), 85.

10. Franz Kafka, "The Truth about Sancho Panza," in *Franz Kafka: The Complete Stories,* trans. Willa and Edwin Muir (New York: Schocken Books, 1971), 430.

11. Jorge Luis Borges, *Collected Fictions,* trans. Andrew Hurley (New York: Viking, 1998), 91.

12. Ibid., 94.

13. Ibid., 324.

14. Américo Castro, "Cervantes y Pirandello," in *Hacia Cervantes,* 3d ed. (Madrid: Taurus, 1967), 480.

15. Tennessee Williams, *Camino Real* (Norfolk, Conn.: New Directions, 1953), vii.

16. Ibid., 6–7.

17. Ibid., 158–60.

18. Johnson, *Don Quixote: The Quest for Modern Fiction,* 11.

19. James Thurber, *My World—and Welcome to It* (1942), in *James Thurber, Writings and Drawings* (New York: Library of America, 1996), 549–50.

Conclusion

1. Mark Van Doren, *Don Quixote's Profession* (New York: Columbia University Press, 1958), 2.

2. Ibid., 3.

3. Octavio Paz, *El arco y la lira* (*The Bow and the Lyre*) (Mexico: Fondo de Cultura Económica, 1956), 223.

4. Simon Jenkins, "A Windmill I Won't Tilt At," *Times Online,* U.K. January 21, 2005; http://www.timesonline.co.uk/printFriendly/0,,1-160-1449680,00.html (accessed January 25, 2005).

Index

Gogol, Nicolai, 166, 176–78, 255
Golden Age, 27, 135, 168; of Spanish literature, 122, 129, 216, 217; "state of nature" as, 156; Walter Scott and, 163
Goldsmith, Oliver, 159
Goya, Francisco de, 59
Grant, Ulysses S., 215
Great Gatsby, The (Fitzgerald), 222–25, 247
Greco, El, 83
Greco-Roman culture, 57, 80, 81
Green Coat, Knight of the, 120–21, 209
Greene, Graham, 225–26, 247, 255
Grimmelshausen, Christoffel von, 46
Grossman, Edith, 5
Guillén, Claudio, 175
Gulliver's Travels (Swift), 199
Guzmán de Alfarache (Alemán), 51–54

Hacia Cervantes [Toward Cervantes] (Castro), 231
"Hamlet and Don Quixote" (Turgenev), 11, 180–81
Hamlet (Shakespeare), 232
"happy ending," 153, 242
Hardy, Oliver, 68, 239
Hawthorne, Nathaniel, 196
helmet, enchanted, 111, 113
Hemingway, Ernest, 148, 202
Henry II, king of England, 43
heresy, 7
heroes: bureaucrats and, 169; epic, 67; flawed, 93, 94, 238; German ideal of, 194; Romantic, 162, 165, 182, 193–98, 200
Hillway, Tyros, 196
Hippocrates, 36
historians, 84, 233
history, truth and, 61–63, 67, 229–30
History of Tom Jones, a Foundling, The (Fielding), 154–55

Hitchcock, Alfred, 116
Holland, 34, 35, 48
Hollywood films, 58, 153, 241–42
Homer, 5, 212, 226
homosexuality, 7, 9
Huckleberry Finn (Twain), 4, 199; construction of, 214–16; critical reception, 202–3; friendship in, 206–7; humor and beyond in, 213–14; social criticism in, 208, 209–10
human nature, 1, 187, 247
humanism, 1–2, 5, 8, 24
Hume, David, 156–57
humor, 28, 119, 192; compassion and, 184; as double-edged sword, 217; in life of Cervantes, 20–21; obsession and, 243; in Twain, 201, 211–14
Humor in Galdós (Nimetz), 187
Hurtado de Mendoza, Diego, 49, 53

identity, 81, 231
ideology, 50, 66
Idiot, The (Dostoyevsky), 184–85
Iliad (Homeric epic), 4
Index of Forbidden Books, 6
individualism, 165, 191, 244
Industrial Revolution, 163
innate ideas, 80
Inquisition, 7, 48, 144, 239
intellectuals, 73
Internet, 219
Ionesco, Eugene, 238
irony, 8, 9, 119, 140
Isabella, queen of Castile, 142
Islam, 63
Italian art, 72
Italian language, 24, 197
Italy, 16, 22, 23, 25, 167, 178
Ivanhoe (Scott), 163

Jansenism, 34
Japan, 198
Jenkins, Simon, 256

Jesuit order, 35, 52, 134
Jesus, 184–86
Jews, 53, 142, 210
Jiménez Aranda, Jose, 167
Johnson, Carroll B., 63, 65, 122–23, 242
Joseph Andrews (Fielding), 151, 152, 159, 183
Julius II, Pope, 8
justice, quest for, 69, 237

Kafka, Franz, 226–27, 228, 247, 250
Kant, Immanuel, 76, 77
Kaye, Danny, 245
Kepler, Johannes, 36, 52
knight-errantry, 12, 83, 180; mockery of, 123; utopianism of, 135; as world of love and beauty, 68

Lafayette, Madame de, 13
language, 2, 5, 24, 63–65, 81, 216
Latin language, 15, 24, 36, 197
Laurel, Stan, 68, 239
Lazarillo de Tormes (attrib. Hurtado de Mendoza), 49–51, 53, 54, 153, 212
Lectures on Don Quixote (Nabokov), 11–12
Lee, Robert E., 215
Leibniz, Gottfried Wilhelm, 36, 52, 135, 144, 145
Lemos, count of, 23–24
Lenin, Vladimir Ilyich, 226
Lepanto, naval battle of, 18, 23, 104, 167
Lesage, Alain René, 46, 130
Levin, Harry, 73, 89, 123–24, 191–92
Lincoln, Abraham, 215
linguistics, 63
Linnaeus, Carolus, 37
lion, symbolism of, 120–21
Lisbon earthquake (1755), 134, 135–36, 156
literature: didactic-moralizing, 66; English, 129; film and, 240–42;

hierarchy of modes of, 152; in Japan, 198; juvenile, 198–201; as labyrinth of mirrors, 216–17; life in relation to, 87–89; realism in, 145, 254; self-conscious, 37–41
Locke, John, 156
Lorenzo, Aldonza. *See* Dulcinea del Toboso (character)
Louis Philippe, king of France, 173
Louis VII, king of France, 43
Louis XIV, king of France, 34, 48
Louis XVI, king of France, 211
love, 1, 25, 158; in chivalric romance, 88–89; courtly, 138; death and, 181; Don Quixote's dreams of, 95, 168; Emma Bovary and, 171; enchantment and, 107; in *Great Gatsby*, 223; pure (Platonic), 68; superficial lives in absence of, 209
Love and Death (film), 241
Luther, Martin, 34
Lutheranism, 8

Machiavelli, Niccolò, 5
McKendrick, Malveena, 16, 26
Madame Bovary (Flaubert), 171–73, 250, 255
Madariaga, Salvador de, 20
magic, 142, 155
Mambrino, helmet of, 111, 113
Man of La Mancha (musical), 237, 238, 239–40
Mancha, La, 84, 177, 188, 216; as poorest part of Spain, 136, 217; as uninteresting place, 86, 136–37
Mann, Thomas, 4, 13
Márquez, Gabriel García, 254
Marx, Karl, 149, 150, 226
masterpieces, literary, 5, 6
mathematics, 35–36
Maupassant, Guy de, 171
Maurois, André, 134
Mayo, Virginia, 245
medicine, 36

medieval world, 66, 155
Melville, Herman, 191–201, 255
Ménard, Pierre, 228–30
Mencken, H. L., 202
Meninas, Las [Ladies in Waiting, The] (Velázquez painting), 38, 254
Merlin (wizard), 61, 99
Metternich, Klemens von, 168
Mexico, 19
Miau (Pérez Galdós), 188–89
Middle Ages, 33, 191, 249
Mignot, Louis Rémy, 171
Milton, John, 129
Minkus, Ludwig (Leon), 250
Mirrors, Knight of, 67, 120
Misericordia (Pérez Galdós), 188
Mr. Pickwick (Dickens), 4
Mitty, Walter (character), 245–46
Moby-Dick (Melville), 191–201
Molière, Jean-Baptiste, 129, 211, 239
Moll Flanders (Defoe), 46, 149–50
monastic orders, 6, 7–8
Monsignor Quixote (Greene), 225–26, 247, 255
Montaigne, Michel de, 5, 6, 10, 12, 157; homosexuality of, 7, 9; life of, 7
Moors, 58, 141, 142, 210, 233
"Moriscos," 141
Myshkin, Prince (character), 184–86

Nabokov, Vladimir, 11–12, 155
Naples, 23, 25
Napoleon I, Emperor, 166, 167, 169, 182
nationalism, 170
naturalism, literary, 37, 46, 165, 170
Nausée, La [Nausea] (Sartre), 242–43
Nazarín (Pérez Galdós), 188
neo-Scholastics, 48
New World, 16, 18, 30, 53; Baroque churches in, 52; news of Spanish

conquests in, 18–19; scientific discoveries and, 37
Newton, Isaac, 36, 52, 213
Niebla [Mist] (Unamuno), 220–22, 233, 247
Nietzsche, Friedrich, 196
Night Watch, The (Rembrandt painting), 39
Nimetz, Michael, 187, 188
novel, modern, 2, 5, 148; Aristotle's influence on, 129; *Don Quixote* as beginning of, 35, 152; epic poetry and, 249; episodic nature of, 212; in France and Russia, 165–66; psychological novel, 130; as travel book, 157–58

"Odd Couple, The" (Simon play), 252
On the Waterfront (film), 238
One Hundred Years of Solitude (Márquez), 254
oral culture, 72–74
Order of Things, The (Foucault), 37, 63
"Orlando Furioso" (Ariosto), 96
Ortega y Gasset, José, 4, 72
Orthodox Christianity, 48, 178
Oudin, César, 130

Pamela (Richardson), 151–52, 154
Pangloss, Dr. (character), 133, 134, 138–39, 147; as cardboard character, 143, 144; as caricature of Leibniz, 135, 145
Panza, Mari (Juana) Gutiérrez. *See* Panza, Teresa (character)
Panza, Sancho (character), 2, 10, 174; common sense of, 24–25, 74–75, 77, 91, 92, 168; as communist, 225–26; as coward, 123; dialogue with Don Quixote, 72–73, 92, 252–54; Dulcinea as problem for, 96–100; as flawed hero, 93, 94; as free spirit, 143; as governor of Barataria island,

Panza, Sancho (continued)
13, 22, 103, 109, 143, 206, 227;
illiteracy and oral culture of,
72–74; introduction of, 90, 91;
language and, 63–64; literary
counterparts, 158, 160, 162, 179,
204, 206, 207; magic and, 106–
7; psychology of, 65; readers'
sympathy for, 11; reality upheld
by, 12, 113; relationship with
Don Quixote, 50, 92–93, 94,
206, 253; role reversal with Don
Quixote, 98–99, 226–27; tossed
in blanket, 106, 212–13; transformations of, 252–53; viewpoint
of, 108–14; as visual antithesis of
Don Quixote, 89; wife of, 101–4
Panza, Teresa (character), 95,
101–4
parody, 44, 89, 145; comedic aspect
of, 152, 192; Fielding and, 150–
53; in picaresque worldview, 130;
weaknesses of works revealed by,
154
Pasamonte, Ginés de (character),
46, 150, 153–54
Pascal, Blaise, 52
pastoral narrative, 2, 18, 27, 43, 55;
fashionable in Renaissance, 32;
static nature of, 44
patronage, literary, 31, 40
Paz, Octavio, 249
Percas de Ponseti, Helena, 121
Pérez Galdós, Benito, 71, 163, 166,
186–89
Persiles and Sigismunda (Cervantes), 27–30, 35, 231
Peru, 19
Petipa, Marius, 240, 250
Petrarch, 68
Petrassi, Goffredo, 240, 250
Philip II, king of Spain and Portu-
gal, 18, 33, 169; criticized in Don
Quixote, 120, 121–22; Invincible
Armada of, 104–5

Philip III, king of Spain, 33, 120,
169
Philosophical Dictionary (Voltaire),
136
philosophy, 52, 76–80, 187
physics, 212–13
picaresque narrative, 2, 32; Defoe
and, 148–50; Dickens and,
160; first-person perspective
of, 48; in France, 130; Guzmán
de Alfarache, 51–54; Lazarillo
de Tormes, 49–51; in literary
history, 44, 46–49; nineteenth-
century naturalism and, 170–71;
as "novel of education," 46;
Twain and, 201, 207–8
Picasso, Pablo, 193, 240, 250
Pickwick, Mr. (character), 157,
160, 161–62, 184–85
Pickwick Papers, The (Dickens),
159–62, 184
"Pierre Ménard, Author of Don
Quixote" (Borges), 228–30, 247
Pilgrim's Progress (Bunyan), 52
Pirandello, Luigi, 231–34, 247, 255
Plato, 62, 75
Plautus, 239, 251
Plumb, J. H., 47
Poetics (Aristotle), 24
poetry, 186, 212; epic, 152, 212, 249;
truth and, 61, 62
popular culture, twentieth-century,
238–40
Port-Tarascon (Daudet), 175
Portrait of Miguel de Cervantes,
after William Kent (Folkema), 17
Portugal, 18
Predmore, Richard L., 107
Princess of Clèves, The (Lafayette),
130
private property, 156
prostitutes, as fair damsels, 87, 138,
240
Protestantism, 34, 48, 52
Proust, Marcel, 165, 175–76

Prussia, 134, 135
psychology, 70-72, 110, 148, 158
puppet-theater, 23
Purple Rose of Cairo, The (Woody
    Allen film), 240-42, 247
Pushkin, Alexander, 176-77

Quevedo, Francisco de, 46, 53
Quijano, Alonzo (character), 87,
    91, 124, 133; "birth" of Don
    Quixote and, 137; death of, 180,
    206; heroic transformation of,
    204; library of, 142; new person-
    ality of, 23; physical weakness
    of, 255; transformation into Don
    Quixote, 215
Quixote of La Mancha, Don
    (character): "birth" of, 1, 137;
    Candide compared with, 135,
    138-40, 146-47, 197; Cap-
    tain Ahab and, 193-98, 255; as
    Catholic priest, 225-26, 247;
    courage of, 69, 90, 120, 168,
    199, 200, 226; death of, 11, 29,
    132, 139, 146, 172-73, 180; desire
    for Dulcinea, 27; dialogue with
    Sancho, 72-73, 252-54; dream
    of, 70-72; encyclopedic knowl-
    edge of, 93; eroding illusions
    of, 213; as eternal essence of
    Spain, 219-20; everyday life as
    literature and, 87-89; female
    version (Madame Bovary), 171-
    73, 255; Gatsby and, 222-24;
    as hero, 120, 165, 173; identity
    and psychology of, 65-70, 124-
    25; Jesus and, 184-86; journey
    through history of, 2; as Knight
    of the Sorrowful Countenance,
    84, 256; language and, 63-65,
    216; library of, 24, 67, 104, 106,
    141, 142, 244; life experiences of
    Cervantes in, 22; as madman,
    123-24, 146, 151, 178, 193; magic
    and, 104-8; Middle Ages pre-

ferred by, 33; noble thoughts
    of, 245; origin and background,
    83-84, 86-87; pragmatism of,
    22; psychological analysis of,
    70-72; quest for justice and,
    237-38; readers' sympathy for,
    11; relationship with Sancho, 50,
    206, 253; as Renaissance man,
    197-98, 219; role reversal with
    Sancho, 98-99, 226-27; Russian
    literary counterparts, 177-86;
    Sancho's common sense and,
    168; Scott's heroes and, 163;
    sensory perceptions and, 79,
    169; suicide wish of, 101; super-
    natural realm and, 77, 97; Tom
    Sawyer and, 204-5; viewpoint
    and, 108-14
"quixotic," as word, 146, 148

Rabelais, François, 6, 12, 157; as
    dissident, 7-8; *Gargantua and
    Pantagruel,* 8; as joker, 10
Racine, Jean, 129
racism, 141
realism, literary, 46, 53-54, 105,
    165; Balzac and, 169; definition
    of, 254; *Don Quixote* as founda-
    tion of, 145, 201; Stendhal and,
    166-69
reception theory, 229
Red and Black, The (Stendhal), 166,
    168
Reformation, 47-48, 51
relativism, linguistic, 64
religion, Twain and, 208
Rembrandt van Rijn, 38, 39
Remembrance of Things Past
    (Proust), 175-76
Renaissance, 5, 15, 31; artists of,
    40; books published in Latin,
    36; Counter-Reformation as
    reaction against, 66; Greco-
    Roman models and, 57; ideal of
    Renaissance man, 197; linguistic